And They're Off!

And They're Off!

My Years as the Voice of Thoroughbred Racing

Phil Georgeff

Foreword by Tom Durkin
Introduction by Jim O'Donnell

TAYLOR TRADE PUBLISHING
LANHAM • NEW YORK • OXFORD

First Taylor Publishing Company edition 2002.

This Taylor Publishing Company hardcover edition of *And They're Off!* is an original publication. It is published by arrangement with the author.

Published by Taylor Trade Publishing
A Member of the Rowman & Littlefield Publishing Group
4720 Boston Way
Lanham, Maryland 20706

Distributed by National Book Network

Library of Congress Cataloging-in-Publication Data Available.

ISBN 0-87833-264-2 (alk. paper)

10 9 8 7 6 5 4 3 2 1

∞™ The paper used in this publication meets the minimum requirements of American National Standard for Information Sciences—Permanence of Paper for Printed Library Materials, ANSI/NISO Z39.48-1992.
Manufactured in the United States of America.

Contents

Foreword

When I grew up I wanted to be Phil Georgeff.

Now, note, I didn't state I wanted to be like Phil Georgeff. No, I really wanted to *be* Phil Georgeff. Somehow, to have morphed into his actual being; to possess his mind and to live, somehow, in his body to produce his words. You see, even at an early age I knew that nobody could ever be just like Phil Georgeff. He was a classic, unique, impossible to duplicate figure.

I idolized him for only a brief while. After that it became something much more. I would go to Arlington and get a spot at the rail right on the wire. Not to see the finish well, but to see him better. I'd turn my back to the races and look upward to his booth, the best seat in the house, five stories above the finish line. I'd bring my first pair of binoculars to the track and focus in on him, watching every move, seeing him articulate the words, then hearing them a fraction of a second later over the echo of the public address system.

I'd regarded exactly how he would hold the program and binoculars, with his right hand firmly round the glasses and with his left thumb and first two fingers curling the program and then balancing the glasses with his fourth and little fingers. It got to a point that I could recognize his ties. On summer days at Arlington he almost always wore white short-sleeved cotton shirts, collar open and double Windsor tie knot drawn down an inch or two. If you were going to be Phil Georgeff someday, you had to know these details.

Thirty-five years later I don't know how to tie a double Windsor but I do have the best seat in the house at places like Saratoga, Belmont, and on special days everywhere from Longchamp to Churchill Downs. And there is only one reason why I've got that seat—Phil Georgeff.

What made him the object of my veneration? I'm not sure there was a sole reason. Was it his boundless energy and enthusiasm? The way he could work the grandstand into a frenzy for a field of $5,000 claimers? That sense of timing? His unquestionable love of the game? Was it the catch phrase "here they come spinning out of the turn!" that never failed to ignite a sense of deep urgency? Was it the way the crowd responded to his sparks of electric prose? Was it the melody of his calls? Was it because he was the first announcer who actually called the finish of the race? Was it the fact that he never, ever made a mistake? Was it his popularity? He was every bit the equal of Harry Caray in the world of Chicago sports.

What made me want to grow up and be Phil Georgeff? To this day I don't know that there is a single reason. But I do know that when I spent my days at rail looking into his booth I saw a man possessed by his work and heard the voice of an incredible, original talent.

TOM DURKIN
Floral Park, NY
January 2002

Remembering Phil Georgeff

By Jim O'Donnell
(Staff Correspondent, *Chicago Sun-Times*)

Michael Jordan has it.
Mike Ditka has it.
Harry Caray had it.
Bill Veeck had it.
Phil Georgeff has it.
Thank God.

Along with the Chicago sports landscape, the "it" of which we speak is that compelling mix of unstated but clearly apparent joie de vivre, a permanently ingrained bonhomie and "the devil's glint," as the old Irish quarryman in a Frank O'Connor tale put it, all adding up to that special attitudinal calling card which the truly invincible of heart present to the world as a reminder of the capacity of the human spirit to survive, reload, and even thrive amid changing times.

Back in 1986, multiple championships and many frustrating nights ago, Jordan lived through the bullspit period of being held out of games until management deemed his foot healed. Inwardly enraged, Jordan bided his time, won his little winnable battles along the way, and came back as the most bankable name ever in American sports.

Ditka refused to accept his status as a volcanic but essentially forgotten assistant coach with the Dallas Cowboys, instead writing a bold letter to the aging George Halas to get remote consideration as head coach in 1981, ultimately to win a Super Bowl and undying fame.

Caray sensed attitudinal conflict approaching the White Sox broadcast booth towards the end of the 1981 season, and rather than sweat out the anticipated meddling of the new South Side management marauders, the Hall of Famer-to-be jumped ship to a better, greener, more secure broadcast roost and thus forever earned the right to thumb his nose at all things baseball south of Madison St.

Against all fiscal odds, Veeck put together an investment syndicate to buy the White Sox in 1976 and made the last comeback of a Hall of Fame career and saved the last vestiges of popular baseball in Chicago in the process.

And then there's Phil Georgeff, a career man with a microphone and a love and knowledge of racing who was about as low as a good person should have to go in mid-August of 1982.

Only 23 years and 70,000 race calls into his historic career, Georgeff awoke one morning to find that his style was no longer in synch with some management type who was then masquerading as the president of Arlington park. With the coiled "help" of a few media friends, Georgeff forced the issue publicly, and was fired.

Dumped on the scrap heap of heartless American business, Georgeff might have been one lost soul except for an ally few outside the realm of Chicago racing could appreciate, a high vocal and visible fifth legion with which the bantam announcer had long before earned—the fans.

"Without the fans, I was a goner, a footnote to the history of racing in Chicago," Georgeff today readily admits. "They were the ones who ultimately sustained me, both in terms of my own spirit, and in keeping my cause alive at Arlington."

The fans responded with petition drives, booing and guerilla heckling and catcalls. But even as the '82 season ended, the chances of Georgeff ever calling another race at Arlington seemed as likely as an Alaskan-bred winning the Kentucky Derby, or a Kentucky-bred winning the Iditarod.

But then, when the Arlington re-opened for the 1983 season, something very strange happened . . . the booing continued!

"That amazed me," Georgeff said. "I figured that after a winter to let the situation flame out, I'd be forgotten. But the fans picked up right where they left off."

Like Jordan, Ditka, Caray and Veeck, Georgeff endured and conquered. A new group had purchased Arlington Park. The former president lost his job, and Georgeff got his back!

The sad and happy tale ended on a glorious September afternoon when Georgeff, borrowing a stride from MacArthur at Leyte Gulf, alighted from a helicopter near Arlington's finish line and returned in triumph to the announcing perch, which was—and possibly may always be—considered his.

The Georgeff legend lives on in this book of memories, of what racing was and could be again. Who better to take us on this wondrous journey through the sport's Golden Age than a man who lived it all. Phil Georgeff's cry of "AND THEY'RE OFF!" remains that of a living legend.

Prologue

Granted, there are dissenting versions about how and where the Thoroughbred got its name—also about how and when it discovered its destiny. But for the sake of argument, let's stick with Adam, who had the job of naming every beast of the field. The Bible story's beauty, you must admit, is perfectly compatible with the love and admiration folks like us have always afforded this majestic animal.

At the risk of stretching a point, consider how the word *upset* gained special meaning when Sam Riddle's fabled Man o' War suffered his only setback in a magical 21-race career (1919–1920), losing only once—to an upstart named Upset. To horse racing fans, *Upset* forever will signify defeat of titanic proportions. The word *Thoroughbred* is similarly enhanced; it has come to depict more than some exotic breed of high-octane horse whose only purpose in life is to entertain spectators with exciting bursts of speed and stamina in hoof-to-hoof combat.

Yes, the Thoroughbred unselfishly shares its name with us humans, particularly its noblest connotation—but only if we prove worthy by displaying those qualities the name embraces: high-spiritedness, elegance, courage, grandeur, and impeccable education and grooming. No mean dossier, indeed. For example, congratulate anyone who excels in business, sports, or play with the words, "Hey, you're a real pro," and you deliver a super compliment. Use *Thoroughbred* and you deliver a superlative accolade, the ultimate kudo, that the honoree is the possessor of class. The words *Thoroughbred* and *class* are synonyms—for a crown of success, the cachet of impeccable breeding, the indelible stamp of extraordinariness.

I firmly believe the Thoroughbred deserves its lofty reputation. Yet I'd be remiss not to admit that the Thoroughbred racehorse probably wouldn't command anywhere near its fame or celebrity were it not for the state-endowed privilege of gambling! This fact is indisputable—the Thoroughbred's fiery inborn abilities have been abetted, coddled, and promoted by indulgent humans eager to back their horse against another, or others. With a wager of a bob or two, we have elevated "bettor" to the status of "participant" rather than that of mere "spectator."

Merry old England for centuries was successful in exalting Thoroughbred racing to almost godlike status as "The Sport of Kings." In the New World, however, the sport seemed to take on the burgeoning democratic spirit of rugged individualism. During its glory days of the 1940s through the early 1980s, the game flourished as "The King of Sports," achieving soaring crowd interest and statistics. Thoroughbred racing was America's number-one spectator sport. I'd have those days again.

But I've meandered enough. It's time to get down to business—the business of Thoroughbred lore.

Historians and archaeologists report that ancient stone carvings prove horse racing is at least 3,000 years old. For some racing fans, it seems that long since they picked their last winner. Thoroughbred racing as most people know it, however, is relatively modern. In fact, practically every Thoroughbred today traces its registered ancestry back to one or more of three sires that arrived in England about 1728 from the Mideast. That trio of sires—known from the names of their owners—were Byerly Turk, the Darley Arabian, and the Godolphin Arabian. Racing then traces its evolution to the English Jockey Club, founded at Newmarket in 1750–1751. The Jockey Club became the official custodian of the Stud Book, also the court of last resort as adjudicator of all turf affairs.

In colonial America, horse racing prospered. Four stallions invaded the United States shortly after the Revolution. First there was Medley. This smallish gray son of Gimcrack took up residence in Louisa, Virginia, and was later renowned as the daddy of Hanover and Domino.

Then came Shark, at home in Fredericksburg, Virginia. The son of Marske and Pigott, by Snap, this stallion epitomized speed, yet he could stretch out 4 miles against formidable foes when asked. Most of his progeny were fillies and mares, among them the propitiously named Black-Eyed Susan (the flower symbolic of Pimlico's Preakness).

Next was the amazing Messenger, whose arrival in America—or so the story goes—was cloaked in mystery. But there was no mystery about his ability to sire champions. In fact, Messenger became patriarch of two breeds and is still famed as the father of the harness breed. He also was known as Lord of the Match Race, so successful had he become when pitted one on one. Messenger stood at stud primarily in the New York–New Jersey area. One of his finest progeny was Hambletonian, the cornerstone of the Standardbred sport.

Horse racing received its biggest lift in 1798, when Col. John Hoomes of Virginia imported the famous runner Diomed, hero of the inaugural 1780 Epsom Derby, with dreams of further enhancing American bloodstock. A son of Florizel, Diomed had piled up an amazing 10-race win, capped by his victory in the Epsom Derby. Before stepping onto American soil, Diomed was considered England's finest colt since the undefeated Eclipse, who himself was lionized as the Man o' War, Citation, and Secretariat—all rolled into one—of his generation.

Diomed was an aged 21-year-old when purchased by Col. Hoomes for $250, and he wasn't an overnight sensation as a sire. He stood at stud for a paltry $25. Many considered Diomed over the hill by the time he took out U.S. citizenship papers. In the long run, however, among his more famed descendants were the wondrous American Eclipse—America's answer to England's wonder horse, Eclipse—and the grand runner, Lexington. For trivia buffs, Diomed lived a long and productive life; he was a robust 31 years old when death called. He distinguished himself as first of the "traveling equine Casanovas," covering mares in England and the United States in the same season. Maybe that's why he lived so long.

Even the most unpracticed racing fan has heard of Eclipse, in whose name American champions, including Horse of the Year, have been singularly honored since 1971. The original Eclipse was the undefeated English superhero, foaled in 1764, whose auspicious birth just happened to coincide with an eclipse of the sun. One need not be a sun-worshipper to know Eclipse's male line remains one of the most prominent in Thoroughbred breeding today.

His United States counterpart, appropriately named American Eclipse, was born 50 years later, a son of Duroc out of the Messenger matron Miller's Damsel. Owner and breeder Gen. Nathaniel Coles was so overwhelmed by the newcomer's beauty and physique that he admitted, "I had no other choice but to name him American Eclipse." Coles believed that not even the Atlantic Ocean would keep Thoroughbred pundits from favorably comparing the two steeds. In fact, American Eclipse disappointed no one. His English namesake would have waxed proud when American Eclipse retired undefeated with earnings of $56,700—tops in America at the time.

For over a half-century, from 1800 to the Civil War, racing thrived in Virginia, North Carolina, South Carolina, Tennessee, Kentucky, and Louisiana. The cry "And they're off!" was a familiar sound. Suffice it to say, the Civil War took a heavy toll on the Thoroughbred. Most of the prominent southern horse centers were destroyed, and Thoroughbreds became a tool of war. Kentucky, which emerged from the bloody upheaval in better shape than the states that had joined the Confederacy, quickly became the undisputed capital, first of breeding, then of racing.

When the Civil War ended, changes in the sport were inevitable, and they came fast and furious. It would be impossible to enumerate all of the changes. A few, however, are sufficient:

- Dash racing—single-race affairs—supplanted heat racing.
- January 1 became the universal birthday of Thoroughbreds.
- The American Jockey Club was formed in 1894 out of economic necessity—"for the purpose of improving the breed of horses," to offer prizes and rewards, to secure the attendance of the general public, and to have "a well-conducted system" by which "sums of money may be handled safely and fairly."
- A growing interest in gambling became a big issue.

American citizens slowly but surely were allowed to participate more fully in racing by betting on their favorite bangtail. New racetracks were built, some of which still exist. As of this writing, America's five oldest racing establishments are Saratoga, Churchill Downs, Pimlico, Fair Grounds, and Hawthorne.

North America's oldest stakes race is the Queen's Plate, dating from 1836 in the province of Quebec, Canada. Oldest in the United States is the Travers, whose inaugural running was in 1864 at Saratoga. The Kentucky Derby, perhaps the most famous horse race in the world, had its inception in 1875. The winner, Aristides, enriched his owner's coffers to the meager tune of $2,850, a far cry from the hundreds of thousands of dollars present-day Derby winners command.

By the time the first Kentucky Derby was run, the Epsom Derby in England boasted nearly a century of Thoroughbred heritage—recall that Diomed won the first Epsom Derby 95 years earlier, in 1780. History confirms that the Kentucky Derby took its sweet time becoming legendary. The title "Triple Crown" as we know it today didn't come into existence until 1935.

I'll be covering the Derby ("the Run for the Roses") and the Triple Crown in greater detail in chapters to come. I'll also recall the many greats—jockeys, trainers, stables, and horses.

I've written three fictional Thoroughbred racing books—*Thoroughbred: In a Class by Himself*, *The Man Who Loved Mario Lanza*, and *The Man Who Loved Eddie Arcaro*. But there's nothing fictional about these memories of racing's glory days.

So read on!

Chapter One

Glory Days

Thoroughbred racing's glory days begin with 1941 and an erratic but charismatic equine named Whirlaway, who also just happened to be the best-named racehorse of all time. My personal opinion, of course. I know of no group that gives prizes for horses with the cleverest names. But in case someone out there does, I'd recommend they convey the blue ribbon to Whirlaway, who scintillated as the 1941 Triple Crown champion. I'd do it with respectful apologies to other remarkably named steeds such as Man o' War, Citation, Secretariat, Exterminator, Buckpasser, and Affirmed, whose owners also deserve awards for creativity in naming their beloved warriors.

Kudos must go also to imaginative owners and breeders of such cleverly named horses as Phar Lap, Equipoise, War Admiral, Count Fleet, Assault, Ponder, Pensive, Bewitch, Armed, Regret, Seabiscuit, Eclipse, Phalanx, John Henry, Cigar, Nashua, Swaps, Round Table, and Native Dancer. Inventive names all—shrewdly crafted, often ingenious—depending, of course, on what word or name combinations strike your fancy or make your day.

I think you'll agree that the name Whirlaway has a unique ring, suggesting the dervish colt that he was: talented, unpredictable, powerful, headstrong, long-winded—and, at times, a bona fide nut case. More importantly, Whirlaway by his deeds came to connote the game's most impelling feature. He was a stretch runner whose affinity for the late charge captivated even the most placid observer, at the same time infused racing—which desperately depended on the galvanic finish to electrify its growing fan base—with uncommon drama and rare theatricality.

Whirlaway, incidentally, served as my personal introduction to the wonderful world of Thoroughbred racing, thanks to my Bulgarian immigrant parents. In April 1941, my father, Sam, confidently predicted that Whirlaway would win the Kentucky Derby, a race he esteemed more than the once perennially popular Irish Sweepstakes—which he also played faithfully. My mother, Mary, loved horse racing as much as my dad. A race prognosticator herself, she went a step farther—predicting without hesitation or doubt that Whirlaway would achieve legendary status as racing's fifth Triple Crown winner.

I was only 10 years old at the time, a fledgling candidate as the city of Chicago's youngest, most avid race handicapper. Neither my father nor mother saw any disgrace in involving their only child as an unwitting—albeit willing—partner in their love for the sport.

Therefore, if selecting Whirlaway's 1941 Triple Crown as the springboard for my account of racing's glory days seems a mite arbitrary, I assure you it is in no way capricious. Had Whirlaway lost the Derby, I may well have turned my back on racing. But he won—won big, too—and he continued to win, capturing the fabled Triple Crown, eventually piling up six straight wins. I was hooked!

I blossomed into a zealous race devotee from the 1940s onward and was a full-fledged track employee and inmate from 1953 through 1992. I made time to thoroughly explore those decades before Whirlaway's rise to fame, gathering a knowledge of and appreciation for the likes of Man o' War, Colin, Sysonby, Seabiscuit, War Admiral, Omaha, Gallant Fox, Equipoise, and Phar Lap; also for jockeys like Isaac Murphy, Earl Sande, Don Meade, Snapper Garrison, Sonny Workman, Jack Westrope, and George Woolf. Collectively, these Thoroughbreds and jockeys forged an essential precursor to the incomparable "winning team" composed of Whirlaway, owner Calumet Farm, trainer Ben Jones, and jockey Eddie Arcaro. This team laid the foundation for what I regard and cherish as the time "when racing was racing."

Those were glamorous days, when the sport glistened with magnificent heroes. Jockeys sparkled like bright new pennies: Arcaro, Johnny Longden, Ted Atkinson, Steve Brooks, Bill Shoemaker, Doug Dodson, Bill Hartack, Joe Culmone, Charlie Burr, Gordon Glisson, Anthony DeSpirito, Walter Blum, Basil James, Charlie

Kurtsinger, Johnny Adams, Nick Wall, Job Dean Jessop, George Woolf, Al Snider, Conn McCreary, Johnny Sellers, Jerry Bailey, Pat Day, and Chris McCaron.

Trainers also shone: Ben and Jimmy Jones, Max and Buddy Hirsch, Bill Molter, Hirsch Jacobs, R. H. McDaniel, William Hal Bishop, John Gaver, Harry Trotsek, Frank Merrill Jr., V. R. "Tennessee" Wright, Meshach Tenney, Tom Smith, Lucien Laurin, Ron McAnally, Bobby Frankel, Joe Pierce Jr., Arnold Winick, Charles Whittingham, Ivan Parke, and Sunny Jim Fitzsimmons.

Among the mighty equines were Whirlaway, Count Fleet, Shut Out, Devil Diver, Pensive, Assault, Hoop Jr., Polynesian, Olympia, Ponder, Capot, Busher, Bewitch, Twilight Tear, Armed, Historian, Pavot, Occupy, Tom Fool, Hasty Road, Cicada, Never Bend, Candy Spots, Phalanx, Hill Prince, Nashua, Needles, Swaps, Tim Tam, Round Table, Bally Ache, Northern Dancer, Majestic Prince, Affirmed, Alydar, Genuine Risk, Winning Colors, Alysheba, Seattle Slew, Carry Back, Stymie, Kelso, Forego, Native Dancer, Spectacular Bid, John Henry, Secretariat, Dr. Fager, Buckpasser, Graustark, Tom Rolfe, and Citation.

Okay, I promise: no more interminable lists, even though I'm sure we missed a few names, unintentionally, of course. But those missing will pop up when least expected as we drift back through the years of racing's glory days. But before we get anecdotally specific, allow me one short segment to acquaint you with the personal background that led me to the announcer's booth—and ultimately to the joy and privilege of calling more horse races (96,131) than any announcer from time immemorial.

I'm a Chicagoan by birth—January 1, 1931. Remarkably, New Year's Day is the universal birthday of all Thoroughbreds. And *Phillip* in Greek means "lover of horses." It's as if my career was destined, or at least strangely coincidental.

I was 10 when Whirlaway ignited my interest in Thoroughbred racing. By age 16—at five-foot-two and 112 pounds—I was convinced I was the next Eddie Arcaro. I considered myself an exercise boy par excellence. By 17, my weight had jumped to 132, so if I couldn't ride 'em, I'd write about 'em. I pursued writing and journalism with a passion. I was sports editor, then editor in chief of my school paper at Austin High School in Chicago. I majored in the radio-TV sequence at Northwestern University's Medill School of Journalism, receiving my bachelor's degree in 1954.

I worked at Arlington and Washington Parks during the summers of my junior and senior years at college, then started as full-time, year-round publicity assistant in 1955. I announced my first horse race professionally on May 18, 1959, at Washington Park, and I called my last race on December 31, 1992, at Hawthorne, bidding adieu to "Here they come, spinning out of the turn!" Bittersweet, indeed.

Now, time for the first of countless gems from those glorious days of yesteryear. We'll take it chronologically when possible.

As a kid in the early 1940s, I truly was in love with Whirlaway and his nonpareil jockey, Eddie Arcaro. To hear my father tell it, Arcaro was racing's greatest money rider, a blue-chip reinsman, a genius with a horse, particularly where stakes races were concerned. Needless to say, I believed every word. It wasn't until a year later that I learned my father's glowing praise of Arcaro's talents was either innocently premature or wistfully misinformed. Years later, Eddie confirmed it was Whirlaway who made Eddie Arcaro a household name, not the other way around.

"I was working as full-time contract rider for Greentree Stable and trainer John Gaver," he recalled. "Yes, I had won the Kentucky Derby, but only once, aboard Lawrin, in 1938. Guys like Isaac Murphy and Earl Sande already had won the Derby three times each. To most owners and trainers I was just another jock, but by record not really in the same league as Basil James, Charlie Kurtsinger, Georgie Woolf, Jackie Westrope, Johnny Longden, Johnny Adams, or Don Meade."

Eddie, however, was gaining wider repute as a stakes rider; he didn't win as many races as his contemporaries, but he more than held his own in features and handicaps. He got Whirlaway as his catapult to fame by strange coincidence. Whirlaway's regular rider was a talented youngster, Wendell Eads, fresh from the apprentice ranks. Eads was under contract to Warren Wright's Calumet Farm, whose stable was awaiting blast-off into incredible orbit as the sport's newest and greatest racing and breeding empire.

Calumet Farm's new trainer was the already accomplished Ben Jones, whose son, H. A. "Jimmy" Jones, wisely rode his father's coattails as dutiful assistant. Ben Jones just happened to have been the trainer of Lawrin, on whose back he hoisted a 22-year-old Eddie Arcaro to annex the Kentucky Derby only three years earlier.

Whirlaway owned every natural talent a champion required. But by rakish behavior, he lost nearly as many races as he won, often bolting the outside fence turning for home, both as a 1940 2-year-old and as a budding 1941 3-year-old. His antics baffled Jones. Jockey Eads, also hopelessly bewildered, was physically unable to get the robust chestnut to keep a straight course.

As of Tuesday afternoon of Derby week 1941—the Roses Run was just four days hence—Whirlaway was just a gleam in Arcaro's eye. Whirlaway was fancied highly in that Tuesday's 1-mile Derby Trial, obviously the colt's final Derby prep. You guessed it. He blew the turn, and the race, too, finishing second to Blue Pair. Jones was livid; Eads, embarrassed.

Eddie was thoughtfully winsome in New York, for two reasons. First, Greentree Stable had no 3-year-old for the Derby, making Eddie available. And second, he already had earned Ben Jones' confidence and admiration when they teamed up to win the Derby three years ago.

"Ben called me." Eddie beamed when recounting what occurred. "He asked me if I wanted to win my second Derby."

"Well, I got a colt here," Jones told him, "who needs your kind of strong but soft hands. He's a world-beater, Eddie, but only if we can keep him on the straight and narrow."

Eddie was on his way to Louisville. He'd smile inwardly when describing Jones' tactics to teach Whirlaway to run straight and true. "Each morning, Ben would sit on a fat stable pony just a few feet off the inner rail, and he'd dare me—hell, he ordered me—to ride Whirlaway through that small opening, anything to keep the bugger from running out. I didn't like the colt at all. Yeah, I knew he had size and skills, but he was nutty. He scared the hell out of me.

"Worse still—we're in the paddock on Derby Day, and I'm still leery of taking him to the gate, and Ben takes out a pocket knife and cuts away the inside, or left, cup of Whirly's blinkers. 'Now he can only see the inside rail—that should keep him from bolting,' Jones said. I hoped he knew what he was doing."

First thing Eddie noticed about Whirlaway was his amazingly long tail; it all but touched the ground when he stood still. "That's how got the nickname Mr. Longtail. It was long, bushy, flaming red," said Eddie, and that tail became Whirlaway's trademark.

Thus were glory days born, a saga inspired by a wonderfully crazy colt and a magical Italian with a big nose and the skilled hands of a young riding wizard. Sports pages came alive that day.

Whirlaway ran true that Derby Day, following Eddie's flawless guidance, threading his way between and around horses, lancing four-wide turning for home with nary a hint of bolting. Striding imperiously, his flashy tail flowing behind, Whirlaway blazed home by eight widening lengths—still the race's biggest winning margin—in Derby record time of 2:01$\frac{2}{5}$. He smashed Twenty Grand's mark of 10 years' standing with a time that itself would stand the test of time. Northern Dancer, 23 years later, became the first Derby winner to hit 2:00 flat. As of these words, Secretariat's 1:59$\frac{2}{5}$ (1973) remains the fastest Kentucky Derby ever.

Turf scribes and radio journalists lauded Arcaro's ride as magisterial. "I got all the credit," Eddie would say, "but it was Ben Jones who straightened Whirly out. And, never forget, Whirlaway did the running. Without him, I'd have been listening to the race on radio."

With Greentree trainer John Gaver's permission, Arcaro swept the Triple Crown, taking the Preakness in typical Whirlaway style—from last to first—and underscoring not only the colt's crowd-pleasing penchant for the late kick, but Eddie's uncanny ability to weave in and out of hot spots, potential pockets, and blind switches to guarantee a thumping, going-away, five-length victory.

But it was the 1941 Belmont Stakes that immortalized Eddie Arcaro, who was crowned "king of racing" by sports writers and columnists the nation over. So awesome was Mr. Longtail, only three starters challenged the Calumet flash at the grueling 1$\frac{1}{2}$ miles distance. Each opponent knew Whirlaway's stoutheartedness for distance; they also knew he needed a fast early pace to set up his fearsome late surge. So the field of four walked out of the gate. No one was going to sacrifice himself on the altar of speed. They'd shrewdly save their best for last, the one weapon they possessed to neutralize Whirlaway's now legendary Sunday punch.

One of Eddie's rarest talents was his ability to unerringly assess running times. He had a clock in his head. Trainer Jimmy Jones told me: "Tell Eddie to work a horse 6 furlongs in 1:12 flat, and you needn't look at your stop watch to tell you he hit the nail on the head. He was that damn good."

Right off, soon as the Belmont barrier was sprung, Eddie sensed the slow pace. He mentally confirmed the snail-like first quarter; he was fourth and last, but only a few lengths off a lead that hardly had broken into a canter.

"Now any late-closer like Whirlaway is disadvantaged by a lack of speed. Speed's what softens up the leaders. They've got to extend themselves, wear themselves out, or you'll vainly wind up trying to catch fresh horses. I had a crucial decision to make."

What Eddie decided was incredible. He spurred his mount, a colt whose modus operandi as late-runner was etched in stone, and they bolted to the fore. Settling up the backstretch with nearly a mile yet to run, Whirlaway left his three rivals in the dust, actually sprinting to a 7-length advantage. It was akin to asking a sprinter famed for high-octane zip to drop back to dead last and try to win from there.

Eddie bamboozled his three rivals, forcing them to react vigorously to answer his bold maneuver. Once in command, he regathered his equally mystified colt, giving him a breather to preserve his vaunted stamina for a more serious challenge as the field passed 1¼ miles.

Just when his pursuers asked the big question, Eddie again roused Whirlaway. The latter responded like a fresh horse, kicking into famed overdrive and galloping into history as Thoroughbred racing's fifth Triple Crown champion and the easiest until then.

I experienced Whirlaway's victory vicariously on radio and in the press. I those days, thanks to Whirlaway's emergence as an incredible athlete, streamer headlines were regularly flashed across the front and back sports pages of Chicago's daily papers. Few days went by in which columnists Red Smith and Joe Palmer—whose stories were often syndicated locally—weren't accompanied by features from the Chicago typewriters of Arch Ward, Warren Brown, Leo Fischer, and John P. Carmichael. These guys loved racing as much as, if not more than, football and baseball. Thoroughbred racing had legitimately become big news, and racetracks flourished from all of the attention.

For example, I was with my folks on July 4, 1941, at Arlington Park to see favored Equifox, Equipoise's most famous son, lose to longshot Steel Heels in the Stars and Stripes Handicap before no fewer than 50,638 fans, the most ever to jam Chicago's most famous racing emporium. There was no TV then, no casino gambling, no riverboat betting. Most fans regarded horses they followed and bet on as genuine athletes, not some numbers game. Anytime a "name" Thoroughbred performed, track management was guaranteed anywhere from 5,000 to 10,000 additional patrons, eager to see racing history in the making.

I can honestly include Whirlaway in my personal account of the glory days, because I did see him perform that summer of 1941 at both Arlington Park and Washington Park (Arlington's sister track, located on Chicago's bustling south side). I saw Whirlaway race three times—sadly without Arcaro—and win twice. The first race was a prep for the Arlington Classic, with Eads back in the saddle; the second win was a powerhouse triumph in the American Derby with a nice jock, Alfred Robertson, aboard. In between, Whirly dropped a heartfelt loss to an upstart named Attention in the Classic. He was ridden that day by jockey Alfred Shelhamer.

I'll have a lot more to say about Calumet Farm, trainers Ben and Jimmy Jones, Whirlaway, and Arcaro throughout this book. They were all part of racing's glory days. Fact is, American Thoroughbred racing was just gathering momentum. War Admiral, a son of the great Man o' War, had won the 1937 Triple Crown and was later defeated by the doughty Seabiscuit in their memorable 1938 match race at Pimlico in Maryland. Whirlaway, by his very name, his fiery countenance, his mode of victory, and a brilliant comradeship with racing's newest jockey phenom, Eddie Arcaro, had rekindled interest in a sport whose greatest days lay just ahead.

We can gloss over 1942 for a more in-depth consideration later on—Arcaro's hapless choosing of Devil Diver over Shut Out in the Derby; Alsab's pulsating, by-a-whisker victory over 4-year-old Whirlaway in their special match race at Narragansett Park—because 1943 would produce yet another Triple Crown hero, the spirited Count Fleet, and one of the most underrated jockeys in American Thoroughbred history—Johnny Longden.

I never saw Count Fleet in person; I saw his Triple Crown via *RKO Pathe News* at the local cinema. But in August 1965 at Arlington, I was privileged to honor Johnny Longden, who at 58 was still active, reigning as America's "winningest jockey of all time" with over 6,000 winners. Bill Shoemaker, who'd later displace Longden in the winners' category (jockey Laffit Pincay Jr. is currently numero uno), also was on hand that afternoon.

Equally significant, I got to discuss Count Fleet with Longden, whose love and respect for the beast had not waned one whit. Naturally, he called the Count the best horse he's even seen or ridden: "the closest thing to him was Citation." It was a biased opinion, of course, but honestly felt. It was Johnny's first and only Derby win, also his only Triple Crown. Count Fleet was so special to British-born Longden that he celebrated his 1943 Triple Crown sweep by becoming a United States citizen. Johnny always looked older physically than his age—appeared a wizened "old-timer" in his thirties when he piloted Count Fleet—but how that "old man" could ride!

I wasn't totally prepared to concur with Longden's cogent assessment of Count Fleet's preeminence among Triple Crown winners. But my appreciation for the lightning-quick son of Reigh Count swelled markedly with each passing year—I just hated to grant any one colt, no matter how classy or fast, the glory of surpassing Whirlaway's overall grandeur, especially in just two short seasons, 1941 to 1943. But Count Fleet was "one of the ones." His greatness cannot be disputed.

A couple of years back, I was commissioned to create an unprecedented "Fantasy Race" marshaling the 14 greatest Kentucky Derby winners of the 20th century. I proudly exalted Count Fleet to an explosive, close-up third behind Citation and Secretariat—ahead of a spate of Louisville sluggers, including Seattle Slew, Swaps, Affirmed, Gallant Fox, Assault, Silver Charm, Northern Dancer, War Admiral, Spectacular Bid, Alysheba, and of course Whirlaway. With humble candor, I placed Whirlaway a somewhat lackluster seventh, though beaten by less than four lengths by Citation, who edged Secretariat by a long neck, that pair finishing only a half-length ahead of Count Fleet. I took rare delight in my integrity. And for the sake of argument—and in stout defense—I stand by that forecast-analysis.

Longden's appraisal of Count Fleet is irrefutable on many levels. The colt was assigned a staggering 132 pounds by renowned racing handicapper John B. Campbell in the latter's Experimental Free Handicap weights for the colt's upcoming 1943 3-year-old season, following a spectacular 1942 juvenile campaign. It was the highest weight ever assigned by way of predicting a young colt's future. In all fairness, that weight assignment measured Count Fleet only against his own seasonal opposition; it was in no way intended as a comparison with other mighty 2-year-olds, like Citation, Native Dancer, or Secretariat yet to appear.

But Count Fleet murdered his opposition as a 3-year-old winning everything in sight and with peerless alacrity, too. The nation went wild over Count Fleet's Triple Crown: he won the Derby by 3, the Preakness by 8, then offered a startling foreglimpse of marvelous Secretariat by running away with the Belmont by 25 lengths, totally demoralizing his peers. Secretariat may have won the 1½ Belmont by 6 extra lengths, and in world record time, too, but Count Fleet compensated by capturing the first two legs of the Triple Crown by bigger margins and with consummate ease.

Much was said decades later when Secretariat, Seattle Slew, and Affirmed won their Triple Crowns of 1973, 1977, and 1978, respectively. These achievements were applauded enthusiastically because 25 years had elapsed between Secretariat's Triple in 1973 and Citation's Triple in 1948. In fact, the 1970s would have achieved a special notoriety all their own had Spectacular Bid, who handily annexed both the Derby and Preakness, not flopped dismally to finish third in the 1979 Belmont. His defeat, concomitant with other major sports changes as the 1980s dawned, all but brought down the curtain on racing's days of glamour and glory.

Hark back to the 1930s and 1940s. Omaha won the 1935 Triple Crown, coincidentally the first time the three-race package was so named by turf columnist Charlie Hatton of the *Daily Racing Form*. War Admiral grabbed his Triple Crown two years later, in 1937; Whirlaway followed suit in 1941; Count Fleet conquered in 1943; Assault scored three years later in 1946; and Citation wrapped up a glorious 13 years of Triple Crown lore with his gallop of 1948.

Much of this action took place during the 1941–1945 World War II years. Racing coverage on radio and in the press—TV had not yet arrived—equalled anything baseball or football commanded. Attendance figures soared at tracks everywhere. When Arlington's wartime meeting, 1943–1945, was switched across town to Washington Park, crowds between 45,000 and 56,000 were commonplace. Same for crowds at Churchill Downs, Pimlico, and New York.

Washington Park wasn't the only Chicago track to prosper. Hawthorne, which was always forced to open the day *after* Labor Day, on a Tuesday—considered racing's true "dog day"—also prospered. Its inner-city location drew 37,792 fans in 1937, over 37,000 again in 1943, and an all-time high of 39,033 in 1946.

Calumet Farm became racing's breeding empire. Its Pensive exploded from dead last to win the 1944 Kentucky Derby with diminutive Conn McCreary aboard. Pensive should have won the Triple Crown—he won the Preakness handily—but dropped a heartfelt half-length decision to Bounding Home after appearing home free in deep stretch at Belmont Park.

Eddie Arcaro ascended to America's jockey throne in 1945 when he guided Fred W. Hooper's Hoop Jr. to a waltzing 6-length Derby victory, tying Earl Sande and Isaac Murphy with three Derby wins apiece. I hoped he'd notch No. 4 aboard Maine Chance Farm's late-running Lord Boswell the following year. All he got was fourth; King Ranch's upstart Assault stunned racing as the game's seventh Triple Crown champion.

By 1947, when Eddie lost the Derby by a scant head on Phalanx to Maine Chance Farm's speed-inspired Jet Pilot, I was head over heels in love with racing—not as some idle observer, but as the sport's next Eddie Arcaro. I used to ride my bicycle 35 blocks at

5:00 each morning from my home a block off the Cicero–Madison intersection to Sportsman's Park and Hawthorne, from 33rd to 35th, in Cicero, Illinois. There I met trainers William Hal Bishop, Angelo Cilio, and Bill Schmidt; also jockeys Tony Skoronski and Red Keene. I exercised horses for three wonderful weeks; my path as the sport's next jockey sensation was set. The dream, as mentioned earlier, was short-lived. By 17, I had grown another inch and was packing 132 pounds. Neither Arcaro nor Longden had anything to worry about.

If racing's glory days needed a defining moment, it happened in 1948. The racing scene erupted sensationally as the names Citation, Calumet Farm, the Jones boys, and Eddie Arcaro combined magically to spell *perfection.* Not since Man o' War mesmerized sports observers in 1919–1920—though not to minimize the impact of Phar Lap, Seabiscuit, Colin, Sysonby, Count Fleet, Whirlaway, and Assault—had one horse inspired such love and respect. His name was Citation. And racing would never be the same, at least not for another quarter-century, until Secretariat came along to make turf headlines the world over.

I discovered Citation—I'll devote more space to our bonding as horse and fan later on—by accident in late summer of 1947. I had driven my parents to Washington Park for the Washington Park Futurity. The big lure that day was Calumet Farm's unbeaten filly Bewitch; she was gunning for her eighth straight victory, her third over "the boys." She got it, too, but had to go all out to preserve her dignity over two male stablemates, Citation and Free America. The trio ran 1-2-3, and Bewitch was hailed as America's top 2-year-old.

The Jones boys loved Bewitch, but they had discovered one better in Citation, who though failing to break Bewitch's win streak slashed 5 lengths off her commanding 6-length lead in midstretch. Citation creamed Bewitch in New York later that fall and was acclaimed the nation's 2-year-old kingpin. He then dominated his 1948 3-year-old division like no horse before or since. He piled up an incredible 19 wins in 20 starts—his lone second an excusable defeat. Citation was forced into premature retirement by leg injuries with 27 wins and 2 seconds in 29 career outings. Trainer Sunny Jim Fitzsimmons, who had saddled both Gallant Fox and

Omaha to Triple Crown glory, confessed: "Citation's done more than any horse I ever saw—and I saw Man o' War!"

The media—press and radio—eagerly gave racing exposure. Let me try, if I may, to recreate how highly the media regarded Thoroughbred racing from Whirlaway onward, covering Count Fleet and Citation, moving on to Hill Gail and Native Dancer with the advent of television, and leading up to Secretariat's emergence as "the second coming" of mighty Pegasus.

There were four Chicago daily papers—the *Chicago Tribune* and the *Chicago Sun* (later called the *Sun-Times*) in the morning, and the *Daily News* and *Herald-American* in the afternoon. Dave Feldman and Elmer Polzin combined to cover racing in *Chicago Today*; Joe Agrella, who adopted the name Bud Doble, wrote for the *Sun*; Maurice Shevlin and Frank Segretti had the *Tribune*'s racing beat; and George Swift both handicapped and wrote for the *Daily News*.

Not a day went by that some news from the Thoroughbred front wasn't spotlighted, often given front-page importance. There were features galore, and every major Saturday stakes—sometimes midweek features, too—received headline coverage. Each paper's sports editors, and all their name columnists, regularly followed the ponies. They were regular press-box denizens at the tracks, as faithful as those at the Cubs and White Sox ballparks.

Before TV, Chicago had daily radio broadcasts of every race day from Arlington, Washington, Hawthorne, and Sportsman's. The broadcasts were delayed a half-hour, except major Saturday stakes, and the races usually were described in "bookie-room" fashion. For example: "They're off . . . at the quarter it's Coaltown by two, My Request is second by two, Citation's third, and Better Self fourth . . . at the half, it's still Coaltown, now by six . . . but Citation's now second by three, and Better Self's moved into third . . . they're in the stretch—now here's Citation taking the lead . . . Coaltown's second, and My Request is far back in third . . . and at the wire, it's Citation by four . . . Coaltown's second, and My Request is third." Exciting, so-so. Informative, yes. And we loved it.

There were no tollways or freeways in those days. Tracks like Arlington and Washington were nearly an hour's ride from the hub of the city. Both also were served by trains. And the fans hungered for racing's special romance, glamour, and action. Within miles, certainly within a block or two before you'd hit track gates, hawkers strode the middle road selling their wares—tip sheets, code horses, *Daily Racing Forms*. It was nothing short of a carnival atmosphere; your heart beat faster, your pulse quickened, and then the track's huge grandstand came into view.

There were no TV monitors, but you could rent binoculars for 50 cents. The public address systems were not all that great, and announcers were not permitted to bring the call of the race inside the final 16th. Mostly because of TV's absence, there were few distractions. No talking heads spewed forth handicapping hints. Every fan had his or her own handicapping system. My favorite fan response: "Hey, a guy doesn't need somebody else's help to lose his money!"

That, of course, didn't prohibit "touting" from seedy insiders who were willing to share "hot inside info" for an equivalent $2 bet on the side. Touting was illegal; the track's private security squad tried in vain to wipe it out. It was all part of the game—or as the Marx Brothers called it, *A Day at the Races*.

Racing was scheduled Monday through Saturday—never on Sunday. Upwards of 30,000 showed up every Saturday. First race was at 2 p.m. With only eight races a program, and as much as 30 minutes between races, it was a slow, leisurely pace that only seemed to intensify the excitement as the bugle sounded each call to post.

The jockeys' quarters were conveniently located behind or under the stands. And the mighty little men in flashing silks would pass among spectators after dismounting in the vicinity of the winner's circle. Each rider was called by his first name, often stopping to sign an autograph or two. They took the cheers and jeers in stride; there was usually some heckling.

Fans didn't have one window at which to both bet and cash. There were separate windows for each kind of transaction. At the windows specifically to cash, there always seemed to be room to breathe and circulate. Each track boasted at least one fancy restaurant, not exactly gourmet, but sufficiently elegant to differentiate from the countless hamburger and hot dog refreshment stands on all floors of both clubhouse and grandstand. Liquor was available, and beer was the biggest seller.

Arlington, Washington, and Hawthorne featured turf, or grass, courses. I favored those because the day's opening and closing races, usually over a distance of ground, were usually on the infield green, a medium, to Chicago's credit, that was pioneered in the Windy City.

Not that hopscotching around is appealing, but I must jump to 1952 for the first Kentucky Derby telecast to a major market. In 1950–1951, a few New York races were beamed experimentally to the Midwest. Often they were preempted locally by ball games or wrestling, but the 1952 telecast of Hill Gail's front-stepping Derby triumph helped solidify the sport's glory days reputation. That day, Eddie Arcaro became the first jockey to win *five* Kentucky Derbys. It certified his fame as the Master, and he'd forever be the absolute against which riders would be measured.

Coincidentally, the sport's first Triple Crown was televised a year later. A gray colt named Native Dancer was crowned the sport's first TV matinee idol despite losing the Derby in one of the great upsets of all time, finishing a neck short of Dark Star. Alfred G. Vanderbilt's Native Dancer would bounce back to win both the Preakness and Belmont, eventually retiring as one of racing's undisputed greats. His Derby debacle was the only blemish on an otherwise invincible career.

Chicago genuinely reigned as the home of America's finest summer racing. No idle claim, since every major stable, horse, and jockey flocked unashamedly to Arlington and Washington Parks, several staying on for Hawthorne's annual fall season. The monarchy that was Calumet Farm—founded by Whirlaway's 1941–1942 Horse of the Year titles, then reaffirmed by Pensive's near-miss Triple Crown of 1943, and solidified by Citation's dominance in 1948—was now an undisputed dynasty, to which American sports did ready obeisance. The stable's Faultless accounted for the 1947 Preakness; Ponder flew from last to first to win the 1949 Derby; Hill Gail starred during the game's first major Derby telecast in 1952.

Arlington–Washington majordomo Ben Lindheimer sprung the coup that certified Chicago's glory days rating when he privately "hired" the services of Eddie Arcaro, convincing the great rider to abandon his traditional New York haunts for two brilliant Chicago campaigns (1952–1953), during which he broke all records for stakes triumphs. It wasn't until a few years ago Eddie intimated to me that Lindheimer had provided a $25,000 annual fee, plus all the purse monies he could garner, to lure Eddie to the Midwest. "There was nothing illegal about it," Eddie said smiling, "but that man simply made me an offer I couldn't refuse at the time."

Hey, $25,000 is peanuts today, but it was real money back then, a time when a $100,000 stakes or handicap was racing's creme de la creme. Parenthetically, I called my first "hundred grander" in 1959, the Arlington Handicap on the grass, won in a daring three-horse finish by the great Round Table over Manassas and Noureddin. I was privileged to call the sport's first million-dollar race, the 1981 Arlington Million. As fans in 34 lands watched the race on NBC TV, John Henry nailed upstart 30–1 The Bart right on the wire for all of the money!

By 1953, when Native Dancer's TV image had made him and racing household names, new Thoroughbred luminaries were hot and heavy. Bill Shoemaker exploded as no rider before, piling up 485 winners—a whopping winning average of 29 percent. He wasn't alone; newcomer Bill Hartack that year rode 350 winners, also a 29 percent rate. Shoe and Hartack would become Chicago regulars.

From 1953—mark it well—America's three greatest jockeys of all time would cement racing's glory days reputation. Eddie Arcaro was undisputed leader of the pack until his retirement in April 1962. Bill Hartack equalled Eddie's record of five Kentucky Derbys, though he'd never threaten in number of Triple Crown scores. Diminutive Bill Shoemaker, who'd retire as the world's winningest jockey, also enjoyed phenomenal Derby success, winning the Run for the Roses four times—but no Triple Crown.

Three great riders. Three distinct personalities. Three different riding techniques and styles. But each knew the shortest route to the winner's circle. Each has a well-deserved chapter in this book to showcase his skills and achievements.

In 1955, Arlington and Washington Parks' Ben Lindheimer achieved another major racing coup—the nationally televised $100,000 winner-take-all Swaps–Nashua match race, ambitiously billed as the "Race of the Century." Nashua, King of the East, had won both the Preakness and Belmont after being upset by Swaps, King of the West, in the Derby. The arch rivals met for their second and last time on the Midwest's neutral battleground at the classic 1¼ miles. Arcaro rode Nashua; Shoemaker was aboard Swaps. Both colts had gone undefeated since their Derby bout four months earlier. Nashua wreaked merciless revenge—and later I'll devote more time to the race—and the event, the last of the great match races, still rates as a timeless reminder of racing's glory days.

Unfortunately, the Swaps–Nashua match race soured Ben Lindheimer and other racetrack impresarios on future racing telecasts. Although a major milestone during the sport's glamour days, the telecast backfired. Tracks, nationally as well as locally, feared live TV exposure. In this they were unlike baseball, which used the coverage—even though it initially ate into live attendance—to popularize the game. The Thoroughbred industry turned down a major network offer to produce a race of the week, saying it would be bad for the gate. What discouraged Lindheimer most was that he was unable to black out the Chicago area; graciously, he wanted the rest of the turf world to witness the event. He tested the waters by scheduling the match race on August 31, 1955, a Wednesday. He knew Saturday's natural appeal would guarantee the customary 40,000-plus turnout. But CBS insisted on having the Chicago market. Lindheimer acceded, and CBS claimed an incredible 50 million viewers. But only 32,000 turned out at Washington Park, in numbers considerably down from what Lindheimer and his people had hoped.

Football and baseball moguls, however, were visibly impressed by the telecast's Nielsen ratings, recognizing what impact the new medium wielded. Thoroughbred racing, however, much as it continues to demonstrate to this day, lacked vision. What had been a monumental TV achievement, acclaimed nationwide, wound up being the sport's first major faux pas.

I grew up loving horse racing. But for most kids, there's no racing kindergarten. Kids grow up with baseball, football, and basketball. Unless they're taken to the track, as I was by my parents, kids get no racing exposure. Regular Thoroughbred TV might have been the answer to making new fans, at the same time continuing to enthrall the old.

Thoroughbred racing's decline as a viable athletic endeavor is undeniable. Tune in any annual or centennial awards banquet and racing is conspicuous by its absence, at times treated no more honorably than professional wrestling. But it wasn't always like that. Gambling, at least on the surface, always took a back seat to the accomplishments of rider and horse. Fans talked about Seabiscuit, Phar Lap, Citation, Native Dancer, Nashua, Swaps. Arcaro, Longden, Shoe, and Hartack; their names were bandied about like DiMaggio, Ruth, Joe Louis, Red Grange, and Muhammad Ali.

Sadly, slowly, and surely, racing deteriorated into numbers, exactas, trifectas, and bald-faced wagering, which held up fairly well until casinos crashed the party. Racing, however, didn't cave in without a fight; there were still a lot of glory days left in the old gal. True, the sport struggled for 25 years without a Triple Crown champ—Secretariat in 1973 would prove a powerful antidote, a veritable shot in the arm—but inflation and postwar prosperity lent financial stability and notoriety, and racing fought back valiantly.

By 1962, when I was in my fourth announcing year, Marje Everett had replaced her deceased father, Ben Lindheimer, as Arlington–Washington impresario and had exalted the Arlington–Washington Futurity to the world's richest race—an unheard of $357,250 pot. It was won by Rex C. Ellsworth's Candy Spots, Bill Shoemaker aboard, over the highly regarded eastern invader, Never Bend. Purses would continue to spiral upward, capped by the 1981 Arlington Million, which I called during my 22nd season. Incidentally, Shoemaker won that one, too, astride the great John Henry.

Fact is, the 1960s were glorious enough to sustain the sport until Secretariat's arrival. The amazing gelding Kelso, who'd sweep five straight Horse of the Year titles, started twice at Arlington, losing both times in major upsets. But he did win the Hawthorne Gold Cup as a 3-year-old in 1960. Eddie Arcaro made one of his last Chicago appearances before retiring atop Kelso; I called the affair on a tape-delayed telecast for CBS.

Hartack, meanwhile, was winning the Kentucky Derby like he owned the race. He scored in 1957 aboard Calumet Farm's Iron Liege, in 1960 astride Venetian Way, in 1962 with Decidedly, and in 1964 with Northern Dancer. Hartack garnered his fifth and final Derby victory in 1969 on Majestic Prince, trained by former jockey legend Johnny Longden.

Shoe's four Derby wins were with Swaps in 1955, Tomy Lee in 1959, Lucky Debonair in 1965, and—as a tender 54-year-old—astride Ferdinand in 1986. Silent Shoe was ageless, indeed.

Not that I'm a name-dropper, but there's an unheralded aspect of racing's glory days that includes a starry galaxy of celebrities from the world of entertainment. From 1955 on, when the Swaps–Nashua match race was arranged by film actor, Don Ameche, and all through the 1960s and 1970s, whenever stalwart Thoroughbreds appeared in Chicago, New York, Florida, or California, you could count on seeing VIPs from film, TV, and radio. I regularly saw and occasionally met, in addition to Don Ameche, movie tycoon Louis B. Mayer, Gary Cooper, Mickey Rooney, Jimmy Durante, Milton Berle, Lucille Ball and Desi Arnaz, and perhaps the most avid horse-player of all, TV's Ben Casey himself, Vince Edwards. Mickey Rooney, whenever in town, spent every day at the track. Milton Berle cheered wildly for his namesake, Uncle Miltie. Desi Arnaz, especially after splitting with Lucy, followed every race with reckless gusto. Jack Klugman visited me in my booth and was also on hand when his Jaklin Klugman teamed up with jockey Chris McCarron to win the 1980 Hawthorne Derby. Betty Grable and Harry James were racing aficionados, as was Bing Crosby.

Equally visible were members of racing's jockey corps, whom I helped expose to their growing fandom. During the 1960s we staged free public softball exhibitions, to which fans were invited after the races each Wednesday. The games usually involved the Jockeys vs. the Press. The latter team was headed by former baseball great Lou Boudreau, retired baseball pitcher Jim Brosnan, and fabled Chicago disc jockey Howard Miller. Also on that roster were turf writers and sports announcers famous in the Chicago area. Upwards of 3,500 fans turned out, cheering mostly for the saddlemites—particularly Hartack, Shoe, and Kenny Knapp, three riders whose competitive zeal carried over to the lighted baseball diamond erected on the Arlington backside.

Even without Triple Crown kings, there were Thoroughbred heroes aplenty during the 1960s. Tom Rolfe, small in stature but gigantic of heart, who swept everything in sight in Chicago following his big score in the 1965 Preakness, could run all day. Shoemaker called him the finest distance colt he had ridden to that time, and that included the stouthearted Gallant Man.

World records at one mile were regularly set at Arlington. After a horse named Intentionally, there was the redoubtable Buckpasser, and racing's newest riding sensation, the stoic one from Panama, Braulio Baeza. The fastest miler of 'em all was Dr. Fager, who, in the 1968 Washington Park Handicap at Arlington, whistled the mile in 1:32⅕, toting a staggering 134 pounds like a feather to a resounding 10-length victory. That record withstood onslaught for 30 years.

The parade of new riders won admirers and influenced handicappers. Walter Blum, Johnny Sellers, Craig Perret, Carlos Marquez, Phil Rubbicco, Dave Whited, Larry Snyder, Earlie Fires, Sandy Hawley, Randy Romero, Jerry Bailey, Pat Day, Ray Sibille, and Laffit Pincay Jr. displayed their wares in Chicago. Elsewhere Bill Boland, Hedley Woodhouse, Ron Turcotte, Jacinto Vasquez, Jorge Velasquez, Eddie Delahoussaye, Angel Cordero Jr., Bobby Ussery, Chris Antley, Kent Desormeaux, Gary Stevens, Chris McCarron, and Don Brumfield vied for turf headlines and honors.

A few equine near-greats appeared too briefly—like undefeated Hoist the Flag and the fabulously quick Graustark, whose rider, Braulio Baeza, once confided: "He might've been better than Dr. Fager were he not injured before Derby Day."

Just when racing had about given up on another Triple Crown champion to complement the great Citation, the clock struck 12, that first Saturday in May 1973. Secretariat emerged as savior, and racing's glory days got a second wind.

Secretariat launched a nonpareil decade of champions, which included back-to-back Triple Crown winners Seattle Slew and Affirmed (1977–1978). There was also Affirmed's undaunted arch nemesis, Alydar, who became the first colt to finish second in all three Triple Crown events. The late-charging gelding Forego swept three straight Horse of the Year titles (1974–1976), and Spectacular Bid in 1979 won both the Derby and Preakness before winding up a disappointing third in the Belmont. The Bid, however, reigned a peerless champ at 4 (1980), going undefeated and eliciting strong raves from Shoemaker, who rated him alongside Swaps as the greatest horse he ever rode.

For the record, I had the pleasure of calling Secretariat's first start following his 1973 Triple Crown sweep, when the flamboyant chestnut son of Bold Ruler invaded Chicago for a special invitational. He won it by 9 widening lengths in record time. It remains one of my favorite thrills. And in 1980, as Spectacular Bid rolled up victory after victory, I was ecstatic to call his Arlington bow. "Here they come, spinning out of the turn—and the Bid is truly Spectacular today!" He won laughing.

Waiting in the wings was the first million-dollar race in Thoroughbred history—August 30, 1981—the Arlington Million. I treasure that call and the excitement it engendered. As far as I was concerned, the sport appeared healthy as ever. But its glory days were actually gasping for air. Happily, the Breeders' Cup was just around the corner.

So much for our general overview of racing's glory days. Time to put this chapter to bed. Now's the time to review those four thrilling decades of fame and glamour in more intimate detail.

Chapter Two

The Thoroughbred Hall of Fame

I'm hardly old enough to have seen the great Man o' War in person, except of course on grainy film, including his match race triumph of October 12, 1920, over Sir Barton, the latter renowned as Thoroughbred racing's very first Triple Crown winner (1919). I did see—but never had the privilege to announce—the equally incredible Citation perform live on four separate occasions: once as a 2-year-old, three times at 3 years, plus his farewell appearance as a 6-year-old before Arlington fans the summer of 1951. I also viewed his Triple Crown triumph on film. I saw and had the pleasure of calling Secretariat's first and only Chicago appearance, June 30, 1973, his first outing since a record-smashing conquest as the game's ninth, and overdue, Triple Crown champ—25 long years after Citation turned the trick. Naturally, thanks to TV, I closely followed his many exploits before and after he achieved Triple Crown acclaim.

No matter how you cut it—whatever your touchstone and by any criteria or yardstick you choose—I'm compelled to define greatness by these three wonderful equine athletes. Yes, I have strong opinions why Citation was a shade better than either Secretariat and Man o' War. But because he who laughs last laughs best, the passage of time most likely would influence pundits and experts today to select the most recent among bona fide legends—namely, mighty Secretariat.

Of course, Secretariat had TV going for him. The sport was in dire need of his brand. Twenty-five long years without a Triple Crown hero was insufferable indeed. He arrived just in time to breathe new life into racing. Yes, he was the fastest 3-year-old I've ever seen. But not the best!

The fastest, but not the best? A strange statement, almost contradictory? Explanations are in order. Granted, Secretariat was speed personified, lionized for his lightning-quick ways, justifiably hailed for his inspired Triple Crown sweep, particularly a Herculean 31-length Belmont victory in world-record time of 2:24 flat, at least 4 seconds faster than Citation's Belmont of a quarter-century earlier. And it's said that "speed's the name of the game," right? Well, yes and no. Forgive my piety, but wasn't it wise old Solomon, the ancient Bible sage, who uttered those inscrutable words (Ecclesiastes 9:11), "The race does not always belong to the swift"? For that matter, Solomon also declared prophetically: "Nor does the battle always belong to the mighty."

The foundation for my argument against pure speed as an absolute indicator of Thoroughbred renown was laid when I was a teenager, orchestrating bicycle races around my Monroe Street neighborhood. Two boyhood neighbors, Tom and Marty Durkin—no relation to announcer Tom Durkin—were eager, daily competitors. We'd hold time trails, trusty stopwatch in hand, as each took a spin around the block as fast as he could peddle. For the sake of discussion, let's say I never broke 2 minutes; they'd regularly go in 1:56 or 1:58. But when we raced against each other, I always managed to whip the both of 'em, although never in times under 2 minutes. They'd wheel around by their lonesome faster than I could, but I'd beat 'em every time we raced competitively. Pardon my immodesty, but in racing, that's what horsemen call "class."

Here's another example. During my nights calling the buggies at Washington Park in the mid-1960s, I knew of a harness horse, a quality Standardbred named Steady Star. He paced like the wind and burned up the track every morning by himself, or with Thoroughbred prompters to bring out his best. They didn't actually race against him; they were there just to egg him on early. But come evening, Steady Star would lose against other pacers in slower times. Go figure. Racing has had its usual share of "morning glorys," those who burned up the track in morning works, but inexplicably proved incapable of duplicating that speed or effort in actual competition.

Now, most of this has nothing to do with Secretariat. Not for one second would I impugn his class or speed. To the contrary, his magnificence is unchallenged; his record is genuine, his glory unsullied. But I'm saying what some horsemen insist is necessary to judge greatness. There are four basic requirements: (1) who you beat, (2) how you beat them, (3) how many times you beat them, and (4) speed. Of these, speed is the least important.

Sacrilege, you cry! But class must come into play, and it's most important. A horse can have everything—speed, stamina, courage—but if he doesn't have class, then he doesn't have enough. But if he has class, an intangible that all but defies definition, he really doesn't need much of anything else.

Sounds too simplistic, doesn't it? That's why the debate continues. Who's greater, Tiger Woods or Jack Nicklaus? Joe Louis or Rocky Marciano or Muhammad Ali? Mark McGwire or Barry Bonds or Babe Ruth? Jim Brown or Gale Sayers? Eddie Arcaro or Bill Shoemaker or Bill Hartack or Jerry Bailey?

We must be honest and start right at the top of Secretariat's pinnacle of success. Owner Penny Tweedy is almost equally deserving of her colt's lofty repute as perhaps the greatest Thoroughbred of all time. She was one of the many fine things he had going for him. She was comely and personable, a socialite whose breeding and upbringing rivaled her classy colt's. She was a whiz at promotion, a brainy, attractive spokesperson for a Thoroughbred who, long before he defeated Sham in the Kentucky Derby, already ruled as darling of the Thoroughbred sports world.

Penny Tweedy's colt had another advantage over earlier equine champions like Citation, Man o' War, Seabiscuit, Colin, Count Fleet, Whirlaway, and Phar Lap. Secretariat had TV on which to strut his stuff. TV earlier made Native Dancer a national hero, but he failed to win the Triple Crown—and was never forgiven that gaffe.

I must admit an amazing affection not only for Secretariat himself, but for his rider, Ron Turcotte, as well as his trainer, Lucien Laurin, whose cozy, gentle ways afforded him a warm limelight wherever he traveled. Ron Turcotte, one of the game's most underestimated riders, often invaded Arlington and Washington Parks in the 1960s and 1970s. Fact is, he was Tom Rolfe's regular pilot, and together they won the 1965 Preakness, but Ron was replaced by Shoemaker later that summer in Chicago. He also plied his trade astride such cracks as Arts and Letters, Damascus, Dark Mirage, and Lady Pitt, and he even had a ride or two aboard Northern Dancer.

Ron was highly articulate and knew his horseflesh. He was particularly fond of Secretariat's older stablemate, Riva Ridge, with whom he annexed the 1972 Kentucky Derby and Belmont Stakes, a forerunner to his Triple Crown score the following year aboard Secretariat. The Canadian-born booter cherished his intimate association with America's superhorse; they were together in all but one of the colt's many stakes wins. Eddie Maple deputized for suspended Ron when Secretariat closed out his career in the 1⅝ miles Canadian International Championship. Ron died that day, "my heart broken," he confessed, "that I couldn't be aboard for his farewell race." But he added, "At least another jockey got to know his greatness." To which Eddie Maple to this very day adds a hearty "Amen."

I had a pleasant meeting with Turcotte the day before he combined skills with Secretariat in the 1973 Arlington Invitational, the pair's initial outing following their Belmont rout. By late June, Ron was overwhelmingly convinced he was aboard "the greatest horse who ever lived." He became a believer, not so much by Secretariat's score over a game Sham in the Kentucky Derby in stakes record time, but rather in the Preakness, when he spurred the sport's newest "Big Red" to power from last to first on the clubhouse turn, then waited for Sham's expected big challenge, which again fell 2½ lengths short.

"We figured the Belmont to be Secretariat's best race, even though his sire, Bold Ruler, never really wanted to go that far," Ron explained. "But our guy was rarin' to go—and we knew he'd have to win it big to make the kind of impression Mrs. Tweedy and Lucien Laurin wanted to make on the racing world."

Now, everybody knows what Secretariat did in the Belmont; his 31-length victory remains one of the most astonishing performances in Thoroughbred history. Inadvertently, however, it was Ron who clued me in on how the colt's superhuman effort came about. "There were only four challengers, and the only one we felt we had to beat was Sham, who we felt was primed for his best effort. However, during the post parade, and in our warm-ups, I noticed that Sham looked a mite shabby—the old sparkle wasn't there. Something was missing. So I decided we'd test him from the get-go."

It's no secret that the other three horses showed up for third, fourth, and fifth monies; they had no delusions of disrupting the highly anticipated Secretariat–Sham match race. Thus, they dutifully dallied and dawdled as Secretariat, starting at breakneck speed, put the issue directly to Sham once the gate was sprung. Sham, obviously hurting, gave chase gamely for a half-mile before capitulating. Sham finished dead last, dead lame—never to race again.

Naturally, this left the Belmont in Secretariat's talented hooves. There'd be no challenges, no bids, and, like the great champion he was, he actually raced against the clock. He was free as a bird after the mile, unharassed and unmolested. The result transfixed the world of racing!

All of the pieces fell together on Belmont Stakes Day. Racing got its long overdue Triple Crown champion via worldwide television for all to savor. Its winner was a flaming chestnut à la the august Man o' War himself, a colt brimming with personality and flair. Not only was the win an unbelievable 31-length triumph, but it was the fastest 1½ miles of all time!

Who could ask for anything more? I, for one, did. I would never detract from Secretariat's speed nor the margin by which he scored. But remember our horsemen's computation of greatness: Who he beat, how he beat them, how many times he beat them, and his speed—the last the least important.

I asked Ron, "who did Secretariat beat?"

He quickly answered, "Sham, three straight times."

So Secretariat qualified by whipping arch adversary Sham in all three Triple Crown classics. The Derby and Preakness were for real, but Sham was eliminated from the Belmont issue virtually before the starting gate opened. That didn't detract one iota, however, from Secretariat's aura of special mightiness. The world took cognizance of his Triple Crown conquest, and by the time he journeyed to Chicago and the Arlington Invitational, he was undisputed Horse of the World.

Arlington put up its 1⅛ miles dirt invitational not to test Secretariat, nor to get him beat, but to showcase the sport's newest all-star. It was a Chicago racing coup, to be sure. But the three opponents marshaled—My Gallant, Our Native, and Blue Chip Dan—were mediocre at best. Still, Secretariat did his thing, vanquishing his rivals with aplomb. He spread-eagled his field leaving the half-mile pole, striding clear majestically by 9 at wire's end.

I called that race. The crowd was enormous and loud. Yes, a packed house cheered "America's superhorse, Ron Turcotte aboard," as I brought him home by 9 in track record time. That race was a genuine work of art by the greatest equine of his era.

Secretariat did whip several fine horses other than Sham and the "unholy three" of Arlington's Invitational. Among them was his older stablemate Riva Ridge, a powerhouse performer in his own right. Moreover, Secretariat's final tally in Canada on the grass confirmed his versatility to tackle all kinds of tracks—and distance was no obstacle. I suppose one could conclude he deserved acclaim as the greatest Thoroughbred of the 20th century.

But one fact remains. All great 3-year-olds must also be judged by whom they met and beat, especially in their inevitable forays against older horses in late summer and fall. Four times Secretariat dared to tackle older steeds—4-year-olds and up—and in two of those contests—inexplicably won by upstarts Onion and Prove Out—he was soundly whipped. This meaningful fact is conveniently lost in the wake of a sports world hungry to crown Secretariat as the greatest thing since the American hot dog.

By comparison, Citation, during his heyday 3-year-old season in 1948, met older horses, seven times including two amazing outings even before seeking Triple Crown renown. Citation won all seven. But if we've uncovered a caveat in Secretariat's record, we must also concede a chink in Citation's armor. Injury forced him into retirement with 27 wins and 2 excusable seconds in 29 starts.

Sunny Jim Fitzsimmons had already acclaimed Mighty Cy as superior to Man o' War. Another renowned trainer, King Ranch's Max Hirsch, who two years earlier had unveiled the great Assault, went on record: "There's never been a horse like Citation!" Of course, that was before Secretariat. More significantly, it was before

Calumet Farm owner Warren Wright decided to "unretire" Citation in an attempt to make the son of Bull Lea the first equine millionaire of all time. Citation rusticated his whole 4-year-old season in Lexington at the home of his birth before trainer Jimmy Jones was ordered to bring him, now a 5-year-old with pardonable muscle and ankle pains, back to the races.

"Citation should have stayed retired," trainer Jimmy Jones told me repeatedly over the decades. "His comeback as a 5- and 6-year-old should not have been made.

"Becoming the game's first millionaire seems piddling today. Sure, it was an achievement back then. But there were no million-dollar pots, no $4 million Breeders' Cup Classic, and no $5 million bonus for winning the Triple Crown. Though he was returning to his great form of old, winning his last three races as a 6-year-old, including a four-length score in the 1¼ miles Hollywood Gold Cup, going after the million mark may have tarnished, not enhanced, his reputation.

"We stopped on Citation when he was hurt at Tanforan late fall of 1948 as a 3-year-old, his 19th win in 20 starts, and 27 of 29 overall. If we stopped right there—and I should have done more to convince Mr. Wright it was the right thing to do—Citation would have been remembered as the greatest horse of all time. No doubt in my mind." How would Secretariat have fared as a 5- or 6-year-old had Penny Tweedy insisted on bringing him back from the farm?

Aches and injuries lead to sad tales in racing's history, and they affect horses and jockeys. Ron Turcotte and Bill Shoemaker both were seriously injured. Five years after his Triple Crown fame, Ron Turcotte, only 37 at the time, was paralyzed in a nasty racing spill at Belmont Park. "It broke my heart when Ron suffered that injury," Eddie Arcaro confided. "Things, accidents like that, are always present. I know, 'cause I've had my share of spills. Injury is one thing, paralysis and disablement something else. Then when Shoe was also paralyzed—and this happened after closing out a career in which he was always in harm's way—a freak automobile accident—you wonder if all the fame and glory were worth it."

Eddie had a good share of fame and glory aboard Citation. But it's time to confess a little chicanery on my part to meet my idol,

Eddie Arcaro, long before I could do so formally as a racetrack employee. I devised the scheme after he and Citation won their 1948 Triple Crown and were en route to Cy's home base in Chicago. I had convinced my English-Journalism teacher, who oversaw sports editorship of my high school newspaper, to write me a letter of introduction to the media boss at Arlington Park, requesting permission to interview Mr. Arcaro if and when he came to Chicago. I was 17 at the time, and my riding hopes were dashed, but my love for Citation and Eddie Arcaro remained unabated. The publicity director at Arlington saw fit to grant that potential interview.

I called in the favor on July 4, when Arcaro flew in to ride Citation in the Stars and Stripes Handicap, 1⅛ miles on the dirt. This was their initial outing since running off with the Triple Crown.

Eddie always held goofy Whirlaway in highest esteem, proclaiming him the best he'd ever ridden. After capturing his fourth Kentucky Derby with Citation that May, when asked on radio how he'd rate Citation against Whirlaway, he answered cautiously: "It's a toss-up, but I suppose I have to give Whirly a slight edge—he did win the Triple Crown, you know."

Following Citation's Preakness romp, Eddie confronted the same question. This time he answered: "I'd hate to live on the difference between the two—they're both great ones."

A week or so before galloping off to an 8-length Belmont Stakes triumph under heavy wraps, Citation visited New Jersey to electrify easterners with an 11-length canter in track-record time for the 1¼ miles Jersey Stakes. In the Belmont charmed circle, on CBS radio—the *Gillette Cavalcade of Sports*—Eddie minced no words comparing the two Triple Crown champions: "Citation could carry the both of us—and still beat Whirlaway!"

Wide-eyed, and impressed by Arcaro's zest and eagerness to be interviewed by a high school student, I reminded him of how he lucked into Citation, much as he did Whirlaway. Citation's titular 2-year-old campaign in 1947 caught many jockeys, their agents, and horsemen by surprise. His paternal half-sister Bewitch was the big draw that August when they ran an unprecedented 1-2-3 in the 6-furlongs Washington Park Futurity, the day I first laid eyes on young Cy. Citation and Bewitch were both progeny of Bull Lea. Free America was third in the race.

Calumet contract rider Doug Dodson rode Bewitch; Steve Brooks was aboard the fast-closing Citation; and Jackie Westrope was in the irons of Free America, who also closed gobs of ground late. Brooks later confirmed that he "fell hopelessly in love with Citation that first time aboard." But contractual ties and racing's unending game of jockey musical chairs wouldn't allow the two of them to get back together for another three years, when Citation was brought back from the farm in 1950.

Calumet had another fine young riding prospect, Albert Snider, who had become Citation's jockey. The two of 'em walloped Bewitch in the 1947 Belmont Futurity, virtually ending her reign and announcing Citation's. A month later, Dodson pulled stable rank, yanking Citation away from Snider to win the Pimlico Futurity. The 1947 2-year-old champion was Citation in a landslide.

But Dodson was also the regular rider for Calumet Farm's rugged gelding Armed, who, thanks to his match race win over a gimpy Assault, was unanimously crowned 1947 Horse of the Year. (I have an interesting story to relate about Armed a little later.) Therefore, as 1948 rolled around, Dodson naturally chose to stick with older champion Armed when Jimmy Jones elected to start him as Citation's entrymate in the Seminole Handicap. Remember, Citation had just officially turned 3 on January 1, the month before, but he was still two months shy of his April 11 foaling date. No young 3-year-old before or since did what he did.

Some details I learned years later from trainer Jimmy Jones, who loves to tell the story: "I had planned to run Citation three times that winter in Florida. The Bahamas and the Everglades were the two warm-up races for the Flamingo, which was a big gun for 3-year-olds back then. But at the beginning of the winter, rival horse owner Eddie Moore was putting the needle into Calumet owner, Mr. Wright. The two of them were drinking buddies, and Mr. Wright had a low flashpoint. He couldn't ever stand much ribbing. So when Eddie Moore told him 'When we get a hold of your fancy Citation with our colt, Relic, we're gonna dump him on his fanny,' naturally, Mr. Wright went bonkers. He told me to get Citation ready, right now and fast, to answer the challenge."

Rather than await his patiently calculated route to the Derby, Jimmy took the order as command, hastily seeking a race or two to crank up Citation weeks before his time. First came a 6-furlongs allowance test against older horses on February 2, which Citation won handily. Nine days later came the Seminole at 7 furlongs, again against older horses, including sprint champion Delegate; Calumet's Horse of the Year, Armed; and the 1947 Preakness hero, Faultless. Snider had returned as jockey for Citation; Dodson, of course, felt he held the edge with the older, undisputed American champion, Armed.

"I told Snider not to hurt him by running him too strongly against such crackerjack older horses this early," said Jimmy. "Well, all three—Armed, Delegate, and Citation—flew to the lead. By gosh, Citation was just playing with Armed and Delegate. He won easily. I said, 'My god, what kind of a horse have we got here?'"

Dodson again demanded Citation be returned to his control for the upcoming Flamingo. Not this time, Jones retorted. "Snider's done great with the colt. Citation's his to keep, come what may." Dodson went ballistic. He quit Calumet Farm in a rage. And from that day on, his life and career, like those of the now jubilant Al Snider, would never be the same.

Back in 1948 when I first met my idol, Arcaro, I knew the bare bones of the story, which I recapped to Eddie. He confirmed the facts. "So far, kid, you've got the story just as it happened," Arcaro complimented me that morning.

As of July 4, 1948, Dodson was still cursing his decision. Calumet Farm had made him a star; now he was forced to freelance. Obviously, I had no idea then how difficult or impossible it would be for Doug to regain national prominence. He never did, and later he was despondent, even suicidal.

Snider, though cheerful beyond speech, hardly realized his great fortune was short-lived. "Al and I were golfing buddies," Arcaro told me. "Now I was riding in California at the time. I knew of Citation, but not that he was so special. On February 28, he and Al won the Flamingo by 6 lengths. Al told me his colt was his 'ticket to the stars,' and that he'd forsake a golf date we had in early March. 'I don't dare want to leave this colt; he's too good to be true,' he told me."

That very weekend, Al Snider, fishing with two other horsemen off the Florida Keys, vanished off the face of the earth. No wreckage. No debris. They were swallowed up in a sea of mystery.

"Once again I was called, this time by Jimmy Jones," Arcaro said. "Just as with Whirlaway, I was tapped to ride another great one—just how great, I wasn't quite sure."

Ironically, the first time Arcaro and Citation got together, the April 12 Chesapeake Trial at Havre de Grace, Citation lost! Victimized by a horse forcing them wide turning for home, Citation and Arcaro recovered sufficiently to finish a closing second to some dude named Saggy—the same Saggy, incidentally, that Cy and Snider had clobbered by 10 lengths in the earlier Flamingo.

Arcaro was shaking his head during our interview, in total disbelief, also chagrin, that he was a party to such a debacle. "I didn't want it to sound like so many sour grapes," Eddie mused, "so I took the blame, promised reporters never to repeat my boner. And I was to blame; it wasn't Citation's fault. Bad racing luck, that's all, that I could have caught Saggy once straightened out, but that I didn't want to abuse Cy with all those big ones up for grabs."

Arcaro kept his vow the very next week in the Chesapeake Stakes. "We went to the lead that day—took no chances. I was getting to know Citation—he was a push-button colt. Go to the front, or come from behind. He was totally obedient to my touch. But I had one anxious moment in the race. Midway up the backstretch, here comes Saggy again. He had something to prove, I suppose. But then, so did we. Saggy actually put a nose in front. So I gave Citation his head—and it was all she wrote!" Citation crushed Saggy unmercifully, lancing to a 4-length victory. Saggy threw in the towel, winding up 15 lengths back up the track.

Citation became the first horse in racing history to win both the Derby Trial—run on Tuesday of Derby week—and the Kentucky Derby. He blew his opposition away in the Preakness and humbled his Jersey Stakes foes by 11 before posting an 8-length gallop over some mighty courageous 3-year-olds in the Belmont. And on Monday, July 5, at Arlington, Citation and Arcaro had something more to prove.

"Everybody who knows horses," Arcaro told me, "calls Citation one in a million. Sunny Jim already rates him over Man o' War, and he's certainly the best I've ever seen or ridden. Remember, he's already beaten older horses twice—no 3-year-old's ever done that before. So we're back against older horses in the Stars and Stripes. I have no doubts about him. Ben and Jimmy Jones say he's the best of all time—and I'm a true believer."

But Eddie wasn't an overnight convert, especially given his shaky start with Cy in the Chesapeake Trial following Al Snider's tragic death. Calumet Farm, always loaded for bear, had another "invincible" one, Coaltown, unraced as a 2-year-old. Coaltown was a legitimate pretender to Citation's 3-year-old throne as Derby Day approached.

"For a moment there," Arcaro recalled, "I would have been pleased to ride Coaltown in the Derby." Like Citation, Coaltown was a son of Bull Lea, and Eddie thought he was the fastest thing on four legs. "He was unbeaten in four straight, including a blowout in the Blue Grass Stakes. And the Jones boys were running him as Citation's entrymate in the Derby. The night before, I asked Ben Jones if I was up on the right horse for the Derby."

Jones was credited by Arcaro with words of utter prophecy: "Eddie, any horse Citation can see, he can catch! And he's got perfect eyesight!"

"I tested his eyesight perfectly on Derby Day," Arcaro said with a smile. "Going to the far turn—and we had a sloppy track that favored speed—Coaltown was bounding along 6 lengths ahead of us. I told Cy, 'you see 'em, now go get 'em.'" Within a quarter mile, Citation ran by Coaltown as if he were glued to the rail, splashing home handsomely by 3½ lengths.

Eddie's favorite assessment of Citation's impact on the world of Thoroughbred racing is the one voiced by a humble groom working for the stylish Alfred G. Vanderbilt Stable following Cy's Belmont victory: "Boss, that hoss, he ain't human!"

Well, Citation was made out of flesh, blood, and bone, and all was not well that July 5 at Arlington. He went into the race perfectly sound and came out of it a near cripple, limping on three good legs—and still he won, tying the track stakes victory with a 2-length verdict over a powerhouse field of older Thoroughbreds.

I was heartsick when Citation limped to the winner circle. I also saw agony on Eddie's face. He leaped from the saddle, gently escorting Cy by hand to where Ben and Jimmy Jones gawked concernedly. Citation had severely wrenched his right hip and suffered a serious ankle sprain. Eddie for the first time had to use the whip to wake up his friend, not realizing Cy had suffered painful injury.

Talk about super horses! Citation would be idle for only six weeks, until August 21, before starting again. He returned a winner in a prep for Washington Park's American Derby. Then he won the actual Derby over stablemate Free America. I witnessed those performances.

He was shipped to Belmont Park for a spectacular series of bouts against older horses, piling up victories in the Sysonby Mile, the 2-mile Jockey Club Gold Cup, and the $1\frac{5}{8}$ miles Empire City Gold Cup, before scaring off all opposition. He won the Pimlico Special in an unprecedented walkover, in which he pranced the $1\frac{3}{16}$ miles all by his lonesome. A tremendous crowd applauded his awesome presence.

Thereafter, Citation invaded Tanforan in California, closing out an indomitable 3-year-old season with two straight wins over seasoned horses. He reinjured himself in his December 11 finale, the $1\frac{1}{4}$ miles Tanforan Handicap, but still he won by 5 lengths. When Citation was sent back to the farm of his birth, having won 27 of 29—with 2 excusable seconds—he was universally acclaimed as the greatest Thoroughbred who ever lived.

I wouldn't sit down with Eddie again until another makeshift interview in 1952, when I was a student from Northwestern's Medill School of Journalism. It was Eddie's first of two straight summer seasons at Arlington–Washington. I'd be with him regularly starting with my Chicago track employment the following summer, in 1953. We naturally couldn't compare Citation with the yet unborn Secretariat, but there was ample opportunity to talk about Man o' War, whose faithful groom had praised him as "the mostest horse."

While on the subject of comparisons, there's always at least two sides to every argument, and Charlie Hatton, the highly esteemed *Daily Racing Form* columnist, always had at least three. But Hatton led such a guardedly concealed life, pinning him down on anything was as tough as catching a slick eel in deep waters.

Hatton was known chiefly as the turf writer who borrowed from England, then coined for America, the term "Triple Crown." That grandiose title was introduced in the United States in time for Omaha's 1935 Triple Crown score. Sir Barton (1919) and Gallant Fox (1930) also won the Kentucky Derby, Preakness, and Belmont Stakes—but no such recognition was available in their day.

I first met Hatton in 1953, during my first summer publicity stint at Arlington and Washington Parks. He was dapper and trim, quiet, properly dignified, and smarmy—an eastern snob, overblown and pretentious. Hatton was ever watchful not to be sullied by mundane midwestern Thoroughbred bourgeois. I give him this: he knew Thoroughbred racing. But he was an ornate, Victorian-type penman; he'd never allow simplicity or lucidity to infest his Shakespearean prose. And, like most vainglorious people, he'd never hesitate to remind you that your humble opinion could not hold a candle to his authoritative one.

I didn't like Hatton, but then, he wouldn't allow a lowly press box inmate, still wet behind his journalistic ears, access to familiarity. To achieve some form of civility, I'd congratulate him on coining the title "Triple Crown" or apply some other complimentary ruse to elicit even the most tepid half-smile. Several times, however, being privy to his daily writings and his inexplicable personal dislike for the late Calumet Farm owner Warren Wright, which carried over into a volatile disdain for Citation, I'd deliberately prod Charlie.

To hear him tell it, Hatton was a kid in knickers when he saw Man o' War do his thing. There was none greater than Big Red. I never really understood why he disliked Calumet Farm's Warren Wright, but that enmity sucked all of the fun and pride out of Thoroughbred racing's noblest dynasty. Hatton died a thousand deaths during those days of wine and roses when Whirlaway, Pensive, Armed, Fervent, Coaltown, Faultless, Ponder, and Citation ruled the game. And he rarely had nice things to say about the Jones boys, Ben and Jimmy.

He swore Citation never had a "snowball-chance-in-hell" to walk in Man o' War's cleats, debunking high praise to the contrary from such revered trainers as Sunny Jim Fitzsimmons and Max Hirsch. Though I resented his scorn, I tolerated some of it because Citation had failed to replicate his former greatness when brought back out of retirement in 1950–1951. And 1953, you'll recall, was Native Dancer's year for TV renown—with some unavoidable disgrace when "the Gray Ghost of Sagamore," as he was affectionately called, flopped miserably in the Kentucky Derby.

For a time, Native Dancer was Charlie Hatton's idol. Charlie waxed eloquent prior to the Dancer's Derby fiasco, and he donned sackcloth and ashes until the colt redeemed himself in both the Preakness and Belmont Stakes. When Native Dancer came, saw, and conquered by 9 gaping lengths in the 1-mile Arlington Classic, it took virtually the whole Chicago press box to pull Hatton down sober from Cloud Nine. Hatton was right: Native Dancer—a son of Polynesian and Geisha—was truly one of the sport's all-time greats. Beautifully named, too.

Hatton wasn't especially a fan of Eddie Arcaro. Thus, when the Dancer's regular jock, Eric Guerin, was set down for rough riding in New York as Washington Park's American Derby came into view, Charlie agonized over the fact that the Dancer's trainer, Bill Winfrey, unhesitatingly chose Arcaro for the ride. Hatton's loyalties were divided. He naturally wanted the Dancer to keep his charge toward racing immortality viable, but he wasn't happy that Arcaro got the nod.

"Any jockey could ride Native Dancer and win," Charlie observed sagely. He was right again. The Dancer, who like most oft-run campaigners was showing signs of wear, nevertheless hauled Arcaro home by 2½ lengths under a heavy 128 pounds, an eased-up 1⅛ miles tally in 1:48⅖, a fifth off the track record.

The Dancer pulled up a little iffy and wouldn't race again as a 3-year-old, though clearly he established his heroism and class. In

1954 he would be selected Horse of the Year, off only three winning starts. Such was Native Dancer's measure of greatness.

But Charlie Hatton wasn't satisfied. Two decades later, a bit shriveled and weary, he renounced Native Dancer as all-time Thoroughbred No. 1, passing the baton to none other than stately Secretariat. By that time, Hatton was no longer a Chicago press box regular—I'll tell why in just a moment—but his languorous prose bespoke "the newest, greatest kid on the block," the awesome Secretariat.

All who came before—Man o' War, Count Fleet, Citation, even Native Dancer—were veritable plugs compared with Secretariat's dominance of the American turf stage, according to Hatton dogma. How he died all over again when Secretariat, whom he formally had knighted and sainted, dropped two of his four starts against older horses. No excuse was viable. Like many high and mighty before, Charles Hatton had fallen.

Hatton had a number of flaws, but during his 1953 Chicago stay, mostly because of his aggrandized *Daily Racing Form* repute, he won uneasy admiration and respect from Chicago's sports media. Because of his isolationist temperament, however, Charlie had erected a social barrier so he wouldn't have to cope with all of us pesky, plebian midwesterners on a day-to-day basis. Feeling sorry for this lonely man, Arlington's director of publicity offered turfdom's most knowledgeable scribe friendship. Well, Hatton not only loved Native Dancer, but he took a shine to the wife of Arlington's publicity director. She and Charlie flew the coop, leaving a shocked husband and two kids behind. The pair fled into eastern exile, never to darken Chicago's door again.

I should be mature enough to objectively appreciate and impartially separate Hatton's racing contributions from his amatory conquests. It was his kind of opinion and diversity—which ran deep and strong—that made horse racing. I was privileged to hear from his very lips the life and times of Man o' War and to appreciate why Sam Riddle's incomparable colt deserved his place in the expanding fabric of Thoroughbred prominence.

Hatton also reminded those among us privileged to be part and parcel of "when racing was racing" of yet another yardstick of

Thoroughbred class—the horse's win streak. My fondness for Olympic swimmer-turned-Tarzan Johnny Weissmuller honed my appreciation for the roles that consistency and record-longevity play in judging the athlete. Weissmuller's swimming records have long gone by the boards, but not his storied consistency, now legendary. He never, not once, finished second. Movieland's most famous Tarzan didn't know the meaning of the word "runner-up." Whether in preliminary or gold medal tests, he won every race. Weissmuller swam only fast enough to remain eternally unbeaten—a true badge of greatness.

Thus, Native Dancer deserved genuine accolade when as a 2-year-old he swept his 1952 nine-race juvenile campaign. Yes, he turned in a clinker, losing to Dark Star in the Kentucky Derby, a race he should have won were it not for a tentative ride by jockey Eric Guerin. He won everything thereafter, including 3 more as a 4-year-old, going into retirement with 21 wins and 1 second in 22 starts.

Man o' War suffered 1 lone defeat in his two-year career (1919–1920), posting 20 wins in 21 starts. It was in his seventh outing as a 1-year-old that Big Red dropped a shocking half-length decision to the aptly named Upset, in the August 13, 1919, Sanford Memorial Stakes at Saratoga. He proceeded to win his next 14, capped by a memorable match race drubbing of the 1919 Triple Crown king, Sir Barton.

Secretariat also underscored consistency as a definitive barometer of nobility, racking up score after score both as a 2- and 3-year-old, worthy of two Horse of the Year titles. He was awesome, to be sure. One scribe penned: "his colossal stride, his huge girth, those steel-tempered legs . . . the pitiful sight of so many splendid horses lurching along in his wake." Secretariat had a strength and fury unheard of in the past quarter-century of Thoroughbred hoofbeats.

But not even Secretariat could quantitatively match either Man o' War or Native Dancer with their final career records of only one defeat during comparable campaigns. Secretariat lost as a 3-year-old prior to gathering the first Triple Crown in 25 years; he also was defeated by both Onion and Prove Out in subsequent races before finishing in 1973 in a blaze of glory.

It was immortal Citation who set the modern-day record for consecutive victories—16 straight, most of which he racked up in Triple Crown action, plus another 5, added to an earlier pair, against older, more seasoned campaigners.

"His record should have read—not 16—but 29 straight," Jimmy Jones often effused pardonably. Jimmy pointed out that Citation's only defeat as a 2-year-old was when jockey Steve Brooks intentionally kept him from beating Bewitch in the Washington Park Futurity. "It was a gift to her, our fault, since we were trying to keep her undefeated. And, the next spring, when that horse carried Citation to the outer rail, the first time he and Arcaro got together after Al Snider's death, it was only Arcaro's lack of familiarity, and faith, in his new mount that prevented him from salvaging that loss."

Citation launched his victory string in the Chesapeake on April 17 and captured his next 14 in 1948, before being forced into early retirement by injury. Returning more than a year later as a 5-year-old, he won a 6-furlongs sprint in the slop at Santa Anita—his 16th straight!

"I'm proud he got the 16," Jimmy told me, "but it'd been a lot better to have had 20 for 20 as a 3-year-old, or 29 for 29 in a finished career. It just wasn't right, bringing him back as a 5-year-old. I tell you, he was just a shell of his old self."

Citation's modern-day record was amassed at the direct expense of a veritable Who's Who of champions from racing's glory days: Armed, Phalanx, Delegate, Coaltown, Bewitch, Free America, First Flight, Stepfather, Better Self, My Request, Escadru, Miss Grillo, Spy Song, Papa Redbird, Volcanic, Conniver, Nathoo, and Bolero. Mighty Cy's record was equalled, but nor surpassed, on July 13, 1996, when Allen Paulson's vaunted Cigar captured the specially created Citation Invitational Challenge at Arlington International Racecourse. Cigar's 16 straight victories enabled him to share the crown, albeit against lesser competition, but a subsequent loss denied him the pleasure of dethroning Mighty Cy.

I'd be foolishly naive not to expect some disputation regarding the comparative merits of those whom I choose to salute as racing's regally knighted Three Equine Musketeers—Citation, Secretariat, and Man o' War. Choice of top billing is yours.

I stepped into the announcer's booth in May 1959, and I had worked full-time at Arlington–Washington since 1955. Even before this time, a mighty swath of stately Thoroughbreds cut across turf horizons everywhere, but particularly in Chicago, where the sport's cream continued its rise to the top. My young head swirled under the hypnotic equine elegance of grand horses joined in combat, not only by jockeys Arcaro, Shoe, Hartack, Longden, and Atkinson, but also Manny Ycaza, Sammy Boulmetis, Dave Erb, Steve Brooks, Bobby Baird, Kenny Church, Conn McCreary, Ismael Valenzuela, and Johnny Adams.

Calumet Farm's hard-knocking Bardstown replaced the retired Armed as the nation's most fearsome gelding. E. Gay Drake's Swoon's Son returned "speed" to its noblest attainment. Calumet's Ponder gave new definition to "the late-run," as did his indefatigable son, Needles, from the D&H Stables. Needles' dramatic Derby charge from 16th in an unwieldy 17-horse field—some 20 lengths back at the half-mile pole—was stretch-running at its textbook best.

We've already touched on Native Dancer's near invincibility. A lot can be said for Joe Gavegnano's fleet Errard King. Let's not forget Greentree Stable's Hall of Fame, C. T. Chenery's Hill Prince, or Calumet Farm's Mark-Ye-Well, who leaped from the bench to spell the stable's 1952 Derby prince, Hill Gail. Also in the limelight were Swaps and Nashua, whose $100,000 winner-take-all match race in 1955 at Washington Park, was a precursor to upcoming personal encounters of such 3-year-old VIPs as Bold Ruler, Gen. Duke, and Gallant Man—all deserving of special consideration on their own.

Straight from the starting gate of my career as announcer, I had a soul-stirring afternoon on May 18, 1959, at old Washington Park. My second call was the day's second race—the second half of my opening daily double announcing effort. The winner was a maiden named Venetian Way, who would team up with Bill Hartack a year later to defeat Bally Ache in the 1960 Kentucky Derby, giving the youthful Hartack the second of five Derby tallies.

Less than two months later—by then I was less anxious, certainly more confident behind the mike—I called my first hundred grander, the Arlington Handicap, at 1$\frac{3}{16}$ miles on the turf, or grass. Grass racing had come of age, and the Arlington prize was being coveted for a second straight year by perhaps the greatest grass horse ever bred in the United States, the Kerr Stables' vaunted Round Table. No account of racing's glory days would be complete without Round Table and the "green"—as in grass and money—he personally helped pioneer.

Chapter Three

Knights of the Round Table

If Thoroughbred racing's golden days were truly as spellbinding as we claim, there had to be a string of years in which America's 3-year-old crop—annually glamorized by Triple Crown action—sparkled radiantly, basking in the limelight of exceptional fame and fortune. Man o' War faced no such grand array of starry challengers. Citation, Coaltown, Bewitch, My Request, Escadru, Volcanic, Billings, Papa Redbird, and Better Self came magnificently close in 1948. Nashua, Swaps, and Traffic Judge gave it the old college try in 1955. Needles, Swoon's Son, Fabius, and Career Boy made it a real horse race in 1956. In later years, such rivalries as Affirmed vs. Alydar (1978), Alysheba vs. Bet Twice (1987), and Sunday Silence vs. Easy Goer (1989) kept our juices pumping.

But it was the 1957 crop that probably took the cake: Bold Ruler, Gen. Duke, Gallant Man, Iron Liege, Federal Hill, and a rough-hewed interloper, Round Table—whose propensity for turf, or grass, aroused coast-to-coast attention. They simply don't make 'em like Round Table anymore, not from what I've seen through my trusty binoculars—and those binoculars don't lie.

How great was "all-horse" Round Table? He was turfdom's King Arthur! Unquestionably, he's one of my all-time Top 10. And I'm not just talking grass. Doubtlessly he was the first great, perhaps the greatest, grass horse bred in the United States. His preeminence, however, far outstrips his grass exploits. A cyclonic son of Princequillo, he was bred, born, and trained to give his all: sprinting a distance of ground, dirt as well as grass.

He feared no man's horse, and he never dodged an issue. You could beat him, yes, but you'd have to beat him honestly—and you could never take victory for granted. He'd be right back at your throat the very next time.

I barely recall Round Table when he was a 2-year-old of 1956. Most of the nation focused on Bold Ruler, a brash, erratic, blue-blooded son of Nasrullah out of the Discovery mare Miss Disco. Bold Ruler's speed was impelling backstretch gossip long before he made his racing debut. Bred by his owner, Wheatley Stable, and trained by icon Sunny Jim Fitzsimmons, the leggy son of Nasrullah—the latter had sired the equally quirky Nashua in 1952—dazzled clockers, effortlessly reeling off quarters in :22 or less without taking a second breath.

Here's a little breeding trivia you may not have known. Both Bold Ruler and Round Table were foaled at Claiborne Farm on the same day, April 6, 1954. Both were weaned, schooled, and trained at the same equine military academy. And they, along with others of their age class—Gallant Man, Gen. Duke, Federal Hill, and Iron Liege—would repeatedly cross swords, satisfying an insatiable appetite for battle that crowned the 1957 3-year-old crop as the most warlike of all time.

Astoundingly, none of the above 1957 stalwart 3-year-olds was enthroned 1956 2-year-old, though their campaigns were nothing short of yeoman achievement. That honor fell to Calumet Farm's Barbizon, son of 1945 Preakness winner Polynesian. It was a strikingly belated title quest, accomplished in less than six weeks. Barbizon delayed his 2-year-old bow until September 15, then streaked to four straight scores in just one month, before dropping a narrow tally to Clifford Lussky's quick-footed Federal Hill—who could sprint with any up to a mile—in the Garden State Stakes Trial. Barbizon, however, saved his best for last. He squeaked out a whisker decision over Federal Hill in what amounted to his sole stakes venture, the rich Garden State Stakes on October 27. Barbizon banked the richest winner's prize until then—$168,430.

Bold Ruler suffered ignominious defeat behind Barbizon that day, finishing a dreary 17th as heavy favorite. He went into the middle-distance affair as the nation's number-one 2-year-old, and he came out of it a leg-weary dud. In fact, he made yet another start that fall but flopped again, a direful last. Still, the enigmatic Bold

Ruler had done enough earlier as a 2-year-old to rate strong comparison to his elder stablemate-kinsman Nashua. He swept his first five starts as a juvenile, including a pair of blue-ribbon stakes for neophytes.

The Ruler wound up with a 2-year-old record of 7 wins in 10 starts—his last fiascos too bad to be true. He went into winter exile in Florida, as one scribe, reported, "something of a question mark (?); but emerged in 1957 as an exclamation point (!)."

And where was Round Table when all this was happening? Blocky at birth, but beautifully symmetrical and unblemished to a fault, Round Table spent his entire 2-year-old campaign finding himself—coming to grips, mostly through trial and error, with his ultimate destiny.

He was fast, but not fast enough for Bold Ruler. Round Table apparently could run all day, but it seemed to take him that long to stay with equally long-winded Barbizon. He knocked heads against the likes of Iron Liege, usually coming up a dollar short. (Gallant Man, meantime, skipped stakes engagements as a 2-year-old, and his quality was somewhat unknown when 1957 dawned.)

Yet in 1958, Round Table as a 4-year-old was unanimously acclaimed Horse of the Year, and Grass Horse of the Year for the second of three consecutive turf titles. Legitimate king of all he surveyed, Round Table destroyed his 1958 Arlington Handicap field under a heavy impost of 130 pounds.

I enjoyed discussing Round Table with all connections concerned: owners Mr. and Mrs. Travis Kerr, trainer Bill Molter, and, of course, jockey Bill Shoemaker. The Kerrs had money to burn. When they learned Round Table, a colt they had taken a shine to, was up for sale in February 1957, they came up with a blank check.

"We were dealing with some shrewd horse people," Kerr always recalled wistfully. "His breeder was Arthur Hancock Jr., and early on, when he sensed we liked the colt, the price tag was $40,000—that's the summer of his 2-year-old season. Well, the price skyrocketed, and by the time I authorized my agent, Dr. John Peters, to buy Round Table, it was up to $175,000, which was as big a sale there'd been up to that time. But I wanted him, but really not on the terms I was forced to accept."

Kerr said Hancock insisted on retaining 20 percent of Round Table as a stallion, a shrewd maneuver in hindsight, since ultimately Kerr's gallant champion would retire with a bankroll of $1,749,869 and the proud cachet of being the world's leading money-winning Thoroughbred at that time.

Trainer Bill Molter at first wasn't all that enthused over Round Table's potential. Molter told me: "He always tried too hard. He'd literally run right off his hocks." Molter pointed to the small joint in the colt's hind legs, just above the fetlock joint (the ankle in human anatomy). "How sore he'd get at times, we could never really know. But I'm sure it cost him many a race. Right away I knew there'd be some tracks that wouldn't suit him.

"He had this powerful forward thrust, and if he couldn't find a track to suit his stride, it had to cause some amount of pain, at least discouragement. In addition, we discovered he overstepped with his hind legs his front hoof prints by about a foot just when walking. It was, to say the least, a strange way of going. We had no idea then that turf, or grass, may prove the answer—at the same time, help correct his stride for the dirt, too."

To this day, the debate over why some horses prefer grass racing to dirt, or vice versa, continues hot and heavy. Of more recent vintage, Cigar was Round Table in reverse. He hated to run on grass, although he didn't mind eating it. Cigar, however, proved near invincible on the dirt.

Over the years, I've had discussions with such turf trainers as Harry Trotsek, Bobby Cramer, Noel Hickey, and Baldy Tinker; with jockey greats Arcaro, Shoe, and Hartack; with renowned grass riders Johnny Adams, Earlie Fires, and Ray Broussard. From these discussions, I've found the following to be the most plausible answer to the riddle: Running on turf, or grass, which should be natural for any horse, more so than dirt, there's less give. It's firmer, deeply rooted, so there's very little ground displacement. Certainly, except for occasional divots gouged during competition, very little soil is kicked back into the animal's face. More importantly, a grassy surface is perfect for horses who skip along, whose action is more of a glide than the pounding thrust that is better suited for dirt. A horse whose stride skips lightly over terrain can improve anywhere up to

10 lengths on grass. When he's paired with that kind of surface, he's capable of a strange, wonderful metamorphosis—greater power and personality.

Shoemaker, not the only rider to handle the Table, told me on the eve of the colt's second Arlington Handicap, in 1959, "Round Table's just as good, I believe, on the dirt; he's just better, a superstar, on the grass, that's all."

Few realize that when Iron Liege nipped Gallant Man in their controversial 1957 Kentucky Derby finish—which Shoe was slammed for misjudging—Round Table was finishing an unnoticed, unheralded third. The favored Bold Ruler, who'd eventually wind up 1957 Horse of the Year, was fourth. One might make a serious case against the Table's dirt prowess when he was upset in 1958 by Hal Bishop's Illinois-bred Bernburgoo in the Warren Wright Memorial at Arlington Park.

By 1959, racing's glory days had expanded to feature competition over the infield green, which gave a fascinating new dimension to the sport. Acceptance of racing on the sod didn't occur overnight, however. Grand old traditions give way grudgingly. It was unthinkable, virtually impossible, too, for Man o' War to depart racing's tradition of dirt racing. Colin, whose remarkable career (1907–1908) ended too soon, was unbeaten in 15 starts, all dirt of course. The brilliant foals of 1928, whence came Mate, Twenty Grand, and Equipoise, also restricted their feats to dirt. Nor would Calumet Farm deign to deploy its mighty troops—Whirlaway, Pensive, Citation, and Ponder—to a battlefield of grassy green.

But by the 1950s grass racing could no longer be denied; it was new, alive, and colorful. First, it would create new equine heroes over a medium all its own. Later, should horses like Round Table and John Henry prove capable of conquering both surfaces, their versatility would be certified beyond doubt.

Hartack rode Round Table to an impossibly close nose decision over Clem in the grassy 1958 Laurance Armour Memorial Handicap. Bill told me in the winner's circle that day: "He's all horse, a real Pro."

"A real Pro" said it all for me in 1959 as Round Table, again in receipt of Shoemaker, packed 132 pounds to a resounding neck victory over Manassas and Noureddin in 1:53⅗, a full second faster than he needed the year before. "He had to keep up with your call," Molter teased the following morning.

I remember the thrill: "That's Round Table leading by a length and a half . . . Manassas is second along the rail . . . Noureddin is closing ground third . . . and Anxious Moment fourth. That's Round Table . . . along the rail Manassas, and on the outside Noureddin . . . they come to the wire . . . Round Table wins it by a neck, Manassas is second, Noureddin third . . . the Arlington Handicap from Arlington Park!"

My Arlington Handicap stretch call, "right down to the wire," daringly broke tradition, ranks, and rules. I refused to shut my mike off inside the final 16th of a mile, as nationwide practice insisted. In those days, track announcers everywhere—Chicago, New York, Florida, California—could bring 'em to the wire in a radio or TV broadcast, but not until they shut off the track public address system. In all fairness, track fans probably rarely noticed. The PA systems for the most part weren't all that great, and crowd noise, as fans got to rooting loudly, would all but snuff out the caller's final moments—when the thrill figured to be the most galvanic.

I argued with the stewards and other racing officials who clung tenaciously to tradition. "What if you call the wrong horse in a photo finish?" they cried desperately.

"What if," I argued, "inside the final 16th, I miscalled the race, calling Bugaboo the winner? Would you pay off on Bugaboo? Of course not." Announcers occasionally make mistakes. Mistakes can be apologized for and corrected by official decree.

Finally, I begged Marje Everett, the Arlington–Washington CEO, to give me a chance to revolutionize the art of race-calling. She had initiated countless innovations, a major one being Chicago's emphasis on grass racing. She consented to my request without hesitation or regret. "Go to it, Phil," she ordained. "The track's ours, not the judges', and as long as there's nothing in the rules of racing that forbids it, let's make it work."

Other tracks at first resisted the change. New York for many years continued to kill the call once the field entered the final 16th.

So short-sighted. As if Luciano Pavarotti were asked to eschew hitting that high C for fear of not conquering the summit.

Naturally, I benefited from approval and sanction. Fans loved it. They could now lounge anywhere—inside, underneath the stands, or in the paddock area—and soak up my call. My style evolved into an even more exciting delivery as I raised my own bar, realizing I was now serving a whole new segment of fans. Bringing them to the wire was not simply a radical departure from the norm, or some experimental novelty to toy with. By smashing a worn-out tradition, it was a modernization long overdue. Thankfully, Round Table's people also endorsed the call to the wire.

Earlier, when I said they don't make horses like Round Table anymore, I wasn't joshing. This top-level Thoroughbred would conscientiously throw in four full-time seasons, ages 2 through 5, and make no fewer than 66 starts, an average of 16-plus each campaign. He posted 43 wins (66 winning percentage), went unplaced only 10 times in big-league company, and earned (wondrous for that period) $1,749,869, displacing the mighty Nashua ($1,288,565) as world's financial czar.

And that's just testimony to his rugged constitution. How's this for brilliance and versatility? Round Table earned his fame as grass great: he made 16 starts on the grass, winning 14. Fifty of his starts, however, were on dirt, of which he won 29. A few of his dirt triumphs, for that matter, dwarfed his grass feats. The fact is, dirt played an ever greater role than grass during one of Round Table's most meritorious periods.

Remember our criteria for equine greatness, including protracted win streaks against the best the house could offer? Man o' War managed 14 in succession; Colin got 15; Citation and Cigar still share the record of 16 straight. Other fine horses posted unbeaten seasons: Native Dancer as a 2-year-old; Tom Fool and Spectacular Bid as 4-year-olds. Well, in 1957, following a record-breaking 1⅛ miles victory in the Blue Grass Stakes at Keeneland in 1:47⅖—after which he was a strong third to Iron Liege and Gallant Man in the Derby—Round Table kicked off the best win skein since Citation, winning 11 straight at distances from 1 mile to 1¼ miles.

"He was fabulous," Shoemaker remarked. "Win after win, getting better with each one, actually defying someone to beat him."

What really impressed me was that only 3 of those 11 were on the grass. The other eight were on the dirt, a medium not considered the Table's cup of tea.

Better still—remember another yardstick for 3-year-old distinction? Taking on and humbling older opponents. Round Table vanquished all comers in the United Nations Handicap at Atlantic City on the turf, humbled older dirt foes in the Hollywood Gold Cup, then returned to Chicago for the Hawthorne Gold Cup, where he subdued the doughty 4-year-old speed demon, Swoon's Son. Shoe couldn't make that ride; Bill Harmatz ably substituted.

Round Table negotiated dirt not only flawlessly, but speedily. Trainer Bill Molter particularly took pride when Round Table galloped off with the 1¼ miles Hollywood Gold Cup, tying the track record of 1:58⅗. When Round Table uncorked his late run to collar Swoon's Son going away, he equalled Hawthorne's Gold Cup standard of 2:00⅕, also at 1¼ miles.

"Twice during his winning streak, it was next to impossible finding opposition willing to run against him," Molter waxed proudly. "They [the tracks] had to card special races in which all starters were guaranteed the same purse awards regardless of where they finished. And in three of those races, Round Table was considered such a standout, there was no betting allowed."

The only black eye Round Table suffered came that fall in the Trenton Handicap in New Jersey. Bold Ruler, who bounced back off his Derby fourth to win the Preakness, wreaking revenge on Iron Liege, once again was a powder keg, swamping rivals left and right. Bold Ruler pulverized them with sheer zip and eclat, including Belmont Stakes hero, Gallant Man, whom many considered unbeatable at distances 1¼ miles upward.

Only three disputed the 1¼ miles Trenton Handicap. Eddie Arcaro predicted victory for Bold Ruler despite the extra terrain. Shoe, for reasons we'll explain later, selected the tireless Gallant Man over the Table. Harmatz again appeared in the green silks of Mr. and Mrs. Travis Kerr.

Round Table, obviously leg-tired from his 11 straight scores, needed suicidal early foot to guarantee his patented late charge. Bold Ruler, on the other hand, benefited from Arcaro's uncanny sense of pace. He stole the lead at the start; led masterfully at every furlong marker; was shown the whip three times, a whip Arcaro never used; then coasted home by 3 over a frustrated Gallant Man in 2:01$\frac{3}{5}$. It was a strategic, jockey-assisted victory. Round Table was 8 lengths farther back.

Consequently, Bold Ruler, despite his many idiosyncrasies, understandably was awarded the baton as Horse of the Year. Round Table was properly assuaged, however, when he was promptly adjudged best grass horse in the nation. Some felt, yours truly included, that Round Table deserved the 1957 Horse of the Year title despite his futile Trenton try. Actually, he returned to California following that defeat and scored smartly under 130 pounds, bagging his 15th win in 22 outings as 1957 rolled to a close. The gutsy performer erased that voting blunder, vindicating himself with an even greater 1958 season, one which would crown him the best anywhere—on dirt or grass!

But I promised to explain Bill Shoemaker's choice of Gallant Man over Round Table. Sometimes jockeys, for whatever reason, jump ship—unconscionably switch mounts—as major stakes loom, particularly during spring Triple Crown action or Breeders' Cup competition in the fall. I was often perturbed when a rider for no apparent reason chose to forsake what had become a winning combination. I now think I know why Shoe in the Trenton selected Gallant Man over Round Table. He did so out of a strange amalgam of loyalty and guilt.

Tiny Bill Shoemaker was a native of Fabens, Texas, which put him in close proximity with Gallant Man's owner, millionaire oilman Ralph Lowe of Midland, Texas. By 1957 Derby Day, Shoe and Lowe's Gallant Man loomed a powerful threat. The threat intensified when the pre-race favorite, Calumet Farm's big hitter, Gen. Duke, came up with a career-ending injury on Derby morning. Bill Hartack then jumped aboard Gen. Duke's lesser-regarded entrymate, Iron Liege; Arcaro, of course, stuck with favored Bold Ruler;

and Shoe sat more confidently than ever in Gallant Man's stirrups as the band played "My Old Kentucky Home."

Hark back, if you will, to the late stretch of the 1957 Derby. Bold Ruler already had removed himself from serious race contention when Arcaro complied with trainer Sunny Jim's command "to rate the so-and-so," an attempt that rankled the sensitive favorite. Bold Ruler spit the bit before the final half-mile, though winding up a decent fourth. Iron Liege took advantage of Bold Ruler's rankness and stole out to an early lead. Nursed patiently by Hartack, he was still in front in mid-stretch when Gallant Man exploded full tilt.

Great riders rarely make mistakes, especially when engaged in Olympian competition. Yet observers say Shoe made an error that day—one that inspired gossip and notoriety during racing's memorable days of glory. When Gallant Man had just overhauled Iron Liege some 100 yards from paydirt, the experts say Shoe misjudged or prejudged the finish line, standing up in the irons for one lousy stride. Realizing his mistake, he recovered instantly and went back to riding, but the damage was done. The mental lapse supposedly enabled Iron Liege to eke out a controversial nose victory.

Rare as it was, it wasn't the first time the accomplished Shoemaker had misbehaved so indiscreetly. He erred a year earlier when he fell asleep aboard Swaps in the Californian Stakes, losing out to a quixotically monikered stakes horse named Porterhouse. He did contribute to Swaps's defeat that day.

I had endless talks concerning the Gallant Man faux pas with Shoe and his agent, Harry Silbert, over the years, including a public interview held when Shoe journeyed to Chicago's Hawthorne Race Course on November 26, 1989, during his nationwide retirement tour. Shoe was riding races and conversing with his army of fans.

I'm definitely in the minority, but my judgment is that his momentary peccadillo had no real bearing on the Derby result. I've watched the incident replay a hundred times, and I'm not convinced he ever took the lead from Iron Liege before bouncing upright for one split second, if that. Having witnessed some 100,000 races, I'm positive Gallant Man never sensed, let alone felt, Shoe's miscue. For sure, Gallant Man neither slowed nor broke stride. Rather he clung doggedly to his task, but he simply couldn't outgun Iron Liege in the final strides.

Diffident and modest as always, Shoe smiled timidly when defended by yours truly before hundreds of Chicago fans eager to pay homage to one of racing's greatest athletes. Incidentally, upon retirement in February 1990, Shoe was the world's undisputed "winningest" jockey of all time—8,833 wins!

What made the 1957 Derby incident even more noteworthy was that owner Ralph Lowe, just a night or two before Derby Day, had a dream—nightmare was more like it—of what actually would happen. Despite being armed with such insight, Shoe committed the unthinkable. Happily, a crestfallen Shoemaker was readily forgiven by Gallant Man's magnanimous owner.

Haunted by that mortifying moment on the track, however, Shoe earned a measure of vindication when he piloted Gallant Man to a monumental Belmont Stakes 8-length victory in American record time of 2:26⅗ for 1½ miles. When push came to shove in the titular Trenton Handicap in New Jersey, Shoe felt compelled to ride Gallant Man, stressing that his choice in no way was based on opinion as to Round Table's and Gallant Man's relative merits.

It's been said that Gallant Man rates the dubious honor of having raced over American soil without capturing a championship ring of any kind. Well, he was a blueblood for certain, having been bred by the Aga Khan. And he did annihilate his peers with a peerless Belmont Stakes victory. And he was regularly hailed by Shoe as "the greatest distance horse I ever rode"—that is, until pint-sized Tom Rolfe came along a decade later.

When assessing Round Table, you have to consider his incredible gift of versatility. All he needed was a surface over which to cavort. Grass became his noted forte. But he'd beat you on the dirt, too, and with amazing consistency. He followed up his 1957 Hawthorne Gold Cup triumph on the dirt with an equally sensational repeat victory the next fall en route to unprecedented honors—Horse, Grass, and Handicap Champion of 1958. With Shoe back in the saddle for the 1958 Hawthorne Gold Cup, Round Table overhauled Swoon's Son, the latter famed as probably the horse who won more Chicago area stakes than any other Thoroughbred in history. As with Round Table, Swoon's Son proved his resourcefulness by demonstrating he too loved the infield green.

Now an unequivocal fact: Chicago racetracks—Arlington, Washington, and Hawthorne—pioneered grass action, championing its cause and effect long before any other major racing center in the United States.

It was during the Lindheimer–Everett reign, particularly in the 1950s, that grass, or turf as it became known, blasted up and away like Superman, lending not only variety but also color and spectacle to a sport that, by virtue of dirt-course domination, had become somewhat dusky, drab, and direly in need of fresh inspiration.

Yes, Chicago had grass racing before the 1950s. Turf racing actually debuted in Illinois at Arlington Park as far back as 1934. As early as 1941, Arlington considered switching its Handicap from dirt to grass. By 1942, the track had substantially banked its grass course turns, maximizing safety for both horse and rider. Hawthorne, in 1947, began construction on a new infield 6-furlongs grass course. In 1948, racing on the sod returned to Hawthorne after a 44-year absence. But for years, horsemen—especially hard-nosed, traditional Kentucky hard boots—gave grass no more than a shrug-shouldered yawn. "Dirt's the name of the game," was their choirlike retort.

If glory days were truly to resonate and flourish, however, the sport needed a potent shot in the arm, a shiny new glow, the kind of colorful zap and vigor only grass could inject. The first thing fans like myself noticed about grass was its required emphasis on distance. For example, Arlington's inner 1-mile turf course—encircled by its spacious 1⅛ miles dirt oval—translated into very few sprints. Five-and-one-half furlongs was the longest dash the track would accommodate. Start distances then had to jump upward to 1¹⁄₁₆ miles to avoid a dangerous early charge into the clubhouse turn. Fans loved to see horses loaded up in full sight; grass racing made those scenes available on a daily basis.

Apparently as I grow older, my hindsight sharpens like iron against iron. In retrospect, I can almost exactly pinpoint when and why racing over the inner oval got airborne.

Citation in 1948 faced a bonny band of top-drawer 3-year-olds, most of whom by mid-summer were enervated, leg-weary, and understandably disheartened, given the futility of chasing after what every horsemen called the greatest colt who ever lived. But I recall one valiant steed in particular: Volcanic, owned by the Walmac Farm, trained by Howard Wells, routinely ridden by Angel Rivera. Wells regularly had been quietly working Volcanic over Washington Park's lush sod so as not to annoy the racing establishment.

Jockey Rivera later revealed: "We knew beating Citation was impossible. Every owner and trainer knew that. Wells said we'd try him one last time in the American Derby. I didn't ride him that day. Bad enough we had to try Citation, but Calumet started him as an entry with Free America." Rivera recalls Volcanic finishing third to Citation and Free America that day. "Hey, we had ourselves a real runner in Volcanic, but we were only breaking his heart against Citation."

Concomitant with introducing Volcanic to "racing over the weeds," as some hard-boiled horsemen called it, Wells chose to go where Citation wasn't. That included Hawthorne's 1949 fall meeting. Citation had retired, and Volcanic promptly won the Bidwill Memorial and Hawthorne Gold Cup. Both were on the dirt, both without you-know-who.

Despite his prowess on dirt, Volcanic broke ranks with craven Class A runners who spurned grass. In 1949 he became the first modern-day grass specialist. He won Arlington's Meadowland Handicap in record time of 1:54$\frac{4}{5}$ for 1$\frac{3}{16}$ miles, then crackled at Hawthorne, annexing the Autumn Handicap in American record time of 1:35$\frac{3}{5}$ for the mile.

Volcanic opened the door. No self-respecting horse need ever again steer clear of grass. The fascinating new medium took on a life of its own, thanks to one valorous pioneer—Volcanic.

Yet the industry dragged anchor. There'd be no formal recognition of grass racing, not until 1953, when Iceberg II gained official notoriety as America's first Grass Horse Champion. But Iceberg II wasn't bred in this country—he was born in Chile. The 1954 turf champ was another foreigner, English-bred Stan, who, prior to

Round Table, was the greatest turf horse in the world. Stretch-rusher par excellence, Stan was last as the field entered the final half-mile in the 1954 Arlington Handicap. Then he detonated from 5 lengths off the race's high-flying leader a furlong out, to 5 widening lengths over the latter at the finish—an unbelievable 10-length exchange in less than 220 yards!

By then, the Hasty House Farms of Allie and Billie Reuben awoke to the fresh brew of grass racing. They imported foreign-bred after foreign-bred—be they South American, English, or Irish—to settle American turf. Hasty House Farms's imported Platan won the 1955 Arlington 'Cap that summer, but, being a foreign-bred, he didn't exactly coincide with Arlington's plan to attract top-class American-breds. In fact, Hasty House was copping virtually every turf stakes in sight. With each victory, the Reubens and trainer Harry Trotsek would return abroad to purchase and import new talent.

British-bred St. Vincent was elevated to turf king in 1955. Finally, in 1956, an American deigned to accept the award. His name was Career Boy, and the barrier was broken once and for all. Round Table thereafter stepped front and center, affording grass racing its overdue legitimacy. Racing's glory days were firmly entrenched!

Give credit where credit is due. Ben Lindheimer and his daughter Marje Everett gave racing spin into succeeding decades. Marje's friendship with owner Rex Ellsworth and trainer Mesh Tenney—they of Swaps fame—helped American Thoroughbred racing turn the corner. Seeking color and diversity for the upcoming Swaps–Nashua match on August 31, 1955, Marje convinced her father to switch the time-honored American Derby to the grass. The Lindheimer–Everett combine knew that grass racing would never achieve true potential unless champion equines were willing to test their wares over the new medium, and Swaps's people consented. When Swaps demolished his opponents, including one of Hasty House Farms's fine imports, Summer Solstice, in the 1955 American Derby, the day of realization arrived.

A few Thoroughbred die-hards continued to balk at Arlington–Washington's renewed grass emphasis, but that was only sour grapes. The die had been cast; more stables, owners, trainers, horses, and jockeys were giving grass a second look.

It wasn't until 1956 that Chicago was finally glorified as the nation's grass capital. Marje Everett knew that to make grass creditable, she'd have to lure 3-year-olds of Triple Crown caliber. Therefore, when late-running whiz Needles from D&H Stables (owned by Oklahomans Jack Dudley and Bonnie Heath) uncoiled from 16th to win the Kentucky Derby over Calumet Farm's Fabius, the latter a quality son of Citation, Arlington's first thought was "We must get Needles here for the American Derby," which was set for the second time at 1³⁄₁₆ miles on the grass.

Fabled Calumet Farm still harbored reservations about grass, so Fabius sat out the American Derby, deferring to E. Gay Drake's lightning-like Swoon's Son, who earlier had vanquished Calumet's best 3-year-old in the 1-mile dirt Arlington Classic. Fabius, incidentally, prevented Needles from sweeping the Triple Crown, whipping the latter in the Preakness, after which Needles restored supremacy in the tailor-made 1½ miles Belmont.

Grass racing had another winning ace up its sleeve, one that attracted smaller stables, less wealthy owners, and shoestring-strapped trainers who never dreamed they'd ever be able to knock heads against "the big boys" in major stakes and features. Grass was racing's Cinderella story! Horses who didn't stand much of a chance against quality opponents on the dirt were now being magically transformed into first-class citizens on the grass.

"Swoon's Son never need apologize for what he's accomplished on the dirt," his husky trainer, A. G. "Lex" Wilson, told me during the summer of 1956. "Hell, he won everything in sight—both Futurities as a 1955 2-year-old, seven races in all, six of 'em in a row. And he was even better as a 3-year-old, again winning everything around, even knocking off Fabius in the 1-mile Arlington Classic. If he had an Achilles' heel, it was a distance of ground. I don't think anybody'd beat him up to a mile or a mile and a 16th. So when it came to a distance of 1³⁄₁₆ miles, I turned him to grass. And he loved it at first sight."

Arlington played up the 1956 American Derby as a true test of speed vs. stamina—Swoon's Son as rabbit, Needles as hound. Dave

Erb, regular rider for both Swoon's Son and Needles, was forced to choose the latter, lest he be crucified by the colt's irascible trainer, Hugh Fontaine. Eddie Arcaro gladly climbed aboard Swoon's Son, who punctiliously led at every marker to register a half-length victory over The Warrior and Toby B. What about Needles? Fifth at mid-stretch, only three lengths behind Swoon's Son, Needles was still fifth at wire's end, still three lengths behind the winner.

Making the ace Swoon's Son even more formidable was only one tasty morsel on grass-racing's mouth-watering menu. It was making "something out of nothing" that became the medium's big headline grabber. There were many examples. I'll relate just three.

Owner Charles Fritz was disheartened with his gray horse, Sir Tribal. Trainer Steve Ippolito searched hard and in vain to find the horse's hole card. It was Chicago-born jockey Tony Skoronski who suggested Sir Tribal should be tried on the sod.

"Grass was just what the doctor ordered," Ippolito beamed. "Sir Tribal not only came to himself by winning, but he improved with every start. We even won a few stakes with him—all because he started to believe in himself."

Sir Tribal's finest moment occurred in the 1956 Stars and Stripes 'Cap on July 4, by which time Bill Hartack had become his regular pilot. Skoronski, however, was in the stands, graciously cheering wildly for Chicago's newest turf discovery.

Morton Johnson's Hard Rock Man belied his name on the dirt. He could run all day, true, but it took him all day to get untracked on the main course. Then, one day, he tried grass. Voila! Hard Rock Man's a winner, a multiple stakes hero.

Among the various tales of metamorphic change is John Zitnik's Manassas, named for the Virginia home of the Civil War battles. Neither Zitnik nor his colt Manassas, however, harbored any such warlike ideas of grandeur. Zitnik looked and spoke like actor Wallace Beery. He owned no other horse; Manassas was his one-horse stable. And Zitnik served as breeder, owner, trainer, and groom. "I would have ridden him in races, too, if I wasn't so fat," he always chuckled.

Manassas was just another Thoroughbred bum on the dirt. "He hated dirt in his face," Zitnik shrugged, "and he had no speed to get out of its way. So he was always far back—far back."

Zitnik said it was trainer Baldy Tinker, himself a grass proselyte, who insisted Manassas be introduced to the infield green.

"Baldy was so right," Zitnik said. "Manassas must've thought he died and went to horse heaven. He kicked and squealed just like a yearling—he was already a 4-year-old, with no real future as a racehorse at all."

Clockers could never really keep a secret, so word got around Arlington. I believe Manassas's first grass start was in a sprint; he uncoiled from dead last to win in a photo. I even bet $2 on him that day, so reliable was the inside track info. A week later, now moved up to 1$\frac{1}{16}$ miles on the turf, Manassas again showed off his new personality. Rallying powerfully from next-to-last, he won going away. Manassas started three more times on the grass—winning all three. The nation's newest Cinderella grass horse was born.

Manassas's incredible win streak was climaxed by his two richest grass triumphs, the 1957 Stars and Stripes and the Arlington Handicaps. John Zitnik's only horse was a national hero—thanks to the miracle of grass.

There's a pleasing sidebar to Manassas's phenomenal grass success story. Remember the hapless jockey Doug Dodson, a national riding phenom in the mid and later 1940s, who quit Calumet Farm in a huff when he couldn't have his way with stable star Citation? By the 1950s, Doug no longer ruled the jockey roost. He was just another journeyman rider. No more days of wine and roses. Oh, he'd get an occasional allowance or minor stakes mount, but no more Armed, no Faultless, no Bewitch, no Pot o' Luck, certainly no more Citation.

Well, Doug rang the bell with Manassas. The corrugated frown he wore since 1948 was finally replaced by smiles. It was good hearing Doug laugh again. He had been out of the spotlight too long. For the record, when Manassas and Dodson registered their 1957 Arlington Handicap score, it was at the direct expense of Swoon's Son, whose lead vanished in the shadow of the finish wire.

Manassas continued a formidable force. He was still winning as a 6-year-old two seasons later. Recall my first hundred grander as a race caller, the grassy 1959 Arlington Handicap won by Round Table under a heavy 132 impost? The horse catching him, but falling a neck short, was none other than Manassas. By then, Zitnik, Manassas, and Dodson were rolling in deep clover.

But our story of the Knights of the Round Table isn't quite over. We lauded Round Table as turfdom's King Arthur; we also applauded him as Master of Dirt when challenged. In his back-to-back Hawthorne Gold Cup victories (1957–1958), he collared Swoon's Son both times. But Swoon's Son proved he could handle Round Table in the roughest of going. Especially at a distance of 1 mile or less.

Swooney won four stakes as a 1957 4-year-old under weight 130 pounds or more, including the Equipoise Mile at Arlington under 132. He was an undaunted 5-year-old in Round Table's 1958 Horse of the Year campaign. Swooney repeated his Equipoise success, this time under an imposing 129 pounds. In a dazzling display of speed and endurance, he outgamed three of America's finest handicap stars: Bardstown, Clem, and yes, mighty Round Table himself!

As racing's glory days sparkled brilliantly through the 1960s, many other outstanding Thoroughbreds capitalized on the dirt-grass crossover, and it was the Lindheimer–Everett–Hawthorne foresight that invitingly opened the door through which a champions' parade, including Round Table, Swoon's Son, Clem, and Manassas, accommodatingly walked. The electrifying speed merchant Dr. Fager, whose world-record 1:32⅕ mile at Arlington Park in 1968 withstood attack for three decades, wore two crowns—Horse of the Year and Grass Horse of the Year. The same could be said for the great Secretariat in 1973, who conquered both mediums to the delight of his myriad of admirers.

Another exceptionally fine equine also caught my eye. The year was 1960. I was in my second of 34 years of race-calling. He wasn't what you'd call "a full horse." He had been neutered. He was an iron-legged gelding, maybe the greatest gelding of 'em all. His name was Kelso.

Chapter Four

Golden Geldings

If humans could talk to horses, how would trainers—such as Wayne Lukas and Bob Baffert of today, or Sunny Jim Fitzsimmons and Ben Jones of yesterday—explain or rationalize the sharpest cut of all, castration? I'm sure they'd say that it helps keep a colt's mind on the racing career for which he was duly ordained at birth. Ungelded males might have other things on their minds.

"Boys," their trainers might counsel, "no distractions. Mind your p's and q's. No witless, pigheaded, or wayward temper tantrums, and, particularly, no ribald or randy behavior around the gals." In other words, "Control your hormones."

A colt can qualify as a "stallion" when his racing is finis. He ascends to the rank of "sire" once he fathers offspring and "sire" is the industry's badge, or ring, of distinction. An intuitive colt need not be an equine Rhodes Scholar to see the wisdom in muzzling his libido, saving his precious virility for when it really matters. As sure as the nostrils on the face, the wise colt realizes that legitimate sexual lust is well worth the wait. A life Casanova would hungrily relish rewards such patience and control.

Some Thoroughbreds, however, much like some humans, must live life minus love's most passionate kiss. Not all that idyllic, true, but where would racing be without its shimmering honor roll of golden geldings—of which Kelso is undisputed bellwether? From 1960 through 1964, the Horse of the Year title went to the powerful and talented Kelso.

Human athletes—baseball, football, hockey, basketball, tennis, and golf—are judged on continuity of performance. Star players return year after year to build interest and sustain momentum. An equine athlete's all too brief track career can fail to generate loyal fan interest. The good or great Thoroughbred—at least, one who wasn't gelded—can ill afford not to succumb to the lure of the breeding shed. The sport is awash annually with new babies, or foals, as racing faithfully renews and reinvents itself.

Sure, Whirlaway raced long enough to garner two consecutive Horse of the Year titles. Same for Challedon those two years before Mr. Longtail. Native Dancer racked up two Crowns, as did Secretariat. Affirmed demonstrated supremacy as both a 3- and 4-year-old. For their ilk, the stud barn wields an irresistible, and rich, influence—and well it should.

It's a different story for geldings. With the exception of Triple Crown champs and near champs, it's the gelding who makes, and keeps making, fans by competing season after season, assuming he remains sound and competitively viable. Let's play Thoroughbred Trivial Pursuit. What do Exterminator, Phar Lap, Cigar, Armed, Bardstown, Assault, Forego, Kelso, Royal Glint, Find, Social Outcast, and John Henry have in common?

If you said they're all geldings, you'd be wrong! But then, it was a trick question. Did you catch the two who weren't geldings? They easily could have been, since both Cigar and Assault proved sterile before or following retirement. They never reproduced their kind. Sad, too, because Triple Crown winner Assault remained a turf terror through age 7, while Cigar, who in 1996 equaled Citation's modern-day record of 16 straight wins, finally retired as the world's leading money-winning Thoroughbred of all time.

Like the others, who were geldings, Cigar and Assault were able to perpetuate fame and sustain notoriety long after colts and horses were routinely retired as "potent progenitors." Unfortunately, some equine champs are retired before their time, their concerned owners and breeders unwilling to chance an untimely defeat or two which might detract from their stallion's breeding promise.

Racing's golden geldings helped solve one pressing concern: how to keep an able equine on the track where he can make fans and retain admirers. Forego, who had the misfortune of being foaled in Secretariat's crop, ripped off three straight Horse of the Year titles (1974–1976). He was famous for courage and stamina. In addition, his late kick—reminiscent of Whirlaway, Pensive, Ponder, Needles, and Carry Back—was crowd-pleasing at its very best.

Kelso shattered all records with his five straight Horse of the Year crowns (1960–1964). Only the most unpracticed sports buff didn't know the name Kelso. Pretty good for a gelding. Pretty wonderful, too, since he was the first 3-year-old in racing history (the polls were started in 1936) to be voted Horse of the Year without having won at least one Triple Crown event. He didn't even try in 1960, his 3-year-old season launched after wins by Venetian Way, Bally Ache, and Celtic Ash in the Derby, Preakness, and Belmont, respectively.

Kelso was my kind of horse, the kind of giving athlete that helped establish Thoroughbred racing as America's number-one spectator sport. Kelso made several Chicago appearances, and it was my pleasure to call 'em all. His daddy was Your Host, noted for speed and alacrity. From his dam, Maid of Flight, a pertinacious daughter of 1943 Triple Crown hero Count Fleet, Kelso probably inherited most of his hardy endurance. Though New York–based, Kelso loved traveling under the artful tutelage of his minikin trainer, ex-jockey Carl Hanford. Carl's brother Ira "Babe" Hanford, a far better rider, won the Kentucky Derby in 1936 aboard Bold Venture.

Kelso was the last great horse that jockey Eddie Arcaro rode regularly. In April 1962, still buoyant and rigorous at 46, Arcaro sent shock waves through the wide world of sports with the news that he was retiring from the saddle! Kelso had just concluded an extraordinary 4-year-old campaign under Eddie, grabbing the second of his Horse of the Year crowns. Why Arcaro pulled retirement out of the hat will be explained later.

Kelso, thanks to Hanford's candor and rare perspicacity, afforded me valuable insight into the Thoroughbred psyche. I became privy to Kelso's soul and attitude, also the physical and emotional forces that drove his fabled spirit. Midway through Kelso's five-year kingly reign, Hanford frankly discussed the obstacles that Kelly had surmounted on his legendary climb to greatness.

"Phil, early on, whether or not it had to do with him having been gelded at an early age, I noticed changes in his personality. He had become a 'get-up-and-go,' a take-charge, bull-headed bloke who'd crouch before no man's horse. And he loved training and racing," Carl told me. "But there were two things that seemed to bother him a bit," he continued, finger to his lips. "One, he had unusually tender hooves. We had to have him shod with great care. Otherwise—you could see it in his eyes—he'd start to hurting. And two, although he had good natural speed, he really preferred to come from out of it. He didn't like to be pushed early."

"I had heard he was a bit moody and uneasy at times, that he needed stable pets to calm him down?" I suggested.

"Naw, not that I know of, certainly not after I got to know him as a 3-year-old," Carl replied. "Yea, I had heard that he had a couple pets, two dogs, when he was a 2-year-old. And Mrs. duPont took those dogs everywhere she went—but not with Kelly, as he was known around the barn or in his stall." Kelso's breeder was Mrs. Richard C. duPont.

Hanford told me, "though he liked the grass, he was somewhat of a disappointment on the turf at first, though he did win his first try on the grass. I was hoping he'd excel on turf the way he did on dirt, since so many rich stakes and handicaps were being offered or switched over to the turf following the grass popularity explosion of the 1950s."

It wasn't that Kelly was a slow learner, nothing like that, Carl verified. "Remember, I didn't have him as a 2-year-old. He was already 3 when I was hired on as trainer. I had no idea how great he'd become. Heck, we had to get to know one another first. But then, one day, late in 1960—I had him then as a 3-year-old—he showed me a special glint in his eye." Carl soon shared this insight with jockey Eddie Arcaro. "I told Eddie about it, and he agreed. Maybe we had something special here?"

Like so many great geldings, past or present, Kelly took his sweet time coming around. "I was hoping against hope that he might be that one in a thousand who'd make you happy just getting up each morning," Hanford said. As it turned out, Hanford would wake up aglow—actually enraptured—every morning right through 1964 as extraordinary Kelso dominated racing with a sustained brilliance unsurpassed during the 20th century.

Which gets us back to the rare notion of what important role geldings played during racing's golden age. The question bears repeating: how satisfying could it be if Mark McGwire, Barry Bonds, Babe Ruth, Mickey Mantle, Roger Maris, or Sammy Sosa performed for no more than a year or two?

Let's consider another factor besides longevity. Let's add "top weight-carrier" to our formula for measuring depth of greatness among Thoroughbreds. Extra poundage isn't normally piled on a Thoroughbred's back until he reaches 4 years of age. By then, most greats or near greats have already sought rich sanctuary in the stud barn, so weight is a missing link in determining just how outstanding a horse might have been.

Geldings, however, can race beyond 4, 5, 6, or even longer, toting high weight in lucrative, definitive handicap stakes. "Weight," it's said around racetracks, "can stop a freight train." True for the most part, but many an august gelding has proved the exception to the rule.

Put my back to the wall and a gun at my head—go ahead, order me to list the Top 10 golden geldings of all time. I'd have to include (not necessarily in order of quality) Exterminator, Phar Lap, Armed, Bardstown, Find, Social Outcast, Kelso, Royal Glint, Forego, and John Henry. Any argument?

Exterminator, lovingly known as "Old Bones," was before my time. The first of the golden geldings I'd see was Calumet Farm's Armed. Had there been a canvass to select the "gelding most likely not to succeed," Armed would have accepted that dubious award, but not without some pardonable embarrassment. Despite regal breeding—like virtually every other Calumet homebred, he was a son of Bull Lea (his dam was Armful)—he neither slobbered nor sucked on any silver spoon at birth. He wasn't downright ugly as a yearling, nor handsome, but he was implacably studdish, violating each and every principle of "decent behavior" laid out at this chapter's beginning.

Armed was a just-turned 2-year-old-in-training when Ben Jones ordered him back to the farm to be gelded. And because Calumet was knee-deep in regal raceable bloodstock, Armed, no longer "a full horse," was all but forgotten as potential racing material. Following castration he was returned to Arlington Park as a lead pony, an unwanted, or unneeded, vestigial racehorse. For several weeks he was used to pony other horses during morning works and trials and to escort the stable's afternoon starters in post parades headed toward the gate.

Jockey Alfred Robertson, whose career was done in by height and weight after riding Whirlaway to victory in the American Derby at Washington Park, remembers Armed "as if it were yesterday."

"Armed was no longer a bad boy," Robertson revealed. "He settled down nicely. He had sorrowful eyes, Armed did, as if wondering why he was nothing more than a lead pony. I told Ben about it, and he agreed to give him one more chance. That was 1944—Armed had just turned 3. And he'd never be a lead pony again—that's for sure!"

Ben Jones took his time with Armed, though the brown gelding was eager to learn, more eager to compete. He started seven times as a 3-year-old and won three, still nothing to write home about. Just how good would Armed become?

As a 4-year-old, after going unplaced in his first start, he unleashed a staggering three-year campaign consisting of 36 successive races in which he never failed to nail down a piece of the pot. During one span, he piled up 11 wins, and in 10 straight races packed 130 pounds of more, conceding gobs of weight to every rival except one—he shared top impost with a horse named Buzfuz in one handicap. During his 1945 season, Armed enriched Calumet coffers by $288,715, equaled or smashed four track records, lost one in record time, another in world-record time. It was a good year for any man's horse, a sensational one for a former lead pony. And Armed was just getting started.

He'd lose occasionally, but never embarrassingly, and he'd always bounce back off the canvas. On August 31, 1946, he dominated the Whirlaway Stakes at Washington Park. I was there, crazy with glee, focusing my binoculars on his every movement, because the former lead pony had just hiked his career bankroll to $342,875, displacing the immortal Phar Lap as the world's all-time money-winning gelding! I was back a week later. This time Armed ran off and hid to annex the Washington Park Handicap. He would turn 6 that January 1—but he still had worlds to conquer!

Armed reigned supreme as 1947 Horse of the Year. He was Doug Dodson's favorite mount, and the sad reason Dodson severed ties with Calumet when he and Armed were whipped so decisively by 3-year-old Citation in February 1948. But by Armed's retirement, his sterling record read 41 wins, 20 seconds, 10 thirds, in 81 starts, with earnings of $817,475. For one brief period, the former Calumet Farm lead pony proudly strutted around Chicago area tracks as the world's leading money-winner of all time!

As testimony to the effect a gelding's tenure-longevity can have on a loyal racing public, Armed had his own fan club, of which I was a card-carrying, T-shirt wearing member. There were hundreds of us, young and old alike, girls and guys. He'd compete, and we'd all show up with banners and cheers. Armed was a national hero; he was even more beloved in Chicago, which was his home base.

And—this is most important—he gained his fame and glory against horses just like him, horses like Assault, the 1946 Triple Crown champ, whose racing career was extended when he was found sterile following early retirement. There was also Stymie, whose forte was distance. Though not a gelding, Stymie generously campaigned beyond his fourth racing season. I recall a rivalry survey-study among the three—Armed, Assault, and Stymie—embracing 11 contests. Armed won four, Assault won four, and Stymie took the other three. Now that's competition, nobody ducking anyone.

I wasn't a Stymie fan. My fault and loss, because he was legitimate, and he could run all day. Assault won me over in 1947 when King Ranch trainer Max Hirsch impressed Eddie Arcaro as the veteran's new jockey to turn around a bad losing streak. It worked, and Assault spectacularly returned to his winning ways.

I was tormented the day—September 22, 1947—Armed and Assault met one-on-one in their special New York match race. Everyone knew Assault was hurting, and Armed demolished a gimpy Assault by 8 lengths, the latter pulled up in the final furlong. It was a hollow triumph for Armed, but it made national headlines. The race was covered like the World Series. Not even an ill-advised stinker of a match race could dampen racing's golden age.

Naturally I never got to call Armed, but unless sick or unavoidably detained elsewhere, I saw his every Chicago appearance. I never saw either Exterminator or Phar Lap, but I know they're among the greatest geldings of all time, horses whose stamina and fortitude set the standard, also raised the bar, for the likes of Armed, Kelso, Forego, and John Henry, among others.

Eddie Arcaro was a 2-year-old kid in 1918, the year Exterminator began a four-year reign as America's top money-winning handicap performer, banking a paltry $26,402. Exterminator would double that check to $52,405 in 1920, the same year that marvelous Man o' War would earn a record $166,140 as a 3-year-old.

No one—well, maybe one—has ever accused Exterminator of being Man o' War. But he was toasted by succeeding fan generations as perhaps the greatest Cinderella turf story of all. He was nothing to look at—not "totally ugly, just unattractive," to hear his critics' descriptions. He was said to be "a huge, angular, lean, and hungry gelding," whose very next race "might be his last." Shows how wrong critics can be. Old Bones fooled 'em all. "Dem Bones" rattled on as if eternally, racing until age 9, starting no fewer than 100 times, of which he won 50! He nickeled-and-dimed his career bankroll to the tune of $252,996.

Old Bones was singularly imperturbable, cool as a cucumber, unless some fool attempt be made to separate him from his stable mascot, a pony named Peanuts. Old Bones and Peanuts went everywhere together. That included 16 different racetracks, in three different countries, where Exterminator ran at distance ranging from 5½ furlongs to 2¼ miles, under weights up to 138 pounds.

For what it's worth, the late Grantland Rice ranked Exterminator superior to Man o' War as an all-around performer! Happily, in those days it wasn't nice for turf heretics, even renowned ones like Grantland Rice, to be burned at the stake.

Phar Lap raced only once in America, an outing immortalized in film and prose. Although I was never privileged to see him race, I learned to appreciate his rare valor and prowess under the most grueling circumstances. My tutors were jockeys Johnny Longden and Eddie Arcaro, who were eye-witnesses on March 20, 1932, when New Zealand–bred Phar Lap unconditionally conquered American soil at Caliente.

"We had all heard of him," Longden recalled, "of just how he murdered his fields in Australia, where he had become some kind of national hero. I was to ride against him in the big Caliente 'Cap. The purse was originally set at a hundred thousand. But Caliente, blaming it on some screwy financial problem, cut it in half. I think the winner's share was cut down to something like $50,500."

Longden was wide-eyed the first time he spied Phar Lap. "My God, he was everything they said he was. Huge, really massive, muscles rippling all over the place. Of course, racing's no confirmation or beauty pageant. But he all but scared us half to death."

Young Arcaro was just a skinny 16-year-old apprentice, who happened to be at the right place at the right time. Eddie talked to me about it in 1996. "I only won 62 races that whole year—I had already gone eight months before scoring my first winner," Eddie remembered. "But I had a couple mounts scheduled that day at Caliente, on the same program Phar Lap would make such a lasting impression that, to this day, he remains among the greatest Thoroughbreds I've ever seen. At least, from his physical being, also from what he showed me that afternoon."

Phar Lap was an undisputed, exalted icon in Australia. I suggest for a genuine treat you buy or rent the 1983 Australian-made flick *Phar Lap*, to more fully appreciate what love and affection the people Down Under felt for their national hero and eventual legend. From what I've read and researched, the movie's every scene, every nuance—even the despicable, overweening jealousy expressed by some of that land's starchy pompous aristocrats—happened as reported.

"Phar Lap," according to the language of the aborigines, meant "lightning." As turf historian William H. P. Robertson zestfully mused: "And that's exactly what Phar Lap was in America—one quick stroke of devastating brilliance!"

Bred by A. F. Roberts in New Zealand, Phar Lap sold as a yearling for $800 to the partnership of Davis and Telford. He had an inauspicious 2-year-old season, spent searching and discovering his latent talents. Then he burgeoned overnight as a 3-year-old, winning no fewer than a lucky 13 races, including the Australian Jockey Club and Victoria Derbies and the St. Legers and the Rosehill Guineas. What won admirers was not only his indomitable will to win and fathomless stamina, but also his amazing consistency. At one stage as a 3-year-old, he piled up nine straight wins.

Better still, he was breaking track records right and left, including 1¼ miles, 1⅜ miles, 1½ miles, on up to a marathon 2¼ miles. Rival owners and trainers refused to mask their chagrin and annoyance; they'd just as well see Phar Lap dead than cede supremacy. Fans, however, saw only sheer elegance and power in their hero. Snooty as Thoroughbred racing had become Down Under, this insuperable rags-to-riches equine had become a personal bete noire to some track owners and judges, who also owned horses—horses constantly being pulverized by the greatest equine machine of his time.

Phar Lap was just getting started. In his 4-year-old season he won 14 consecutive stakes, including the prestigious Melbourne Cup under 138 pounds. His green-eyed detractors concluded that, if he were ever to be derailed, weight and more weight was the only answer. And still, Phar Lap's brilliance shone. Bigger, and growing stronger, at age 5 he rolled up eight wins in nine starts, packing on more weight with each triumph. How overtly scurrilous his antagonists became was borne out in his sole defeat. He was forced to shoulder an unbelievable load of lead, 150 pounds, conceding—are you prepared for this?—an unheard of 52 pounds to the winner, the latter scoring under a feathery 98 pounds!

"When we heard he was coming to America," Arcaro and Longden told me, "he'd already won 36 of 50 starts, and, we think, something like $282,000. They said, should he win the hundred grander at Caliente, he'd become the world's champion money-winner."

Surprisingly, some American horsemen also refused to hide their contempt when Phar Lap arrived in California a few months before his March stakes date. There were others, however, who marveled at his magnificence, though some disagreed openly with the training regimen used by Phar Lap's young conditioner, Tommy Woodcock, who doubled as groom and tripled as exercise rider.

Longden remembered how the late starter Marshall Cassidy pleaded with Woodcock to school his gelding "at the starting gate," since Phar Lap had no experience with the American-type apparatus. Woodcock just gave a friendly smile and said, "No, he'll do just fine, you'll see."

Phar Lap rarely appeared on the track. No fast workouts, no spirited drills or trials, just leisurely jogs up and down sandy hills and knolls. "I've never seen anything like it," Arcaro shook his head.

The Mexican sun scorched Caliente the day of the race. Imagine the inconceivable sight of trainer Woodcock hoisting jockey Billy Elliott aboard Phar Lap an hour before post time, proceeding to parade the gelding in full sight, and under full sun, around the infield under his full complement of 129 pounds, so that, to recall his trainer's words, "he'll get used to the weight."

"I looked at him walking around that day," Arcaro recalled. "He stood nearly 17 hands tall and he weighed something like 1,400 pounds, a good 400 pounds over Wizardry, a horse I was riding that day, not in the handicap, but on the same card. I suppose after carrying 140 to 150 pounds back home, 129 seemed no more than a feather to Phar Lap."

As the 11-horse Caliente Handicap field lined up in the starting gate, Arcaro made a private vow: "If, after all that's said and done, if, after his weird training schedule the past weeks, with what seemed like no real concern for his well-being, if Phar Lap can even finish the race, let alone win it, he's one helluva great animal!"

Eddie recalled uttering, "Oh, my God," as Phar Lap broke promptly only to dive immediately to the outside, and assuredly behind his field. "Going past the stands the first time, Phar Lap was last, maybe 50 yards behind the 10th horse. 'What a bust!' I thought. Then, without batting an eyelash he loops his field, like they're standing still. He's in sixth after the first half-mile. Two furlongs later, believe it or not, he's in front. Now Reveille Boy makes his bid, flying up right alongside him as they turn for home—and Phar Lap's giving him 11 pounds. Reveille Boy looks Phar Lap right in the eye—and I figure the gelding's crazy training schedule by now is taking its toll. Would you believe, without even a crack from his jock's whip,

Phar Lap laughs off the challenge, then proceeds to draw out by 2 open lengths. And the time, 2:02⅘, only a new track record!"

What made the occasion particularly special for Arcaro was that Eddie won the very next race on Wizardry as complement to Phar Lap's memorable performance. "It was at the very same 1¼ miles distance," Eddie reminisced, "but it took 2:07⅕, if that's any indication what kind of horse Phar Lap was."

One robin does not spring make, and Caliente spectators, including Arcaro, Longden, and Marshall Cassidy, believed Phar Lap was just the start of something special. There was talk of matching him against America's "Chocolate Soldier," Equipoise. Tracks everywhere vied with one another to tempt Phar Lap. One track, Bowie in Maryland, put up $10,000 if he'd just gallop around the oval under silks.

Almost two weeks later to the day, Phar Lap was dead! There was talk of poison; or that he had ingested bad feed, infested by insecticide; or that disgruntled gamblers and mobsters wreaked deadly revenge for bets that went awry.

Phar Lap's fairly-tale legacy is more sensational than ever. Recently, Secretariat's greatness was credited literally to his big heart, which weighed over 22 pounds at autopsy. Phar Lap's heart topped 14 pounds, while the heart of another Thoroughbred in post-mortem comparison weighed 9 pounds. Whether literally or figuratively, heart is what makes the great ones tick!

Kelso's heart ticked without interruption or hesitation five wondrous years in a row. Were mighty Forego a little more physically able, the long-winded bay gelding—a son of Forli out of the Hasty Road matron Lady Golconda—could have approached, if not threatened, Kelso's five world titles. But then, taking down three straight heavyweight belts was nothing to sneeze at. Forego, however, never really had a chance to cop top prize as a 3-year-old in 1973. That year's award was a shoo-in for an even greater equine pugilist named Secretariat.

I followed Forego's magical career with as much zeal as I could muster, considering he concentrated for the most part in New York. Turf historians Richard Stone Reeves and Patrick Robinson described Forego as "a fairly typical New York millionaire—high powered, a bit gruff in manner, and very absorbed in his career." They added, "you would not have described him as good looking, but he was big and immensely strong, with a curious aristocratic way about him, possibly inherited from his South American father."

I would have loved to announce one of his daring stretch runs, but unlike other golden geldings—such as Armed, Kelso, Royal Glint, and John Henry—Forego eschewed Chicago. I forgave him that dereliction. I settled for television and what his trainer Frank Whiteley Jr. and jockey Bill Shoemaker had to relate.

Although I didn't call him, I did see Forego perform live as a just-turned 1973 3-year-old. I believe it was the 7-furlongs Bahamas at Gulfstream Park in Hallandale, Florida. I was visiting my father and mother—they had retired to Hollywood, Florida, in 1970—and I wanted my dad to see a lightning-quick sophomore named Shecky Greene, who the year before starred at Arlington as juvenile with the most promise.

Shecky Greene breezed with lengths to spare at Gulfstream, but an awkward, late-running Forego swept from far back to take second. "I doubt I'll ever be able to beat Forego again," was the honest assessment by Shecky Greene's veteran trainer Lou Goldfine.

Fact is, on Derby Day 1973, Shecky Greene led turning for home, gave way readily to both Secretariat and Sham, and fully confessed that distance was his bugbear. Forego, unheralded that day, finished strongly to grab fourth, only a half-length back of third behind Secretariat. Despite defeat, Shecky Greene and Lou Goldfine embraced more than just a consolation prize that year. Shecky won the 1973 Eclipse Award as Sprinter of the Year.

Forego added fuel to the inevitable opinion that racing fans love stretch-runners. He gave new meaning to "the late kick." Capitalizing on front-runners' speed, he usually angled out toward the middle of the track, sometimes 5, even 6 wide, mowing 'em down à la Whirlaway, Needles, and Carry Back. He did it with class, and when it counted most. In 1976, at age 6, Forego was a bona fide legend. He uncorked a magical late surge to win the Metropolitan Mile under 130 pounds by a desperate head. Following Forego's victory in the Brooklyn 'Cap under a pressing 134 pounds, trainer Frank Whiteley, who had taken over from trainer Sherrill Ward, tapped Bill Shoemaker for the Woodward Stakes, in which Forego accepted top impost of 135 pounds.

"As far as pickup riders go, I thought I'd fill the bill," Shoe told me. "Forego and I got along just fine. In fact, I think, considering the weight and all the hubbub, we won it easily. Farther he went, stronger he'd get."

It was after Forego's impossibly electric whisker victory in the 1976 Marlboro Cup—he toted 137 that day, in the slop and mud—that Shoe was quoted as praising Forego as "the best horse I've ever ridden!" I'm certain Shoe meant it at the time, so enthralled was he with the gelding's heroism and class. Shoe vacillated at times, but so did Arcaro when we discussed Kelso and Citation—and well the great jockeys might, as memories fade and are replaced by the fresh thrills of new ones.

Shoe was equally proud of Swaps and Round Table at the top of their game. He also said Candy Spots was special and called Tom Rolfe a shade better than Gallant Man as marathon king. Sometime after his hit success with Forego, he told me that Spectacular Bid, whom he rode exclusively as an unbeaten 4-year-old, was "without doubt the best horse I've ever been around." So much for opinion, without which racing would lose its punch. The diversity of opinion, in which riders like Shoe, Hartack, and Arcaro are forced to choose from among a host of glory days all-stars, gave the game controversy and a litigiousness that kept the home fires burning, or at least kept the media from nodding off in boredom.

Perhaps not as highly regarded as Forego was Dan Lasater's regally bred gelding Royal Glint, a 1970 foal by Round Table, out of the Hail to Reason broodmare Regal Gleam. Owner Lasater was a self-made midwestern millionaire, who started out selling hamburgers at McDonald's in Kokomo, Indiana; later he founded his own restaurant chain, the Ponderosa Steak Houses. Just as he turned out hamburgers and steaks with thundering speed, Lasater wasted no time building a gigantic stable—he had no less than 100 horses in training, and he topped the nation in four separate years as America's number-one money-winning owner, also in races won.

But it was Royal Glint who lent legitimacy to Dan Lasater as a recognizable force during those declining days when racing was racing. Royal Glint traveled almost as extensively as Marco Polo. He'd pop up unexpectedly in California, New Jersey, Ohio, and especially in Chicago, where he performed superbly at both Arlington and Hawthorne. His regular rider was a hard-knocking South American, Jorge Tejeira, whose low profile smacked closely to that of Master Arcaro. Sometimes I think I respected more how a jockey looked—his "seat"—than the result he generated.

Tejeira promised me he'd win the 1975 Arlington Handicap, which had been returned to the dirt at 1$\frac{3}{16}$ miles. "Nobody beats this gelding today," he told me that Saturday morning, "and he wins it big, too!"

Winning "big" translates into a galaxy of "if's and but's," as far as horse folks are concerned. Usually it's defined as: "We can't lose, go ahead, bet the ranch." In this case, it meant Royal Glint at his finest, and fastest, as he and Jorge Tejeira annihilated a good field under top weight of 125 pounds to win going away, in track-record time of 1:54$\frac{4}{5}$, a record that I think still stands.

I called it "the easiest kind of victory, Royal Glint spread-eagling his field, Jorge Tejeira standing proud in the saddle." Tejeira gave me a whip salute following the customary one to the judges—and all was well with the world.

A month or so later, Royal Glint was back in town, this time to covet the $100,000 added Hawthorne Gold Cup. He accepted his top impost of 124 pounds and, again with a grinning Tejeira in the irons, vanquished a good field in 2:02$\frac{1}{5}$. Tejeira doubled his 15-minutes of fame—he'd never win a Gold Cup or an Arlington 'Cap again, but he'd forever owe Royal Glint for those 1975 wins.

A year later, the gelding already was approaching a million in purses won. Sadly, while contesting the Massachusetts Handicap, Royal Glint hemorrhaged profusely before half the race was run. He fell heavily to the earth as blood spurted from his nostrils. Lasater, who had fallen in love with his gelding, as most owners do, spared no expense for his care.

Sent to the Bolton Center for Equines near Unionville, Pennsylvania, Royal Glint was found to be suffering from a bleeding lung. Successfully treated, he returned to the races. When he won his next outing, the Salvator Handicap at Monmouth Park,

Royal Glint formally became the 19th millionaire in Thoroughbred history.

But tragedy was just around the corner. When he fractured both sesamoids of his left front ankle in Detroit, his career ended grievously. Worse, Royal Glint was in distress. But Lasater pulled out all stops short of euthanasia. "Spare him, if humanly possible," Lasater begged, "but only without his pain continuing."

As days rolled by, Royal Glint's condition worsened. The situation, explained tenderly to Dan Lasater, was hopeless. On October 26, 1976, Royal Glint was humanely destroyed. Lasater—much like Phar Lap's grief-stricken trainer Tommy Woodcock—the latter cried inconsolably, gently rocking his gelding's limp head in his hands following his friend's death. As Lasater walked away from the headstone marking Royal Glint's grave, he wept unashamedly.

Another great equine athlete—one that many still consider the "last of the sport's golden geldings"—was Dotsam Stable's living legend, John Henry. An obscure son of obscure sire Ole Bob Bowers, bred by the Golden Chance Farm of Kentucky, John Henry marked the end of an era, that of racing's golden days of yesteryear, a time during which the Thoroughbred's aura and persona would not only elicit, but demand, generous feature-story media coverage.

John Henry emerged bigger than life in 1981, the year of Thoroughbred racing's first million-dollar race, three full years before the opulent Breeders' Cup would grab the nation's turf spotlight. Like Round Table before, John Henry was renowned for turf prowess; like Round Table before, John Henry also excelled, though not as effusively, on the dirt, underscoring his versatility. Twice he was crowned Eclipse Horse of the Year in 1981 and 1984.

My first glimpse of John Henry—he was an unsung 3-year-old of dubious promise—occurred in 1978 when he first invaded Arlington Park for, would you believe of all races, the Round Table Handicap at 1⅟16 miles on the grass. I pride myself for total recall when it comes to certain races I've called over my 34-year announcing career. For some reason—and I had no prior knowledge of John Henry the day he coveted the Round Table 'Cap—the gelding caught my eye. I remember bringing him home, suddenly impressed with his verve and smooth stride: "And here he is, John Henry, all by himself . . . remember that name, John Henry . . . yes, it's John Henry in a runaway . . . John Henry, a name for the future."

He won by 11 or 12 lengths. Someone said he could have been bought as a 2-year-old for as little as $2,500. Well, not anymore. He was just 3, and he had just discovered turf, and another potential switch-over champ had been unveiled!

Here's an interesting sidelight. As emcee for Arlington's weekly Breakfast-Railbird Fan Club, I interviewed John Henry's trainer of note, Ron McAnally, the morning prior to the 1984 Arlington Million. During our conversation, McAnally suggested jokingly that John Henry had "a thing" for my announcing.

"You called him back in 1978 when he won the Round Table, Phil," McAnally quipped. "And when he won the first Arlington Million as a 6-year-old in 1981, in a race that really was too close to call, you were the one who brought him home a winner."

Ron reminded our audience that I had been fired by Madison Square Garden, which owned Arlington, just one week prior to Million II in 1982, and did not return until the day after Million III in 1983. (We'll discuss my being fired a little later down the line.) "We didn't contest the second Million, but we tried the third and just failed to catch Tolemeo. I was sure were you calling the race, we'd have won!"

I didn't have to remind McAnally that I was back on the mike for the next day's Million IV. "As much as owners Mr. and Mrs. Sam Rubin, as well as you, Ron, and of course, John Henry, want to win tomorrow, I certainly have no intention of jinxing your gelding. I'll get him home for you, okay?" We shook on it. The fans cheered.

Let's backtrack a moment. First time I saw John Henry, I was impressed not by his size, but rather by his smooth, nimble stride, the kind of skipping stride that characterized other grass titans of the past. He was a dark bay, long and lean, packing none of the charisma or magnetism of, say, Secretariat, nor the bulk and substance of rugged Forego. He was almost effeminate by comparison; graceful not formidable; sleek not muscular. But for innate competitive spirit, John Henry took a back seat to none—not even Phar Lap, Armed, Exterminator, Royal Glint, or Kelso. John Henry loved to race; better still, he loved to win. He may have been a gelding, but by every other touchstone, he was "all horse!"

He chose the 1981 inaugural Arlington Million to turn in what I have to feel was one of my top two racing calls, as judged by sheer drama. Twelve contested the first 1¼ miles grassy Million, and Big John, ridden that day by Shoemaker, dawdled in eighth as the field curved into the backstretch. Key to Content was cutting out a blistering pace, stalked by 30-1 longshot The Bart. England's Madam Gay, Lester Piggott up, pushed the leaders in third, followed by Match the Hatch and Argument.

As they left the half-mile pole, I said, "John Henry scoots through down along the rail fifth . . . The Bart, racing strongly on the outside, puts his head in front, Key to Content battles back second . . . Madam Gay closing ground third, followed by Match the Hatch fourth and John Henry . . .

"Here they come, spinning out of the turn—The Bart has it by two . . . Madam Gay now second, Key to Content coming back third . . . but here's John Henry closing ground fourth . . . with Match the Hatch . . . The Bart is under a heavy whip, but John Henry is charging . . . a final move by John Henry, but The Bart is still there . . . here's the wire . . . The Bart . . . or . . . is it John Henry on the outside?

"Can't split 'em . . . either John Henry or The Bart . . . this one could be a dead heat . . . it can go either way . . . John Henry or The Bart!"

At that very moment all hell broke loose—a monumental brouhaha! NBC, whose telecast was being sent to 34 lands, foolishly on screen called The Bart first the unofficial, then, shockingly, the official winner—while the "Photo" sign remained posted.

In all fairness, it was that close! Impossible at wire's end to accurately judge who won. As they hit the wire, I thought perhaps The Bart had held on. A second later—my experience taught me always to give the outside and closing horse a nostril's edge—I felt, no, I knew, John Henry had gotten up in the very stride.

I pleaded with NBC over our communication hookup not to declare The Bart even as "unofficial" winner. "Let's not split 'em," I begged. In effect, they told me to shut up and mind my own business.

Well, John Henry won it fair and square. Shoe told me afterwards: "John Henry was in front for only *one* stride—not the stride before, or after, the wire—but *on* the wire. That little guy knew where he had to be to win it all!"

Okay, fast forward to 1984. John Henry is making his fourth Arlington appearance. He had won the first two—the Round Table and Million I, both of which I called. He lost 1983 Million in a photo finish. Now, at age 9, he would become the first Thoroughbred in racing history to win a Grade I Stakes at that age, equivalent to a 45- to 49-year-old human athlete. The next to do it, I believe, was John's Call, who won the 2000 Grade I Sword Dancer at Saratoga, albeit against lesser-quality opponents.

The 1984 Million rates as my second favorite call. Not that it could get any closer than the 1981 Inaugural—that was impossible. But John Henry's unprecedented triumph, achieved as an ageless 9-year-old against a power-packed field, remains one for the books.

"John Henry like a bullet . . . here he is, John Henry, a living legend . . . it's John Henry by two . . . you're looking at the living legend, John Henry . . . and the beat goes on . . . Thoroughbred racing's *first* five-million-dollar baby!" I still get chills.

In scoring his second Million victory, John Henry became the first Thoroughbred in history to exceed $5,000,000 in earnings. Fact is, he'd have over a record $6,000,000 at year's end.

Now that was before the Breeders' Cup, which debuted that fall, to which, because his sire was so nondescript, John Henry was ineligible. His owners decided against putting up an extra $400,000-plus to supplement him to the Cup's big race, the Classic. All this, of course, was prior to the Classic being enriched to $4 million, or the day of a $5 million bonus to any 3-year-old good enough to sweep racing's Triple Crown. Inflation actually proved no true boon to racing, not with greenbacks flowing all over the place.

Alysheba subsequently topped John Henry's earnings. As of these words, Cigar reigns as the leading money-winning Thoroughbred of all time. Both would have their hooves full messing with John Henry.

Money has always been a cogent denominator in determining a professional athlete's success. Today, a horse's financial statement seemingly carries more weight than the weight the champion carries. During the sport's golden days, however, the Thoroughbred's class, record, longevity, and personality formed the true criteria.

Which brings us back to Kelso, our undisputed king of racing's golden geldings. The first time I spied Kelso through my binoculars was at Arlington the summer of 1960. He was parading postward in the 1-mile Arlington Classic, just another eastern threat, but given a speck of added notice because he was a gelding testing such 3-year-old stalwart colts as Kentucky Derby champ Venetian Way and long-time Chicago favorite T.V. Lark. The Classic was brimming with 3-year-old talent.

"He'll be lucky to take third against their kind," I predicted confidently, prior to the field leaving the gate at the head of Arlington's famed 1-mile chute. Smugly, I actually took delight in Kelso's failure. He never fired, winding up a lackluster eighth under Steve Brooks. T.V. Lark out-pointed Venetian Way at the wire. How was I know that would be Kelso's sole defeat as a 3-year-old? Mine was a stupid rush to judgment, a mistake I swore I'd never make again.

Returned to New York, trainer Carl Hanford immediately turned Kelso over to Eddie Arcaro. Like so many times before, whenever a promising or once-successful equine failed to perform as expected, Eddie was asked to step in and help. And the magic worked again!

Kelso shot into orbit, flashing across turf's celestial high, posting victory after victory, including the Choice Stakes in a romp, the Jerome in a photo, and the Discovery in track-record time at Aqueduct. He capped his New York supremacy by equaling Man o' War's 1⅝ miles track standard of 2:40⅘ in the Lawrence Realization.

I witnessed three of those remarkable wins via TV, and I was so impressed—seeing Arcaro aboard did much to sway my allegiance—all at once I realized I was privy to grandeur in the making. When I called Arcaro in New York, he confirmed Kelso's meteoric rise to power. "There's not a 3-year-old in America—nor any older horse—who can hold a candle to him."

"Then why not bring him back to Chicago and atone for his Classic fiasco?" I argued.

"I understand trainer Carl Hanford is thinking just that," Arcaro answered. "The Hawthorne Gold Cup—it's against older horses—will be his next start. Okay by me, too, since I've never won that Gold Cup. See ya in October."

Now, I wasn't Hawthorne's official caller then. I was under exclusive contract as track announcer to Arlington–Washington. But I had been okayed by Marje Everett to do a tape-delayed call of the Gold Cup for the CBS local affiliate. One thing dampened my zeal—all-night rains. Gold Cup day came up ankle-deep slop. Classic winner T.V. Lark loved the goo, as did Mary Keim's Heroshogala and Calumet Farm's On-and-On.

So what! Kelso was fast becoming the gelding of the ages. Distance certainly was no obstacle, nor were horses. Why should an "off" track pose any problem to a potential great? He wallowed in the mud and slop. Others were slipping and sliding. Not Kelso. Yes, Eddie was covered with mud from head to toe as he maneuvered Kelso from off the pace. By midstretch, they wheeled to the middle of the track, and, with nary a crack of the bat, Kelso splashed home by 6 widening lengths.

I saw it all through my binocs. I said it with words, too: "Here he is, Kelso, America's newest superstar, and if he isn't Horse of the Year, then there just ain't no such animal." Kelso wasn't finished either. He had expiated his Classic debacle; he had crushed young and old alike. And he did it over "off" going, exploding from off the pace, scoring with speed and energy yet untapped in his wallet of reserve.

He returned to New York, again caught a sloppy course for the lucrative Jockey Club Gold Cup, and again played with his mud pies, scoring laughingly by 3½ lengths. Kelso stopped the timer in 3:19⅖, a new American standard for a demanding 2 miles of rugged terrain.

Nine starts as a 1960 3-year-old. Eight wins—that unaccountable flop in the Classic his sole blemish. Undisputed Horse of the Year for the first of five straight seasons.

Someone caught Eddie Arcaro at an unguarded moment. "How does he rate among your all-time mounts?" they asked.

"He may be the best I've ridden," Eddie replied. Then, rethinking his response: "I'll let you know next year—ask me then."

Arcaro would modify his praise of Kelso to this extent: "Had he won the Triple Crown, I'd have a better handle on him. I sometimes forget how great Citation was as a 3-year-old. His so-called comeback as a 5- and 6-year-old diminished so many great memories. Why, as a 3-year-old, Citation could fall down at the eighth pole, get up again, and win it all!"

What impressed Eddie most about Kelso was the ease by which he totally demolished older foes as a 1960 3-year-old. Winning eight of nine was praiseworthy, indeed, but it really wasn't until his last five outings that he vanquished older horses.

Eddie said: "I kept reminding myself that Citation as a 3-year-old won 19 of 20—and that one bummer, which should never have been, was my fault—including 15 straight. And as a 2-year-old—and Kelso at 2 was nothing special—Citation won eight of nine."

Eddie, not realizing that 1961 would be his final year in the saddle, had that season to "really get to know Kelso, and firm up how I really felt about him." At age 4, Kelso came back stronger than ever, adding on to his 1960 victory streak, remaining unbeaten through a total of 11 straight races, packing on more weight with each encounter. He successfully shouldered 130 in the Metropolitan Mile. Later he celebrated July 4 with victory in the Suburban Handicap under 133 pounds.

Though Arlington wasn't taking bets on out-of-state stakes in those days, Marje Everett pioneered the notion that local fans deserved a look-see at other major national stakes. The Suburban Handicap was carried live on network TV, and she had me call it live for patrons at Arlington. I'd use an ear-piece, follow the New York announcer's call, then translate it live over the Arlington public address system. It took a little more work and application than a regular track call, but the experience alone was worth the effort.

Kelso won the Suburban in a gallop, giving the runner-up, Nickel Boy, 21 pounds. I waxed ecstatic! America had a new super horse, and it all started only the year before, when he humbled older horses in Chicago's own Hawthorne Gold Cup.

But the best was yet to come. Three weeks later at Aqueduct, this time under a crushing 136, Kelso won the Brooklyn Handicap. Kelso had thus swept New York's handicap triple crown—in those days consisting of the Metropolitan, Suburban, and Brooklyn Handicaps.

Unfortunately, Kelso's people were still smarting over the gelding's defeat by T.V. Lark as a 3-year-old in Arlington's Classic, the only blemish on his 1960 campaign. Not even Kelso's subsequent 6-length Hawthorne Gold Cup triumph, in which he creamed T.V. Lark, could assuage owner Mrs. Richard C. duPont or trainer Carl Hanford. So Kelso, bent on revenge, returned to Arlington Park for the Washington Park Handicap, and he bravely accepted top weight of 132 pounds, despite being inactive for more than a month following his New York successes. The distance that year curiously had been reduced to a flat mile, in keeping with the Lindheimer–Everett theory that the middle-distances were conducive to larger, more competitive fields.

Kelso's fan club, hundreds strong, showed up a the track only to retreat back to New York, tails between their legs. Once again, Chicago proved his Waterloo. "I didn't like him dropping down to a mile," Arcaro said following the debacle. "He'd been going a distance of ground all year, so his speed wasn't all that sharp."

Kelso could do no better than fourth, giving 20 pounds to the winner, Chief of Chiefs, whose best distance was the mile. Kelso did what Citation never did when right—he threw in a clinker. To be fair, Hanford blamed the poor effort on Kelly's aching tender hooves.

My binoculars trained on him before, during, and after the race, I saw no valid reason for so slothful a showing. I know Eddie was puzzled. Hanford concluded, "He just didn't like the track, I suppose. And I'm sure his hooves were hurting."

But mighty Kelso bounced back brilliantly, humiliating Kentucky Derby champ Carry Back in the Woodward Stakes. He was back at 1¼ miles, and he sizzled the classic distance in 2:00 flat. He also captured the 2-mile Jockey Club Gold Cup for a second time (he'd win that coveted New York stakes five years handrunning)—and now he had only one more world to conquer. Grass!

Though Hanford disagrees to this day, grass racing remained Kelly's sole bugaboo. The theory laid out by a spate of brainy horsemen is that grass suits horses with a skipping, not pounding, motion or stride. Well, Kelso let it all hang out every time. He'd dig deep within, hitting and striking the ground with vigor and grit. Grass apparently slowed, rather than speeded, his progress.

At any rate, in the 1961 Laurel Park International, he finished a so-so second to T.V. Lark over Laurel's inner green. This was the same T.V. Lark who whipped him silly in the 1960 Arlington Classic—though Kelso subsequently dumped T.V. Lark unceremoniously in their Hawthorne Gold Cup return match.

Jockey Johnny Longden rode T.V. Lark in the 1961 Laurel International. Four years later, Longden and I talked about the race, and the craggy Britisher put the happening in proper prospective: "Kelso simply wasn't all that great—at least not then as a 4-year-old—on the grass. And I know T.V. Lark wasn't no Kelso on the dirt, though he did beat him at Arlington the year before. But T.V. Lark was a terror on the grass. That surface moved him up 10 lengths easy."

In fact, T.V. Lark ruled the American turf as 1961 Grass Horse of the Year. Kelso, despite his Laurel loss, again was unanimously acclaimed overall Horse of the Year.

Then, things happened rapid-fire. Eddie Arcaro shocked the racing world, announcing his retirement prior to the 1962 Kentucky Derby. (Why he ever considered retirement with a horse like Kelso at his beck and call will be revealed in Chapter Six.) For Kelso a 5-year-old in 1962, retirement was the farthest thing from his mind. Hanford, dismayed at losing Arcaro, asked the Master to recommend a replacement. "I like Shoemaker and Valenzuela," Eddie said. Hanford ultimately selected Ismael "Milo" Valenzuela. And for Kelso, and for a grateful Valenzuela, the beat went on, as if interminably.

Parenthetically, Arcaro, so wonderfully linked to an endless list of Thoroughbred greats—Citation, Whirlaway, Nashua, Bold Ruler, Native Dancer, Sword Dancer, One Count, Hill Prince, Devil Diver, Real Delight, Mark-Ye-Well, and Kelso (just to name a few off the top)—finally put his stamp of approval on his personal champions:

Greatest 3-year-old ever—Citation, bar none.

Greatest 4-year-old, or older horse—Kelso, no question.

Greatest filly or mare—Real Delight.

Fastest of all—nutty Bold Ruler.

Most rugged—Nashua.

Greatest "one-ride" champions—Native Dancer, Swoon's Son.

Kelso, meanwhile, continued to galvanize Americans. Racing fans again had a perennial champion, one they counted on, for five marvelous years. His historic duels with the amazing speedster Gun Bow, ridden by Walter Blum, are legendary. When he finally hung up his cleats in 1964 after an incredible five-year monarchy, he did so as world money-winning champ with over $1,900,000 swelling the duPont coffers, as if they needed the extra change.

By the way, yes, Kelso did get to master grass. On November 11, 1964, following three straight seconds in prior Internationals, Kelso heartlessly KO'd Gun Bow, donning the laurel wreath with lengths to spare. He set a new American turf mark for 1½ miles—startling experts by running the final quarter in faster time than the opening quarter.

Thus, in the 1960s, the sport bid goodbye to its most decorated golden gelding, Kelso; also its greatest jockey, Eddie Arcaro. Why Hollywood never made "The Eddie Arcaro Story" I'll never know, but before Chapter Six atones for so glaring an oversight, let's take a side trip to examine how and why Thoroughbreds got their names.

Chapter Five

"Here Comes SheSellsSeaShells!"

Which came first: the name or the horse? Who made whom famous?

From my viewpoint—after 96,131 calls over TV, radio, and track public address systems, calls that included some of the most inventive, crazy, crude, funny, lewd, and marvelously crafted monikers in the creative art of naming Thoroughbreds—I can't imagine Citation, Secretariat, Man o' War, Phar Lap, Equipoise, Seabiscuit, Whirlaway, Kelso, Cigar, Count Fleet, or Affirmed being forced to race under any other name. Could you? How strange and unimposing it would be to have Triple Crown kings named Boo-Boo, Hopeless, Hypocrite, Big Mouth, and Useless Fred. There, but for the grace of clever owners with causative souls, would dwell anonymity at its dullest.

My toughest name challenge—SheSellsSeaShells—came during the 1980s at Sportsman's Park. Her owner wittingly, and wittily, chose the name to torture me. SheSellsSeaShells isn't that difficult that it can't be said flawlessly, if it is done slowly. During a race, when an announcer is relying solely on memory and binoculars, the name can surprise and intimidate. So I wrote it at the top of my program. Each time I had to call it, I'd drop my binocs and simply read the name: "And there goes SheSellsSeaShells with a flourish . . ."

Hey, I got away with it. Not a slur nor a stumble. Fans on the apron below literally applauded my performance. They'd been amply warned; the announcing attempt was chronicled by sports writers that very morning. That's how involved the media were, even into the 1980s. Thankfully, but sadly—true mixed emotions—the filly was injured the very next week, never to race again.

My least favorite name—Soon to Be Glue—also raced that spring at Sportsman's Park and actually belonged to one of the track's owners. Insensitively derogatory, the name lacked any redeeming feature. He raced only once before being sidelined.

Some of my favorite names—not so much from a beauty standpoint but from how they resonated over the horns and incited fan reaction—included Beep-Beep and Whoop. Each time I delivered "And Beep-Beep is on the move," the fans echoed it en masse. Same for Whoop. The fans would chant the names before and after each race, especially during post parades and when Beep-Beep and Whoop returned to the winner's circle.

One Standardbred owner named his every horse with a dexterous sense of crassness: Dumpy Dan, Grumpy Gabe, Nasty Nancy, Pesty Peggy, among others. Another harness owner went a step farther, naming a peppery pacer Filthy McNasty.

Some names I believe were deliberately concocted to fool the Jockey Club, which must pass on all names. Last time I looked, no name could exceed 18 characters (which included spaces). No names could have immoral overtones. There could be no names referring to vile, despicable people or things. Nor could you use names honored in racing's Hall of Fame, such as Secretariat, Man o' War, Citation, Whirlaway. The legitimate name Harass got by, however. The only time Harass proved a bit ticklish was when she was injured during the post parade and I was forced to inform my public: "Please scratch Harass!" On another occasion, I had to tell the public to "scratch Cerasus."

In the mid-1960s, a filly was named Marje Everett, after my boss at Arlington and Washington Parks. Owners could name horses after celebrities, VIPs, stars of stage, screen, and radio, but only with written permission, and Marje permitted her name to be used. In the filly's second start, a bit skittish, she unseated her jockey as they were being loaded up at the gate. The boy was shaken up badly. The jocks' quarters called me. "Phil, we need a new jock. Page the trainer, please."

Bill Hartack agreed to deputize for the fallen rider, and I announced the change in jockeys: "Ladies and gentlemen, we have a change of riders on No. 4 Marje Everett." Then, unconsciously:

"Put Bill Hartack up on Marje Everett. I repeat: Bill Hartack will ride Marje Everett."

The crowd roared; I blushed; the phone rang. It was the real Marje Everett. Fortunately, my boss enjoyed a sense of humor.

For every fun name, there've been hundreds of clever or meaningful names. Ponder, Pensive, Fervent, Armed, Bewitch, Coaltown, Bardstown, Faultless, and Citation—each name was an absolute, active, forceful, or melifluous signature, and a sound of unforgettable impact. Credit Calumet Farm with such ingenuity and originality. But Calumet wasn't alone. Many owners and breeders particularly enjoyed combining meanings implied by the progeny's sire and dam.

Shut Out was smartly named, the son of Equipoise out of a mare called Goose Egg. The latter is a sports term used in connection with a baseball team's inability to score a run. Using the baseball reference, what might a cagey owner call another offspring of Shut Out? One Hitter.

How about the offspring of Reigh Count and the dam Quickly, by Haste? John D. Hertz was duly inspired to name the colt Count Fleet. Card players will see the subtlety in naming Capot after his dam, Piquet. A capot is a win in the game of piquet. And if Gaga, which implies something excessively foolish, dropped a foal, why not name the new colt Tom Fool?

Allow me pride of authorship, not in the naming of mercurial Ridan, but in the pronunciation of "Rye-*dan*," not "*Rie*-den," when the gigantic son of Nantallah tore up Arlington as a 2-year-old in 1961. Seeing the name Ridan for the first time, I checked with trainer Moody Jolley about how to say it. Jolley told me Ridan reminded his owners so of Claiborne Farm's 1957 champion juvenile, Nadir, they just spelled Nadir backwards—Ridan. But how to pronounce it? Jolley dismissed my concern for accuracy. Being a made-up name, it could be pronounced anyhow. Now, I'm an avid movie buff, and though it was a terrible excuse for a Sci-Fi monster film, the Japanese import *Rodan* had been making the rounds. I liked the emphasis on Rodan's second syllable—Ro-*dan*. Consequently, since I was Arlington's official voice, I claimed poetic license and Ri-*dan* was born.

What about mighty Seabiscuit? Would you ever wonder why he was so named if you knew his sire was none other than Hard Tack, the latter a hard, saltless *biscuit* used as rations for ships at *sea*? Pompey was a son of the race mare Cleopatra. Sun Beau, erstwhile leading money-winning Thoroughbred in the late 1920s, came about as a product of *Sun* Briar and *Beau*tiful Lady. If a son is born to Flying Ebony and Silencia, what better name than Dark Secret? And why not Eight Thirty for a colt out of a mare called Dinner Time?

One name—Dogoon—fooled me completely. He was by The Doge and Swoon, and he was an older full brother to the redoubtable Swoon's Son. The name seemed to begin with the "Dog" from Doge, an Italian magistrate, and end with the "oon" in Swoon. Everybody called the colt Daw-*goon*. I was floored one day to discover owner E. Gay Drake meant for the name to be pronounced "Do Go On." "As long as you guys keep calling him a winner," Drake smiled graciously, "call him anything you want."

Sometimes I got myself smack dab in the middle of some mighty crazy personality clashes over names—like with a horse named Natego. I called the paddock prior to the colt's racing debut at Washington Park in the early 1960s. "He's named for me," said Chicago businessman Nate Pearlstein, so it's "*Nate*-go." Gotcha, I obeyed, and *Nate*-go it was. I think he finished a so-so third that day. Two races later, dropped in a claiming race, he was haltered by another Chicago entrepreneur, B. W. Landy, who just happened to passionately dislike Nate Pearlstein. Before the colt's first outing for his new owner, the latter's trainer, Steve Ippolito, sheepishly called me.

"I'm embarrassed," Steve said, "but Mr. Landy will go bonkers if you call his new horse, '*Nate*-go.' He asked me to tell you to change his name, to call him '*Nat*-a-go,' if that's okay with you."

No problem. "*Nat*-a-go" it was. But it didn't end there. Although raised 25 percent in price, Natego was racing again in a claiming race. Guess who claimed him back? Right, Nate Pearlstein. Again I was politely flogged, this time by his original owner. "Don't forget his *right* name next time," Pearlstein reminded me. Thankfully, I don't think the colt ever started again in Chicago, whatever they wanted his name to be.

Neither Harry Caray nor Jack Brickhouse, Chicago's top two baseball announcers in history, are with us anymore, but it was a joy to call their namesakes: "Hey! hey! it's Jack Brickhouse in a gallop" and "Here comes—holy cow!—it's all 'Harry Caray' today!"

The temptation to have fun and to laugh with, not at, a horse's fresh, queer, or novel name is an irresistible must among race callers everywhere. We instinctively find pleasure and amusement in their names, adding extra oomph to a race where proper and reasonable. Here are a few examples:

"And in the Arlington Classic, it's Attention standing tall over Whirlaway . . ."

"Here comes the wire, and it's all Smile, yes, it's Smile a laughing winner . . ."

"That's Gum Chewer, sticking to the rail . . ."

"And Lover Boy continues to hug the rail . . ."

"In the winner's circle, Sanhedrin is holding court . . ."

"And Cigar remains undefeated . . . Cigar is great—no butts about it!"

"Here comes Jetaway, and it's all Jetaway like Whirlaway in the straightaway!"

"And there's no stopping Adios today . . . here's Adios bidding adieu, saying goodbye, to one and all at the wire . . ."

The opus on Thoroughbred names remains endless. One of my all-time picks for cleverness and ingenuity goes to a horse owned and named by Jacnot Stable in Illinois. I called all his races in 1961, including a searing come-from-behind victory in the July 4 Stars and Stripes Handicap on the grass at Arlington Park. He was a stakes-winning son of the fine sire To Market. Remember the nursery rhyme: "To market, to market, to buy a fat pig"? Well, this equine went through life named Oink.

Chapter Six

The Master, Eddie Arcaro

Since 1941, and my first visits to Arlington and Washington Parks in Chicago, I have gazed in awe at the very heartbeat of Thoroughbred racing through a constant friend and partner, my faithful pair of binoculars. Most spectators at the track today have a plethora of individual TV monitors and handy gigantic infield matrix screens to relay the race to them. Binoculars are virtually passe, unless you are an announcer or race caller.

I rented my first pair in July 1941 for 50 cents. My father picked up the tab. By 1943 I had purchased an inexpensive pair for $10. I improved my vision in 1953, my first season as a track publicity assistant, with a $50 set, 7×40 magnification. I hiked my investment to $70 for a pair of Bushnell optics, 7×50, to call my first race on May 18, 1959, at Washington Park.

That summer, duly intimidated by Arlington's spacious 1⅛ miles main track oval, I made a $100 purchase of 10×50 binocs. Eventually I'd lose three sets of Bushnell glasses in unexpected, tragic fires. Washington Park burned down in 1977, Hawthorne's grandstand was destroyed in 1978, and a towering inferno totally razed Arlington Park on July 31, 1985.

I finished out my 34-year announcing career the proud owner of $1,000 pair of exquisite German-made Carl Zeiss glasses, which Chicago racing fans had presented me with on one special day at Arlington in 1978. I never intended to use so priceless a gift on a daily basis; three devastating fires, however, convinced me their time had come. Through these binoculars brightly, and through all their predecessors, I witnessed exciting turf lore not only in the form of magnificent horseflesh, but also in the grand parade of accomplished jockeys pridefully plying their trade.

Among the first authentic jockey greats I trained my binoculars on was Georgie "Iceman" Woolf. The "Iceman" tag indicated that he was cool under fire. He had the ability to relax both himself and his horse early, calmly awaiting the precise moment to fire. By the time I got to watch Woolf in the early 1940s at Arlington, he was somewhat past his prime, he didn't win often. When least expected, though, he'd flash a token genius that smacked of his former excellence. I'm sorry I wasn't around to see him at his best.

Through my binocs, up close and intimate, I saw other participants in the grand parade. I saw Teddy Atkinson, Steve Brooks, Johnny Longden, Johnny Adams, Warren Mehrtens, Conn McCreary, Bobby Ussery, Basil James, Sammy Boulmetis, Jackie Westrope, Doug Dodson, Eric Guerin, Avelino Gomez, Braulio Baeza, Manny Ycaza, Joe Culmone, Tony DeSpirito, Johnny Sellers, Johnny Rotz, Ralph Neves, Kenny Church, Walter Blum, Laffit Pincay Jr., Carlos Marquez, Phil Rubbicco, Larry Snyder, Eddie Delahoussaye, Earlie Fires, Shane Sellers, Bill Shoemaker, Bill Hartack, Sandy Hawley, Craig Perret, Ray Sibille, Randy Romero, Steve Cauthen, Jorge Valesquez, Ron Turcotte, Angel Cordero Jr, Ismael Valenzuela, Pat Valenzuela, Chris Antley, Mike Smith, Chris McCarron, Lester Piggott, Kent Desormeaux, Gary Stevens, Jerry Bailey, and Pat Day. Wow! What a roster! I'm breathless!

But, best of all, I saw the Master, Eddie Arcaro! Go ahead. Ask me. What three things do I remember most about Eddie Arcaro? First, he earned, and deserved, sacrosanct lordship as the Master, the greatest jockey who ever lived!

Second, he was always preceded, and announced, by his nose, the most celebrated schnozz this side of the mythical French swashbuckler Cyrano de Bergerac and the beloved entertainer Jimmy Durante. And Eddie's disarming, boyish smile wasn't all that shabby either.

Third, he owned a big, wonderful ego—"wonderful" in that he rarely angered, or intimidated, or alienated. The Arcaro ego was masterfully contrived to soften enmity and mollify jealousy. It electrified and won over competing riders and eagle-eyed members of the fourth estate. Eddie Arcaro genuinely believed he could outthink, outride, and outfinish any jockey alive. Unless professionally challenged, however, he quietly kept that conviction to himself. Nonetheless, he felt no one could ride a better, smarter, tougher race than he. He was, because he willed it, the world's greatest jockey. No brag, just fact.

Fact is, Eddie not only looked great winning, he also looked great losing. He once confided: "Win or lose, especially when you lose, you just gotta look good. It's the one sure way to get people to remember you. Never forget, we usually lose three out of every four races. Looking great is the honey that makes losing bearable."

Truth be told, I was probably Eddie's easiest convert. I became an instant fan when Whirlaway crushed his Derby opponents; Mr. Longtail's Triple Crown triumph wasn't hard to take either. At age 10, I declared myself "the next Eddie Arcaro," my sights firmly affixed on a jockey career that would unashamedly copy his in style and substance. As you know, except for three wondrous weeks as exercise boy, my riding career never left the ground. But Eddie's riding, his "seat," in effect his riding style—which I came to appreciate and describe as "power with panache"—was burned inextricably in my mind and heart.

His look was so cleanly defined, so aesthetically pure, so anatomically and aerodynamically perfect, even the most judgmental critic was compelled to take notice. It wasn't until decades later, in the 1990s, that I came to appreciate his whole-souled dedication—first to create, then maintain, that noble look. That look and the shimmering mystique he guarded and cherished selfishly, and privately.

Eddie Arcaro's monumental role in racing and his impact on the sport account for much of what we proudly refer to as racing's luminous golden age.

His unexpected retirement shocked the world of Thoroughbred racing. It followed a second sensational year aboard a bevy of stake stars, not the least of whom was mighty Kelso, the latter rolling to his second of five straight Horse of the Year titles. Eddie had just turned 46. Other riders, like Johnny Longden, R. L. "Bobby" Baird, Earl Sande, Earlie Fires, and the world's current "winningest" rider of all time, Laffit Pincay Jr., all remained tall in the saddle years after turning 46.

Eddie Arcaro retired suddenly because his wonderfully big ego would allow no alternative. "Winning, it's been said, is everything," Eddie humbly shared with me, "but they're wrong. I never intended to stay one moment longer than I could without looking good. I never wanted anyone to criticize: 'Hey, Eddie's lost a step. Why doesn't he quit while he's ahead?'"

Arcaro still had Kelso, though a horse's future is as uncertain as the next day's weather forecast. "I owe my decision to retire—which I never regretted—to my agent, Bones."

Bones LaBoyne noticed it before Eddie. Eddie was bouncing inordinately in the saddle during crucial stretch drives. "Bones got me to look at films of myself, some back in the late 1950s; others in late 1961. The difference was obvious. I looked terrible, to me anyway," Eddie said.

"Simply put, my legs were gone. No more strength, stretch, or elasticity," Eddie explained. "Like any fighter, once a jocks legs go, so goes his riding career."

Eddie barely hesitated a second, only one brief pause to wipe his fingers across a dry mouth. He told his agent, "You're right, Bones, my time's come. And I thank you for pointing it out to me."

We must never forget that although Eddie Arcaro was born to be a small man, he wasn't necessarily born to be a jockey. Unlike many infants and youngsters born into established racing families at farms or tracks dotting America's turf map, Arcaro was born in Cincinnati, Ohio—near Latonia Racetrack, true, but with no racetrack knowledge, certainly no ties to the racing community.

Born on February 19, 1916, he grew up poor but proud—his father was a cab driver—and early on, Eddie had no idea what a racehorse even looked like. More than anything else, his first love, from his earliest recall, was the game of golf. "I was a caddy, only 13, earning my first few bucks as a hustling kid," he laughed. "I loved golf, still do, when some trainer playing golf said I was too small to be hauling golf bags around. 'You should become a jockey; you're small enough,' he told me. Hell, I didn't know a thing about horses or the races.

"In fact, my father told me 'All horse-players die broke.' But he said if I wanted to, go take my best hold. So I did. I learned everything from the bottom up. For the longest time, I thought my father was right. But I stuck to it—that much gumption I got from him."

At his retirement announcement in April 1962, when asked what the future held, Eddie replied coyly: "Hey, golf was always my game from the beginning. Now I'm gonna concentrate on golf until I get it right."

That he did, until his death, November 14, 1997, three months shy of his 82nd birthday. The little Italian who initially couldn't tell a Thoroughbred from a jackass had personally rewritten the book—its final edition—on the art of race-riding.

He rode to the top of his profession, much like Babe "Sultan of Swat" Ruth, or Joe "Yankee Clipper" DiMaggio, or Joe "Brown Bomber" Louis, or Red "Galloping Ghost" Grange, or Michael "Air" Jordan. Through a career of 31 seasons encompassing 4,779 winners, Eddie Arcaro wore not one but three distinctive nicknames, each a decade-long descriptive tag.

New Yorkers especially bombarded Arcaro as "Banana Nose" from the mid-1930s through the early 1940s, a period which included Whirlaway's 1941 Triple Crown and Eddie's year-long suspension (1942–1943). The motive for "Banana Nose" wasn't all that benign; often it was bandied about amid derisive overtones.

During those 12 long months Eddie was exiled by track stewards to a breeding farm, where he toiled as a lowly exercise boy, railbirds discovered how dearly they missed his electric presence. He was promptly elevated to "Heady Eddie" by way of officially celebrating his Calumet Farm years with Citation and Hill Gail.

He was regally crowned the Master—a most deserving cachet—during his final decade. "I was indeed proud," he confessed privately, "but I didn't want anybody to know how really proud I was. That's why I had to leave the game on my terms. I intended to stay around not one little second longer than I felt I had a right to."

Now my binoculars weren't glued to my eyes in the spring of 1938 when Eddie rode Lawrin for trainer Ben Jones, winning his first of five Kentucky Derbys. But from what I've seen on film, plus Eddie's own candid analysis, it wasn't the prettiest of rides.

"Every time I see myself on Lawrin in late stretch, I shiver; actually I cower in shame," Eddie would shake his head. "I was whipping like an old lady, right-handed, an ugly, stiff-armed swing of the whip, at the same time drifting out in front of the horse who was closing ground on my right.

"Seeing how awkward I looked made me go back to the drawing boards. I not only improved my right-hand whip, making sure I tattooed the rump, not the flank, where you could do damage, even cause your horse to sulk, but I started using my left hand more. I concluded, being ambidextrous gave me a considerable edge over jocks who could whip only with one hand—it was like having a two-shot derringer up your sleeve."

But it was Eddie's "hand-ride" that immortalized the Arcaro style of power with panache. "Nobody, and I mean nobody, today or in his day," said former Calumet Farm trainer H. A. Jimmy Jones during a eulogy to Arcaro in 1997, "could out-finish Eddie. And when he put his whip away, you were in for the treat of your life, watching him pump and push to the wire like there was no tomorrow!"

Fellow reinsman Bill Shoemaker said, "Amen, to that. He hand-rode a horse better than anyone I ever saw."

Perhaps the finest compliment was paid Eddie by another hard-finishing jockey, Conn McCreary, who won two Derbys—with Pensive (1944) and Count Turf (1951). "It was at Belmont, the early 1950s, and Eddie and I were ding-donging it right down to the wire. He was screaming like a banshee, his whip flailing, then he bent low, riding like a madman, using both hand and heel. I actually paused, stopped riding, for just a second, mind you. I never saw anything like that man on a horse. I suppose you could say he just grabbed my attention. I had to stop, just to admire his work!"

Sure, Eddie was the first American-born jockey to win 3,000 races. I was there when he was honored for that in 1953 at Arlington. And he'd win another 1,400 races before retirement—4,779 in all from 24,092 mounts. Yet those numbers pale in comparison with Johnny Longden, Bill Shoemaker, and Laffit Pincay Jr. In fact, each of them has banked more purse money than Eddie, some surpassing him as the first jockey to earn more than 30 million in purse monies. Some jockeys can outstrip him in no more than three or four seasons, what with million-dollar pots galore, plus bonus incentives, not to forget the Breeders' Cup and its annual greenbacks explosion.

One sports scribe, Michael Mayo of the *Miami Sun-Sentinel*, summed it up, encapsulating Eddie's glory days: "Eddie Arcaro ruled in a time when sports had a soul. The days (and nights) of Damon Runyon and Toots Shor. When friendships were lasting, and there was more to life than ESPN highlights and Nike endorsements."

When racing was racing, Arcaro was Thoroughbred racing's most recognizable byword. He was interviewed by Edward R. Murrow. Twice that I know of, he exchanged TV dialogue with a young Mike Wallace. He also talked on TV with Hy Gardner. Several times Ed Sullivan, a sports and racing addict, proudly announced: "Ladies and gentlemen, here in our audience, the world's greatest jockey—stand up please, Eddie—ladies and gentlemen, Eddie Arcaro!" He joked alongside Milton Berle, too, whose fine namesake colt, Uncle Miltie, ranked among 1950's most promising 2-year-olds.

Eddie and Joe DiMaggio were golfing buddies. The fact that they were two of the most famous Italian-American sports icons of all time made for a comfortable comradeship. When DiMaggio was approaching his 83rd birthday and in the twilight of his earthly sojourn—enervated, hunched with age, yet as dignified as ever—he paid his respects during Eddie's 1997 interment.

But it was Eddie Arcaro's life and career we celebrate, and racing's Triple Crown has been the standard by which the sport's legend is judged. Arcaro won 5 Kentucky Derbies, 6 Preakness, and 6 Belmont Stakes—an unparalleled 17 victories in Triple Crown events! Oh, yes, he also won two Triple Crowns—with Whirlaway (1941) and Citation (1948). Not bad, considering there have been only 11 Triple Crown champions in American history. No other rider has won it more than once.

Racing is blessed with a brilliant jockey corps. There are none better than Pat Day, Jerry Bailey, Chris McCarron, Laffit Pincay Jr., Eddie Delahoussaye, and Kent Desoremeaux. Gary Stevens, Bill Shoemaker, Bill Hartack, Angel Cordero Jr., Ron Turcotte, and Earl Sande all rate a share of the Triple Crown limelight. Many of these riders, retired or still active, have enjoyed careers that were as long as, if not longer than, that of Arcaro. So the game's an equal opportunity sport—win what you can? Let's compare.

Shoemaker almost doubled Arcaro in races won. He managed no fewer that 11 Triple Crown winning rides, including 4 Derbies, but no Triple Crown sweep. He's second best, but a distant second-best, six Classic wins behind Eddie.

Bill Hartack, who equaled Eddie's record of five Kentucky Derby wins, won the Preakness three times and has a lone Belmont—but no Triple Crown. His nine Triple Crown races rank him a distant third to the Master. Sharing that plateau is the late Earl Sande, with three Derbies, one Preakness, and five Belmonts, also a total of nine. Currently hottest among jockeys today is the irrepressible Pat Day, who also has nine Triple Crown tallies, but no Triple Crown. Fact is, Pat owns one lonesome Derby, in 1992 aboard Lil E. Tee.

Gary Stevens sports eight, including three Derbies (Winning Colos, 1988; Thunder Gulch, 1995; Silver Charm, 1997). Chris McCarron's two Derbies (Alysheba, 1987; Go for Gin, 1994) are the nucleus for six. Ron Turcotte also won six Triple Crown races.

Eddie Delahoussaye, who won the Derby back-to-back with Gato Del Sol and Sunny's Halo (1982–1983), is next with five. With his 2000 Preakness win aboard Red Bullet, Jerry Bailey also sports five Triple Crown race wins, including two Kentucky Derbies.

The strangest fact of all is that Laffit Pincay Jr., the newly crowned all-time world champion in races won (he surpassed 9,000 wins in late 2000), is low man on the Triple Crown totem pole: only one Kentucky Derby (Swale, 1984), zero Preakness, but three straight Belmont Stakes (Conquistador Cielo, 1982; Caveat, 1983; Swale, 1984). But in no way does that diminish his skill or accomplishments.

Of course, racing's Breeders' Cup, which had its inception in 1984, is another touchstone of success, and its jockey roster, brimming with the likes of Bailey, Day, McCarron, Perret, Delahoussaye, Shoemaker, Cordero, Pincay, Mike Smith, and Pat Valenzuela, is a whole new ball game. Sadly, the Breeders' Cup came too late for Master Edward. Imagine the demand for his services; imagine his impact on titular honors in all divisions, especially with all that loot for the asking, and taking! But those same successful Breeders' Cup jockeys also covet Thoroughbred racing's Triple Crown, still the sport's mightiest draw; it remains the absolute by which riding greats will forever be measured.

Always the gentleman, and shrewdly masking that big, wonderful ego of his, Eddie occasionally would remind those who asked, or showed interest of any kind, that he'll always regret "the Kentucky Derbies that got away." Frowning shyly, he would say: "I should have won a few more, and maybe, just maybe, another Triple Crown."

"Another Triple Crown" has reference to Nashua in 1955, when Eddie misdiagnosed the Derby's ostensible game plan in prerace conference with Nashua's mentor, Sunny Jim Fitzsimmons. "We both blew it," Eddie explained. "We figured all we had to beat—on paper anyway—was Summer Tan. Somehow, we overlooked Swaps. I'd never do that again, not ever, not a colt with Shoemaker at the controls."

Swaps, as a result, was allowed to bounce along leisurely on an uncontested lead; Nashua lay third, Eddie's eyes glued to Summer Tan, keeping the latter a length or so back in fourth. "By the far turn, I knew Summer Tan couldn't get us. Lo and behold, up front I had forgotten about Swaps—and Shoe was sitting chilly."

Eddie was still confident Nashua could overcome his blunder. "I got into him with all my might. Now, Nashua, as everybody knew, was some kind of screwball, a nut case, temperamental when he wanted. But not that day; he fired, and he fired big. Our only problem was that we were trying to collar a fresh colt.

"Swaps, under wraps for nearly a mile by Shoe, rolled with Nashua's Sunday punch—we got right to his neck at midstretch—then sprinted clear. Beat us just over a length. It was all my fault."

Swaps, of course, went back home to California, where he cleaned house like the great colt he was. Nashua bounced back, winning both the Preakness and Belmont authoritatively. Later he trounced Swaps in their world-famous $100,000 winner-take-all match race in August. All that action was in range of my trusty binocs, and I called the race to an overflow press assemblage that historic day at now defunct Washington Park. We had no speakers for our makeshift accommodations for some 120 invading media, so they relied upon my call. It was great practice!

"Had I not messed up with Nashua, I'd have had a sixth Derby, and a third Triple Crown!" Eddie would chuckle down alibi lane.

Seriously, I think Eddie should have won nine Derbies and four Triple Crowns. I know. Give you a break. The guy's from Ohio, not Krypton. But you gotta hear me out. It could have all happened with just a little bit of bloomin' luck!

Take 1942, for instance. Eddie had just swept the Triple Crown the season before (his second Derby win) with bull-headed Whirlaway. He was still riding first-call for Greentree Stable's John Gaver, the gentlemanly trainer who loaned Eddie to Ben Jones to ride Whirlaway. It wasn't until years later that Arcaro shared a little-known secret with me. "All along it was said I had my choice between Devil Diver and Shut Out—and they were pretty even-steven at the time—but Gaver really preferred Devil Diver. Privately, he suggested I should string along with him for the Derby."

Record books are aglow with Devil Diver's flop, tiring to finish sixth as stablemate Shut Out, a gift by Arcaro and Gaver to jockey Wayne D. Wright, scored a decisive two-length decision in the 1942 Derby. Arcaro was livid; Gaver, nonplussed.

"Gaver," Arcaro recalled, "was none too public. He said nothing, so I decided to take the blame. It was like a flip of the coin—I took my best hold, and lost! Gaver never said another word, but his sad eye told me he felt as badly about the choice as I.

"Now, he told me I could have Shut Out back for the Preakness if I wanted. 'No,' I said, 'he belongs to Wayne Wright.' John agreed, because we all felt Shut Out a shoo-in for the Triple Crown. Well, the colt got in all sorts of trouble and gets beat by Alsab, actually is floundering at the end, finishing an inexplicable fifth. Naturally, poor Wayne Wright got all the blame.

"So now I'm back where I belonged all along, on Shut Out, for the Belmont. Shut Out does his impersonation of Whirlaway, and we win it going away by nearly three. Shut Out should have won the Triple Crown that year. Again, proof that you can't win 'em all." Had Heady Eddie chosen Shut Out as he really wanted, it seems likely he'd have won another Derby and maybe another Triple Crown.

Phalanx, a beautifully named late-running son of Pilate, owned and bred by C. V. Whitney, should have given Eddie another Derby score in the 1947 edition won by a scant head by Maine Chance Farm's front-stepping Jet Pilot. Phalanx, who had more traffic problems than an inexperienced motorist on Chicago's Kennedy Expressway during rush hour, was second, a head before an equally closing Faultless.

"I just couldn't strike any rapport with Phalanx," Arcaro said. "I don't think I ever had so much trouble trying to get to know a horse and his quirks. Honestly, I don't think Phalanx liked me at all. Still, we only lost the Derby by a head; we'd have won it in one more jump. But then its distance isn't 1¼ miles and a jump, is it?"

Eddie gave Phalanx one more try, the upcoming Preakness, to ascertain whether they belonged together. Phalanx's trainer was Syl Veitch. "I told Syl, as much as I admired his colt, I just didn't think we're making the right kind of music together."

Phalanx ran a lack-luster third in the Preakness as Faultless upended Jet Pilot. Arcaro voluntarily disconnected with Phalanx—hindsight says it was premature—handing him over to Ruperto Donoso, a hungry South American rider who got to know Phalanx in morning workouts. "I think they'll get along beautifully," Arcaro grinned.

They did. Phalanx crushed his Belmont field by 5, kept on winning, and later ran away with the 2-mile Jockey Club Gold Cup, belatedly nailing down honors as America's 3-year-old kingpin. "He's one that got away, that's for sure," Eddie philosophized.

So Eddie should have won the Derby (also the Triple Crown) with Shut Out, and the 1947 Derby with Phalanx, not to forget the 1955 Derby with eccentric Nashua. Those three would have made eight. We still need, by way of speculation, at least one more. Hey, possibly two.

"Hill Prince for some reason didn't decide to do any serious running in his 1950 Derby until it was too late," Arcaro reminisced.

"Maybe it was my fault. I was so anxious, I pushed him hard early. He was a one-run kind of horse, and finally when he gets to running late, we were forced to the inside, trying to catch Middleground, who was on the outside under a full head of steam. We got beat little over a length."

Hill Prince, who'd wind up that year's champion 3-year-old for Eddie, gainfully avenged his Derby loss, trimming Middleground by 5 open lengths in the Preakness. "By then I was convinced the Derby was the toughest race in the world to win," Arcaro confirmed.

"But I was confident, actually too confident in hindsight, with Bold Ruler in 1957," he continued. "Again, just as with Nashua two years earlier, trainer Sunny Jim and I screwed it up. This time, Sunny Jim must take most of the blame."

By way of memory refresher: 1957 was the year of racing's most phenomenal 3-year-old crop, headed by Round Table, Gallant Man, Gen. Duke, Federal Hill, Iron Liege, and Bold Ruler, the latter ultimately crowned 1957 Horse of the Year.

"Sunny Jim and I all along figured we had to beat Gen. Duke to win the Derby," Arcaro recalled. "The two colts were fairly evenly matched, but Gen. Duke seemed to have the edge going 1¼ miles. Gen. Duke comes up lame Derby morning. Trainer Jimmy Jones is down in the dumps—but Sunny Jim and I are high as kites. Oh, Jones still had Iron Liege, but Bold Ruler had proved several times before that we had his number.

"So, old man Fitz tells me—now he's never really ordered me around before, and that included the match race of 1955 when we whipped Swaps. This time, however, he insists I rate the Ruler, something we've never really attempted before. 'Otherwise,' he tells me, 'Bold Ruler won't get the Derby 1¼ miles.'"

Bold Ruler, like so many other progeny of the great sire Nasrullah, wanted no part of Arcaro's early constraints. "He fought me from the moment we left the gate," Eddie said. "He was shaking his head, swishing his tail, all but turning sideways into the first turn, laying second behind Federal Hill, who figured to set the pace. Midway down the backside, I realized we had made the big mistake. Meanwhile, Iron Liege, beautifully ridden by Hartack, takes command with Gallant Man right behind him.

"I finally gave the Ruler his head, but the damage was already done. Iron Liege staves off Gallant Man by a nose, Round Table passes us to take third, and we blow the Derby in fourth."

According to Eddie, "Old man Fitz took the blame. He was a great trainer, and a gentleman, all bent over with arthritis. Never forget, he had already won two Triple Crowns, with Gallant Fox and the Fox's son, Omaha. Nashua (1955) could have been No. 3. And Bold Ruler might've been another feather in his Derby cap."

Sunny Jim returned Bold Ruler to Eddie's good judgment for the Preakness two weeks hence. Arcaro doubtless ruffled Hartack's feathers, publicly predicting a reversal of fortunes in the Preakness, that the "Derby fiasco should never had happened."

This time, there'd be no coercion, no attempt to rate; Bold Ruler, who in the Derby was at his rankish worst, vetoing Eddie's every command, nixing his every directive, was docile as a lamb Preakness Day. "I don't know if he understood me," Arcaro related, "but I told him to do things his own way."

Bold Ruler was sharply roused at the start, outbreaking Iron Liege. Hartack knew the score; he'd have to stalk, then collar Bold Ruler early. It proved an impossible task. Given his head as Arcaro promised, Bold Ruler clung to the bit and, racing like the wind, never looked back. He scored handsomely by 2 lengths. Redemption, indeed!

"I never chided Fitz about our Derby boner," Arcaro mused. "We were both happy to make amends. Horse of the Year wasn't hard to take either."

Now Eddie wasn't always that polite or philosophical. Nor was his temper always that bridled. His full-year suspension, from September 1942 through September 1943, was a result of uncontrollable passion—built and aggravated during his thermal, turbulent years as a skinny teenager forced to defend himself against neighborhood toughs and bullies. "I was a dumb, stubborn ass," Arcaro admitted, "especially in 1942, the year after I had just put the world in my pocket, thanks to Calumet Farm, trainer Ben Jones, and Whirlaway."

The date was September 19, 1942; the occasion, the Cowdin Stakes in New York. Eddie was riding the favorite, a spunky 2-year-old named Occupation. Stupidly—"I was an ass"—Eddie boiled out of control when knocked off stride early by a colt named Breezing Home, in rein to jockey Venancio Nordase. It wasn't the jostling that angered Eddie; it was Nordase's smirking nonchalance following the collision.

Arcaro spurred Occupation, not to win the race, but to run down Nordase, viciously slamming Occupation into Breezing Home, scattering horses all over the place. A spectacular pile-up resulted. Eddie and Occupation recovered to finish second but were promptly disqualified, and Eddie was immediately called on the carpet by the steward. In retrospect, Eddie called the stewards' inquisition "justified, but I didn't have the good sense—nor did I want to—to keep my big mouth shut."

When queried whether his role in the melee was intentional, Eddie impulsively blurted: "If I could have, I would have killed the sonofabitch!" The Judges threw the book at Arcaro. Case closed. he was banned from Thoroughbred racing "indefinitely!"

Arcaro remembered: "And they didn't just say 'for a year'; they said 'indefinitely!' That meant, if they so desired, that I may never ride again. I worked on a farm that whole year. I couldn't go near the track. Just made a few bucks each week. God, what a comedown."

Eddie vowed never to make the same mistake twice. He exorcised the demon within, emerged chastened, humbly apologized for his asininity, and when he reentered the racing arena, did so as a new man. His temper was truly haltered, his very juices of life firmly redirected.

How often Eddie and I relived those crazy days of uncertainty, which served to qualify him for induction into that esoteric club reserved for the rich and famous. Eddie was quite a raconteur. Self-educated, he spoke fluently, careful to articulate clearly when interviewed. With his ego skillfully subdued, he honestly, and ethically, always credited the horse with the success he achieved.

When asked which horse he'd like to ride in a given race, he'd always reply: "The best horse, that's who!" He differed radically in this respect from most jockeys, who sincerely felt they contributed more substantially to a race's outcome than, say, the horse, or even the trainer.

I remember a 1961 visit to my announcer's booth by tall and lean Johnny Sellers, fresh off his superb winning rides aboard stretch-running Carry Back in both the Kentucky Derby and Preakness. They ran afoul of that year's Triple Crown, going unplaced behind a colt named Sherluck. But Sellers, like all Derby-winning jocks, was a national hero, also a Chicago mainstay at Arlington, Washington, and Hawthorne. Our conversation turned to the relative importance of horse and rider to a winning performance.

"I'd say it's 50-50," Johnny said without hesitation. Other jocks, including Johnny Rotz, agreed. A few, like Johnny Adams, Shoe, and Hartack, lavished a lot more praise the horse's way.

Arcaro's assessment: "It's 95 percent horse, 5 percent jockey, and sometimes I feel that's not being totally fair to the horse."

He always maintained there was little difference among the nation's top 10 riders. "All I'd ever want was to ride the best horse, that's all," he concluded. "But assuming all 10 horses were absolutely equal, that's when a rider's judgment is called into play. That, of course, would include things like courage and experience, the instinctive ability to out think the other nine jocks, to maneuver smoothly, to move at exactly the right time, and, of course, to stay out of trouble."

Unsaid, as you may have guessed, was "looking great," that inscrutable, arcane obsession Eddie cleverly hid as pivot to his private vanity and psyche. But then, looking great, even in defeat, was a given whenever Arcaro took to the track.

Eddie's reign as master reinsman also embraced a rare talent to rescue, salvage, and revitalize a horse's career, whatever the reason for the horse's decline. An SOS to the Master helped beautify the glory days. Among those equine stars were Sword Dancer, High Gun, and Career Boy—horses with which Eddie wasn't originally aligned, but was later paired with to inject new life. From Arcaro, each would discover new worlds to conquer.

King Ranch's Assault—called the "club-footed comet" because of an injury to his right hoof when but a yearling—became racing's seventh Triple Crown champion under jockey Warren Mehrtens in 1946. Arcaro started admiring the horse, but from afar. Fresh off his

Triple Crown sweep, Assault, flopped dismally in the Arlington Classic. I was there, a tender 15-year-old, cheering home the winner, an upstart Illinois colt named The Dude, whom I had seen win a Classic prep only the Saturday before.

Assault returned home to New York, was diagnosed with a kidney ailment, and rested for six weeks. He came back, but not as a winner. He started losing, tailing off unaccountably as if stale, which he wasn't, or hurting, which he wasn't.

After six straight losses, trainer Max Hirsch, with a nod of approval from King Ranch owner Robert J. Kleberg Jr., sought Dr. Eddie Arcaro for serious consultation. "We've got to turn things around, and right now," Hirsch told Eddie. Poor Warren Mehrtens was sent to the showers.

Arcaro was the prescriptive answer to Assault's problems, or so the results indicated. Their first dance together was a 6-length waltzing victory over arch rival Stymie in the Pimlico Special. A week or so later, Eddie and Assault humbled their field in Jamaica's Westchester Handicap. Eddie had saved and revitalized Assault to the tune of deserved honors as 1946 Horse of the Year.

But the best was yet to come for Assault and Arcaro. I was in the stands, binoculars strung around my neck, July 12, 1947, at the Jamaica track in New York, one of my rare forays outside Chicago, to see the Butler Handicap at $1\frac{3}{16}$ miles. My folks had permitted me to accept an invitation to visit Jamaica in the company of two Illinois owner-trainers for whom I had worked that spring as exercise boy, William Hal Bishop and William J. Schmidt. They were looking to purchase an eastern sire to bolster Illinois' struggling Thoroughbred breeding industry.

I saw Arcaro hoisted aboard Assault by trainer Hirsch in the paddock. Assault's saddle pads carried enough lead weight to sink a battleship. The colt was packing a staggering 135 pounds, giving 9 pounds to Stymie (126), 14 to Rico Monte (121), and 18 pounds to the brilliant race mare Gallorette (117).

I saw brilliance that day, horse and rider. The race's big contenders, particularly Assault, were late-runners, which meant a snail-like early pace: 6 furlongs in 1:14$\frac{4}{5}$, the mile in 1:38$\frac{3}{5}$. At that juncture, the three favorites, Assault, Gallorette, and Stymie, moved in unison—Assault tightly sandwiched between his arch rivals. Assault was in such tight quarters that, to win, he and Eddie would have to bull their way through. I feared a spill in the making!

There was no spill, but Assault did bull his way through the narrow opening, flinching not as equine bodies bounced back and forth off one another those final 100 yards to paydirt. And there was Arcaro—Heady Eddie—wincing not in the melee of the challenge, pushing, shoving fiercely—how he ever unhoused his whip, I'll never know—dropping Assault's photogenic nose ahead of Stymie right where it counted, on the wire!

Earlier, Eddie had authored his proverbial triple-negative axiom: "Don't Never Get Beat No Noses." It was a pledge he upheld gloriously that day.

Another of Dr. Arcaro's success stories was Sub Fleet, back home at Chicago's Washington Park. The vehicle was the 1952 Sheridan 'Cap, a mile affair limited to 3-year-olds. Top-weighted was Sub Fleet, owned by Dixiana—the same Sub Fleet who months earlier was a closing second to Hill Gail in the Kentucky Derby.

Calumet Farm's Hill Gail, you'll recall, gave Eddie his fifth Derby triumph in the spring of 1952. Eddie rode cunningly, stealing off to an 8-length bulge approaching the final quarter-mile, at which Sub Fleet, under rousing encouragement from hard-hitting Steve Brooks, took serious chase. Hill Gail was put to a typically powerful hand-ride, for which Eddie was famous, to preserve a clear-cut 2-length victory, a defeat for which Sub Fleet's trainer, Jack Hodgins, unfairly blamed Brooks.

Later that summer, still smarting from that Derby loss, Hodgins in a fit of rage replaced Brooks with Arcaro for the Sheridan, hoping to return his long-winded steed to his winning ways. Eddie mollified Brooks the best he could, assuring the latter the Sheridan was "a one-ride only" ticket, that Eddie had Hodgins' promise the colt would be returned to Brooks for future rides.

The Sheridan still rings true in my binocular sights. Sub Fleet, as usual, bided his time early. The speed belonged to Eljay, who cut the corner into America's longest homestretch—1,531 feet—with a commanding 2-length lead. Sub Fleet, at Eddie's insistence, barged through between horses, but not so rudely as to incur the stewards' wrath.

At midstretch, Sub Fleet was at Eljay's throatlatch. Then, from the proverbial blue, bounded the filly Aesthete, and three horses fanned out across the track with 100 yards to come. All three riders went to work. I like to think two of 'em stopped for just a moment to see the Master do his thing.

Trainer Jack Hodgins tells it best: "I've never seen nothing like it before. Arcaro was so smooth, so professional, you'd have missed it if you blinked twice. I know Sub Fleet flinched, startled like, when whipped—I bet he thought Arcaro had whips in both hands! Two whips, that's it. Sub Fleet thought his jockey had two separate whips—Arcaro hit him that fast, that often, first left-handed, then right-handed, like magic, a thing of beauty!"

Sub Fleet and Eddie Arcaro prevailed by a whisker! One railbird yelled it best when Hodgins led Sub Fleet and his accomplished jockey into the winner circle: "You told 'em, Eddie—'Don't Never Get Beat No Noses!" And again Arcaro dogma was validated.

True to his promise, Arcaro returned Sub Fleet to Steve Brooks. The following year, at age 4, Sub Fleet combined talents as usual with his old buddy Brooks to capture the rich Hawthorne Gold Cup at 1¼ miles.

Eddie wasn't the only jockey squeaking out unbelievable photo victories in major stakes. However, because he always flashed uncommon verve and esprit with each new miracle—and so many times in major affairs with big money on the line—he became popular fodder for sensational headlines across the country. Two months before his death, we were still making plans for another Eddie Arcaro appearance at Hawthorne's annual Jockey Hall of Fame Banquet in late fall of 1997. I told him I was researching and confirming dates and events in which his "Don't never get beat no noses" motto held sway.

"My Alzheimer's shouldn't affect my long-time memory, should it?" he kidded candidly. "I do remember something like that happening, and it made big news, too, but for the life of me I'm not able to pinpoint it."

"You wrote something similar to it in your five-part *Sports Illustrated* article back in 1957," I replied. "You spoke of how excited and animated you'd get during the late stages of a race." I read him the quote: "'Doing something completely unorthodox might do the trick,' you wrote. 'I remember one finish at Santa Anita; I switched whips six times between the 16th pole and the wire. I lost the reins completely, I think, and went across the line all-out—look no reins!' Remember that?" I asked.

"Yes, I remember writing that," he said. "What else did I say or do?"

"Okay, Eddie, sit back, listen, and concentrate. It was a big race, yes, at Santa Anita. You were riding one of the favorites, and you, and two others, were locked in a hammer and tongs struggle—life and death—you know, mortal combat, that sort of stuff."

Eddie said nothing. I heard him breathing, then a slight chuckle.

"Anyhow," I continued, "you were sandwiched between the two and you went to whipping like a madman, right, then left, right, and left again. But you gained no advantage. The three of you fought desperately right to the wire—a triple dead heat was in the making.

"In the last, heroic stride, yes, you dropped your reins; you slid your right hand high up on your horse's neck, inches from the top of his bobbing head. You shoved mightily, forward and downward, adding unexpected thrust and push to his final lunge. Three horses hit the wire as one!"

"Chanlea!" Eddie shouted in my ear. "The Santa Anita Derby, 1953, right? With Chanlea!"

"You got it—Chanlea and you, fighting it out in the 1953 Santa Anita Derby by a thrusting nose, rammed forward by your spontaneous shove to win it all!"

"You should write a book about me," Eddie sighed.

"I intend to," I answered.

"Maybe I should write one all my own?" he suggested.

"You did once, didn't you?"

"Naw, some ghostwriter did. He got a lotta things screwed up, too. Especially the title: *I Ride to Win*. That was stupid. All jocks ride to win, unless they're loony, or don't mind losing, or both. But I'm proud of that stuff I did for *Sports Illustrated*."

Well he should be. The *Sports Illustrated* five-part cover article began June 17, 1957: "The Art of Race Riding," by Eddie Arcaro, with turf columnist Whitney Tower, and drawings by Robert Riger. It was an analytical, anecdotal masterpiece by the greatest jockey who ever lived.

That, of course, occurred when he rode the absolute summit. Five years later, at retirement, he would statistically reign as America's number-one money-winning rider six times, with a record 17 Triple Crown events, 2 Triple Crowns, 10 Jockey Club Cups, 8 Suburbans, 5 American Derbies, and virtually every "name" stakes known to man.

More amazing, as we've seen, he rode more great or near great Thoroughbreds than any other jockey in history. Yes, Ron Turcotte had Secretariat and Riva Ridge; Jerry Bailey had Cigar; Pat Day, Easy Goer; Johnny Longden, Count Fleet and Noor; Ted Atkinson, Tom Fool and Capot; Laffit Pincay, Affirmed and Swale; Steve Cauthen, Affirmed; Georgie Woolf, Seabiscuit; Jacinto Vasquez, Ruffian; Clarence Kummer, Man o' War; Randy Romero, Personal Ensign; Billy Elliott, Phar Lap; Earl Sande, Gallant Fox; Hartack, Northern Dancer and Majestic Prince; Shoemaker, Swaps, Round Table, Tom Rolfe, Forego, and Spectacular Bid; Braulio Baeza, Dr. Fager and Buckpasser; Jean Cruguet, Seattle Slew; Angel Cordero Jr., Spend a Buck and Bold Forbes.

But Arcaro had Citation, Whirlaway, and Kelso. Also Nashua and Bold Ruler. Assault and Hill Prince, too. Not to forget High Gun and Sword Dancer. Or Real Delight and Hill Gail. Also Nellie Flag, One Count, Swoon's Son, and Native Dancer. Plus First Flight, Bold, and Hoop Jr. Plus scores of equines eager to partake of his artistry.

He had some one-ride tickets aboard Native Dancer, Sub Fleet, and Swoon's Son. Fact is, a few detractors felt compelled to castigate Eddie for what they called "pilfering" or "stealing" mounts, seizing potential stars or already established cracks he had not ridden before. Balderdash!

Jockey Eric Guerin bristled when trainer Bill Winfrey selected Arcaro to ride Native Dancer, TV's 1953 matinee idol, in the American Derby at Washington Park. What was Winfrey expected to do? Guerin had been suspended in New York for rough riding and Winfrey wasn't going to entrust the nation's finest Thoroughbred to just any jockey. He wanted the Dancer to win. He had the best horse in America; why not the best jockey? His choice seemed logical.

What some failed to appreciate was that in accepting his role as savior or preserver of the status quo, Arcaro not only elicited national attention, but also the weighty pressures that came with such renown. The nation's sports spotlight focused on Eddie. Could he deliver? He simply had to deliver. He had more to lose than gain. But he always came through.

I'd be remiss not to tell you about Swoon's Son and 1956. As related earlier, jockey Dave Erb, a fine gentleman and a brilliant but underrated jockey, was the rider for both Needles and Swoon's Son, both 3-year-olds of an exceptional generation. Swoon's Son was noted primarily for speed, so he bypassed the Triple Crown. That left Needles as hero of both the Derby and Belmont Stakes—Needles lost the middle jewel to Calumet Farm's classy Fabius. Swoon's Son returned as a world-beating 3-year-old in mid-summer at Arlington and Washington Parks, winning a string of lofty events, including a whopping victory over Fabius in the 1-mile Arlington Classic on the dirt.

As time and circumstance would have it, Needles was shipped to Chicago to dispute the 1$\frac{3}{16}$ miles American Derby on the grass at Washington Park. Recall earlier, Marje Everett left no stone unturned to make turf action an important appendage to Chicago racing. Swoon's Son already was committed to the American Derby. Erb couldn't ride both colts, and because he feared trainer Hugh Fontaine's wrath, he discreetly chose the stouthearted, better-known Needles.

Being a year-round Arlington–Washington publicist—and practicing daily as a race-caller wannabe—I was privy to A. G. "Lex" Wilson's private musings over whom he'd get to deputize for

Erb on Swoon's Son in the upcoming American Derby. Only the year before the race had been switched to 1$\frac{3}{16}$ miles on the turf as part of the Lindheimer–Everett emphasis on grass racing. Swaps won the 1955 race.

Erb, of course, wouldn't have minded a bit had Wilson selected any of a spate of local jocks to ride Swooney. The latter actually didn't figure to defeat lion-hearted Needles going a distance of ground, grass or dirt. Wilson, however, wanted the best for his colt. So in flew Eddie from New York. Years later I recall Erb muttering under his breath how "clever that Eddie Arcaro is to steal away someone else's mount when you least expected it." That was a bunch of hooey; Erb felt compelled to choose Needles. He probably hoped Lex Wilson would scratch Swoon's Son, since the colt was minus his regular pilot.

It had rained continuously for some 20 hours. In those days, unless Noah and the flood appeared unannounced, or some Lake Michigan tidal wave found its way as far south as Washington Park, no race scheduled on the grass was ever—and I mean *never*—moved to the dirt. Those switches are routinely done today to appease horsemen increasingly concerned over their horses' safety, because the surface can become dangerously slippery.

Washington Park's turf course that Saturday was a marshy swamp, water sloshed up out of the sod and up over the horses' ankles as they jogged postward. Track condition alone would seem to favor Needles's stamina over Swooney's penchant for early foot.

Arcaro, however, knew of the "one, full quarter-mile burst of electrifying speed" that Swoon's Son possessed. In past races, Erb used that "speed blast" when leaving the half-mile pole, often losing pursuers in his dust and all but demoralizing the opposition, discouraging any attempt to play catch up.

You already know the outcome. Eddie rode Swoon's Son flawlessly, made every pole a winning one, waited up front with the patience of Job. He saved Swooney's quarter-mile surge, not for customary ignition at the half-mile pole, but for the final quarter-mile, totally neutralizing Needles's patented late kick. The Master had carried Swoon's Son the full 1$\frac{3}{16}$ miles over a track not suited to his colt's usual style and against the most feared stretch-runner of his day. Needles made up nary an inch on Swoon's Son, from the furlong pole at midstretch right down to the wire.

Eddie could have insisted Wilson ride him back on Swooney, having helped the latter's cause so brilliantly against all odds. Wilson himself could have resented Erb's snub, deciding to stick with the magician who miraculously got Swoon's Son over a distance of ground every expert felt impossible. None of that happened. It was one-ride ticket only, just as Eddie had promised, and had done three years earlier with Native Dancer. It was similar also to Arcaro's wonderwork with Sub Fleet in 1952. Erb got Swoon's Son back, and they continued to register major scores in seasons to come.

A similar incident comes to mind. It was 1953, the second of Arcaro's back-to-back Chicago riding seasons. The Hasty House Farms of Allie and Billie Reuben had a flock of promising 2-year-olds by the speed sire Roman—including two of the noblest Romans of 'em all, the colt Hasty Road and the filly Queen Hopeful. Both ruled midwestern racing with regal splendor.

Johnny Adams was contract rider for Hasty House Farms. But the Reubens, like so many other Arlington–Washington owners, were bewitched by Arcaro. They publicly sought his riding skills. This rankled Adams, as well it might. I know for a fact that it was Arcaro who arbitrated a fair and just settlement: he would ride either Hasty Road or Queen Hopeful, not both; Adams would ride the other. Whether by secret parley or coin flip, Eddie drew Hasty Road.

The teamwork orchestrated by Eddie proved a master stroke. Hasty Road blossomed into a 2-year-old stakes star of the first water. With Eddie barely moving a muscle, Hasty Road was selected as Juvenile of the Year in one poll. He certainly won more money in 1953 than any other youngster in America. Among his four Chicago scores—Arcaro aboard in each—were victories in both Arlington and Washington Park Futurities, annexing each with speed to spare.

And Queen Hopeful and Johnny Adams? They also proved virtually unbeatable. They dead-heated Greek Lady early in the Mademoiselle. Then they captured the 2-year-old filly counterparts to the Futurities, the Arlington Lassie and the Princess Pat. There was joy and riches and fame for all involved!

Adams got Hasty Road back for the latter's 3-year-old season. They finished a powerful second to Determine in the Kentucky Derby, and they came right back to register a start-to-finish, front-stepping triumph in the Preakness, a magnificently timed ride by the veteran Adams. Hasty Road retired to stud with earnings of $541,402; Queen Hopeful retired with $365,044. Maybe Arcaro, the little Italian with the big smile and generous heart, was really the noblest Roman of 'em all.

My out-of-state journeys were few and far between, but in March 1957, I witnessed the coveted Flamingo Stakes at Hialeah for 3-year-olds at 1⅛ miles. The turf world abounded with the kind of torrid rivalries that characterized its golden age—in this case, a sorta rubber match between two potentially great 3-year-olds, Gen. Duke and Bold Ruler. Recall, if you may, that 1957 was the incredible year that also included 3-year-olds Gallant Man, Iron Liege, Federal Hill, and Round Table.

At Flamingo time, that stakes stacked up as a veritable match race between Calumet Farm's Gen. Duke, with Bill Hartack aboard, and Wheatley Stable's Bold Ruler, Eddie in the saddle. Now, parenthetical to the Flamingo, Eddie Arcaro went to his grave singularly disturbed by a deteriorated professional and personal relationship with jockey Bill Hartack. "I just don't understand Bill," Eddie often remonstrated privately. "He's told people he doesn't like me, saying some nasty things. Heaven knows, I've always spoken well of him. But he won't crack at what I've done or said that irritates him, if anything. I'm at a loss, sad, too."

I can verify Bill's unpleasantness. Hartack was serving as Illinois senior state steward in the early 1990s, and we were at a holiday dinner, sharing a table with retired sports writer Elmer Polzin. I naturally brought up Arcaro's name, careful to remind Bill that in my opinion, he, Arcaro, and Shoe were the three finest jockey's I'd ever seen. Polzin concurred. Bill, at mention of Arcaro's name, curtly replied: "I'd rather not talk about him." Period.

Maybe this 1957 Flamingo of which we speak played some kind of hidden role? At any rate, Bold Ruler earlier, January 30, had whipped Gen. Duke in the 7-furlong Bahamas, conceding 12 pounds to the latter and tying the track record of 1:22 flat. Two weeks later in the 1⅛ miles Everglades, Bold Ruler again conceded 12 pounds to his rival, but this time Gen. Duke turned the tables, scoring in a photo finish in a blazing 1:47⅖.

I sat in the stands on Flamingo day, chilled to my very marrow with anticipation, my binocs aimed at Eddie as he and Bold Ruler braced for the start. Every ingredient of this contest suggested match race, one-on-one, with Gen. Duke playing catch up. This time each colt carried equal weight of 122 pounds.

The gate clanged, the gates swung open, and Eddie, fully aware of the Ruler's unpredictable ways, immediately put him where he always wanted to be, "on the engine." Federal Hill, also quick on the draw, was among the first flight, but all eyes were on the Ruler. Gen. Duke, who was improving with every start, was content to stalk his quarry, Hartack displaying inordinate confidence in the explosive son of Bull Lea.

Federal Hill tried vainly to stay with Bold Ruler as the Flamingo field left the half-mile pole. Gen. Duke was roused by Hartack—and the chase was on!

Here's what I discerned through by binocs—later confirmed by Arcaro: Eddie deliberately, but without fanfare, allowed Bold Ruler to drift away from the rail, inching out with every stride toward the middle of the track. Gen. Duke—I'm sure Hartack felt he could corral Bold Ruler whenever he wanted—continued to the leader's right flank, racing even wider as they curved for home.

Bold Ruler wasn't guilty of herding his opponent, which could be construed as bothering or impeding, but quietly had maneuvered the two of 'em farther out from the inner rail. Now, it's no big thing for the inside horse to gain a momentary advantage by dropping over to the rail. But Eddie had subtly built to that moment, so he didn't just drop, or glide, to the inside. It was as if he and Bold Ruler literally dove to the rail, leaving Gen. Duke hung out to dry. Gen. Duke was caught napping, dangling out there for a split second while Bold Ruler shot to the rail, adding measurably to his lead. What was no more than a half-length lead ballooned to nearly 1½ lengths. Hartack's and Gen. Duke's dander were up. It was crunch time!

Hartack was no slouch when it came to finishing a race. A natural southpaw, blessed with strength, intelligence, and competitive fire, he unleashed a mighty, protracted challenge. Gen. Duke was all out—so was Bill—charging alongside Bold Ruler, only a neck away, with a 16th of a mile to travel.

There was Master Edward Arcaro, all over Bold Ruler—hand, arm, heel, and whip. Like Gen. Duke, Bold Ruler was fully extended. Both colts were running on heart and class.

No craziness for the Ruler this time. He was full-out; no need for additional whip encouragement. So Eddie sheathed his crop and, settling deep into that picture-perfect, low-profile hand-ride—a sight for these eyes—he once again displayed the power, style, and grace that were his alone.

Bold Ruler still had his neck in front at wire's end. And he'd still be in front if they had to go around the track again. With the Flamingo televised nationally, Arcaro's brilliance blazed anew. Halley's Comet had nothing on him. The Master again taught; his student again learned.

Eddie Arcaro's legacy, to my way of thinking, confirms what many astute turf historians preach today: "Thoroughbred racing's future lies in its past, and in its rich history." I've tried in vain to get the sport's newest, sometimes myopic, industry-oriented promotions organization, the National Thoroughbred Racing Association (NTRA), to help perpetuate and celebrate the game's proud heritage. They don't return my calls nor answer correspondence. Perhaps to them I'm just a relic of the past. I'll bet Master Edward Arcaro just turned over in his grave!

Chapter Seven

Bill "Silent Shoe" Shoemaker

When I first laid eyes on Bill Shoemaker—who at the time was called "Wee Willie," a nickname he disdained—I thought he was the most perfectly proportioned, albeit diminutive—and I mean "tiny"—human being I had ever seen. Thereafter, thanks to a Midas touch with Thoroughbreds, he'd always stand tall as the jockey giant from Fabens, Texas, worthy of Hall of Fame acclaim.

At first glance, I had no expectation that Bill (he also despised his given name "William," as did riding contemporary Bill Hartack) would ultimately prove heir apparent to Eddie Arcaro's crown as America's premier jockey. "Big things do come in small packages," I'd later fondly reminisce. A package that stood a good two inches under five feet, and if he weighed 95 pounds "soaking wet," then I was the circus fat man.

Oh, Shoe was still growing. Maybe he'd grow another inch, and living the good life expected of a world-class jockey millionaire, he'd easily balloon up to perhaps a fat 105 pounds after downing a two-inch thick porterhouse steak with all the trimmings. We should all have his weight problems.

When all was said and done, Shoe may have lacked Arcaro's style, power, and charisma, but he lacked nothing in ability, talent, courage, or insatiable appetite for success. His hands, like those of the Master but perhaps not as strong, had mandatory softness, enabling him to control 1,000 pounds of volatile horseflesh with threadlike reins of silk. Shoe was strongly delicate—how's that for an oxymoron?—maximizing his mount's performance with what deceptively appeared minimum effort. Guys like Arcaro "made" their horses run; horses seemed "eager" to run for the Shoe.

But he was a tough guy to get to know at first. He rarely spoke or smiled. Once folks discovered how he abhorred "Wee Willie" or "William," they naturally gravitated to "Silent Shoe," much as Thoroughbred fans in the 1930s and 1940s referred to Seabiscuit's trainer, because of his famed taciturnity, as "Silent Tom" Smith.

What most folks didn't know was that young Bill Shoemaker started out dirt poor; he was plagued with bad, or missing, teeth. That's one reason Shoe rarely spoke or smiled, self-consciously keeping his mouth shut. Soon as he could afford proper dental care, he became as affable as his innate diffidence allowed; he'd talk, intelligently, too, with the best of 'em.

He was so tiny I often feared an energetic trainer, not realizing his own strength, might literally toss Shoe over the saddle while affording him a leg up in the paddock. Never happened, of course. With Shoe nothing more than a squat on a horse's back, I think some horses went postward barely aware that Shoe was aboard. I have a theory on the subject of Shoe's hardly noticed presence astride a Thoroughbred.

First, countless times I've seen a starting gate mishap—a horse rearing, stumbling, often dumping his jockey. Hopefully the rider escaped unscathed. That riderless horse is automatically disqualified, but he's still there on the track. Because he's minus the jockey's weight and totally without human direction, if he's in a running mood, that horse without fail will pick up his field, effortlessly too, threading his way in, out, and around horses, bolting to the fore. I can't remember the last time I saw a riderless horse get himself into trouble. He might unintentionally interfere, crowd, or intimidate another horse and jockey, but he unerringly will steer clear of pockets, blind switches, and other horses.

Allow me to offer living proof from a dead jockey, the late Chicago-born Tony Skoronski. Tony was "All-Chicago" in every respect; he never won the Kentucky Derby, or any Triple Crown event for that matter, but he amassed more than his share of winners at both Hawthorne and Sportsman's Park and even a few major stakes at Arlington and Hollywood. I knew Tony fairly well, especially during my three-week jockey wannabe effort at Sportsman's and

Hawthorne in 1947. Tony drank and gambled freely with Chicago's finest. And they respected him, especially the workmanlike way he handled the hairpin turns at half-miler Sportsman's Park, Chicago's premier (and only) bullring establishment.

"Give your horse his head completely," Tony told me. "Sure, you don't want to clip heels, or run into someone, or get carried wide by another frightened horse. But if you get scared yourself and snatch up or yank back in fear, you'll get yourself in a whole lotta more trouble. May get yourself killed, too."

Now, Tony Skoronski had terrible eyesight. Contact lenses weren't that practical or perfected back then. Many times, he rode virtually blind, especially on rainy or foggy days or when the track was sloppy. I noticed he rode with loose, dangling reins, his hands high up on the horse's neck and mane. Tony encouraged his mount to "do his thing," particularly into and around those sharp turns. Know what? The horse did all right, rarely got into trouble, picked his own spots, and ran on his own courage—virtually unbridled and untrammeled.

You've seen dog racing, I'm sure. The dogs have no jockeys. Sure, they can get bumped or carried wide. But a dog whose modus operandi is the late spurt will split dogs, save ground inside others, and then, all on his own, swing three wide in upper stretch to notch the win. Now, I'm not advocating that horses compete riderless against one another with reckless abandon. I'm just suggesting that sometimes "less"—as in less rigid control and direction—is actually "more." It's only a theory. But think about it, okay?

Shoe's magic, in addition to an overall genius for horse-backing, was in his hands, also his long rein. His soft hands possessed no jerk or pull. He turned his horse's neck reins into silky strands, a magical line of communication horses obviously loved. Bill Shoemaker was truly special, and from where I sat—first, as a turf devotee from April 1949 when he won his first race; second, as a track publicist from 1953 through 1958; then as race-caller from 1959 onward—Shoe gave incalculable heart to Thoroughbred racing's golden days.

What griped me most about Shoe was that, in day-by-day racing, especially during the winter months at Santa Anita, he always seem to out-win Arcaro. Eddie certainly more than held his own in stakes, for years in a class by himself. But every time Eddie managed two or three winners on a program, Shoe seemed to come back with three or four.

"I never had a hankering to win individual track seasonal titles," Eddie insisted. "Yes, there were days when I'd out-point Shoe, and it'd make me feel good. But Shoe was tireless. If I had five mounts that day, he'd have seven or eight. I could maybe beat him on a race-for-race basis. But he'd always have more chances, and he'd never let one slip by." Eddie Arcaro freely called Bill Shoemaker the "best rider I've ever seen or competed against."

Maybe that was one reason Hartack took a dislike to Arcaro? Yet, in all fairness, Shoe made headlines several years before Hartack emerged a serious factor. It was 1950, and 19-year-old Shoe burst upon the racing scene like an insuppressible champagne cork, scoring an unbelievable 388 winners. He shared that total with another youngster, Italian-born Joe Culmone—but the big news was that 388 winners had been unapproachable for 44 years, a record set back in 1906 by Walter Miller. By comparison, Eddie in 1950 won only 195 races, but that year he topped the nation in stakes and money earned, with $1,410,160.

But Shoe was just getting started—he was a house afire! He was out-pointed for winners by Charlie Burr in 1951, the latter bagging 310. Yet Shoe was developing a new talent for winning stakes and rich pots, actually topping Eddie in money won—$1,329,890 to $1,265,455—not by that much, but enough to wake up Eddie to the new kid on the block.

"Hey, Shoe made me sit and take notice," Arcaro recalled. "So I went to work with new zeal and gusto." It paid off, too. Eddie the following year smashed his own money-earned record of $1,686,230 in 1948 by earning $1,859,491 in 1952. "I just wanted to remind Shoe who was still boss." Eddie quipped. "But that little guy was cooking, and, like Satchel Paige warned, I didn't want to look back, 'cause I knew who it was who was gaining on me."

Shoe came into his own in 1953, reigning supreme as the nation's winningest jock (a record-breaking 485 wins) and his second money-winning title ($1,784,187). What made Shoe's 485 winners all the more phenomenal was that he totally annihilated Tony

DeSpirito's brand-new record of 390 winners of only the year before, by no fewer than 95 winners!

"I couldn't believe his productivity." Eddie shook his head. "Shoe never had much to say, but when he said it, everybody in the game listened. He raised the bar. That year he nearly tripled my wins"—in 1953, Eddie collected 167—"though my stakes scores gave me second-best earnings of $1,647,666."

Arcaro remained undisputed king of stakes jockeys, but Shoe was no idle pretender. Fact is, Shoe repeated his 1953 successes. In 1954 he was tops in races won (380), also money earned by mounts ($1,876,760). That year Arcaro upped his wins to a meager 178, but his stakes and money earned amounted to $1,661,640. Eddie was still winning big money with far fewer mounts and winners than Shoe.

Meantime, Bill Hartack erupted as a major riding force. His apprentice year was 1953, the same year Shoe amassed an unbelievable 485 wins for an amazing 29 percent winning average. Hartack himself crashed the charmed circle 350 times, also a winning 29 percent average.

Hartack, whose competitive fire was second to none, proved his "bug boy" year no fluke, piling up 417 winners in 1955. So if two were company—Arcaro and Shoe—three—in the inevitable person of Hartack—had now become a crowd. And Thoroughbred fans loved every moment of it! Sure, in recent years the sport had delighted in Jerry Bailey, Pat Day, Chris McCarron, and Gary Stevens. And when the latter retired temporarily, he was instantly replaced by Kent Desormeaux. But their domination—races won and stakes scored—failed to match the sparkle and drama of the Arcaro–Shoemaker–Hartack era.

As if to prove he still ruled the roost, Arcaro magically reestablished his preeminence among America's riding elite in 1955, the year of Hartack's prodigious 417-winner season and Shoe's match race shipwreck on Swaps against Nashua. Eddie thoroughly outshone his brilliant antagonists by banking $1,864,796 for his sixth money-winning title. But the writing was on the wall. Shoemaker's time had arrived. The tiny giant with soft hands and long rein, whose riding style Arcaro himself freely lauded as "smooth as silk," just like the genie loosed from Aladdin's lamp, was now free to forage the sport's golden pastures at will.

How well I recall Shoe's impact on racing in general, Chicago in particular. Shoe usually reserved his Chicago campaigns until late summer, following the early summer Hollywood season. By then, Hartack, who always made Chicago his spring–summer headquarters, was swallowing up riding titles at will, winning three straight at Arlington, including a track record of 75 winners in 1956. And how well I recall daily programs in which Shoe and Hartack won the day between them. It was a bettor's delight. The only challenge was whom do you bet—Shoe or Hartack? Shoemaker would win four of nine; Hartack, the other five. Or vice versa. Oh, they'd often leave a few races for other jocks, like Johnny Adams, Kenny Church, Steve Brooks, Ovie Scurlock, Johnny Sellers, Bobby Baird, or Lois C. Cook.

Many dyed-in-the-wool handicappers deplored their dominating ways, complaining that Shoemaker and Hartack too often rode either or both the heavy and second favorites, making price-shots few and far between. Real fans, like yours truly, loved it. Shoe and Hartack were two of America's three finest riders, and to see them slug it out on a daily basis was a treat for the ages.

Some horsemen complained, too. If through Shoe and Hartack's agents—Harry Silbert and Chick Lang, respectively—they couldn't line up either jockey to ride their horses, they had to rely on others to break the stranglehold. Those horsemen sadly forgot Arcaro's formula for a rider's success: 95 percent horse, 5 percent jockey. Yes, Shoe and Hartack piled up the winners, but they couldn't go without the best horseflesh available.

There was one stratagem I heard rumored about that, even though I never personally saw it executed, I found distasteful. If a horseman thought he had better than an outside chance to win, and he seriously sought Shoe's services—and we're talking ordinary, run-of-the-mill races, not major stakes, which spoke for themselves—he'd voluntarily come up with a $50 win ticket for the agent, in addition to the regular jockey fee and winner's fee. Easy money. Tax free, too, if true. I have no reason to believe it wasn't so.

From a stakes standpoint, Shoe was a stickout. For example, he captured the Washington Park Handicap three straight years, 1955–1957, with Jet Action, Swaps, and Pucker Up. Then he skipped a year, winning it in 1959 with Round Table. He returned to annex it again with Prove It in 1962, and to prove age no barrier, he won it all over again, for a sixth time, in 1980 with the great Spectacular Bid. Shoemaker was Marje Everett's favorite little big man on campus.

On June 5, 1960, track owner Ben Lindheimer was mortally felled by a massive heart attack. Daughter Marje Lindheimer Everett—she earlier had married nationally known race official Webb Everett—took charge, and I mean took charge.

For years the twin tracks of Arlington and Washington Parks shared Chicago glory. Arlington had ties with the Windy City's upper crust, best exemplified by its swanky Post and Paddock Club, an exclusive building immediately west of the clubhouse portion of the track's furlong-long grandstand. The cream of Chicago society for decades had luxuriated there in opulent splendor during the sport's glory days under Ben Lindheimer's regime as beneficent despot. Among Marje's first major changes was to confiscate the Post and Paddock building as part of her personal environs. She then built a plush, upscale, glass-enclosed restaurant, the Classic Club, extending across 60 percent of the upper grandstand. A small portion was assigned to the city's social elite, a change they disdained. She couldn't care less.

Marje's new domicile, the former Post and Paddock, became a popular hangout for special socialities, like Donald McKellar of the Field Enterprises of Marshall Field and friends; socialite Charles Wacker III; catalog sales magnate Modie J. Spiegel; and Crowdus Baker, president of Sears and Roebuck. Each, incidentally, also owned and bred Thoroughbreds, their interest in Arlington both business and social. Shoe and his first wife, Babs—a statuesque blond who lent a Mutt and Jeff look to their relationship and could give any runway model a run for her money—lived the good life at Marje's exclusive rendezvous.

Marje and husband Webb lived and breathed Arlington. They considered sister track Washington Park expendable. In 1961, south-side Washington Park, which like Arlington boasted a 1⅛ miles dirt oval, a 1-mile inner turf course, and America's longest homestretch—1,531 feet—was streamlined into a full mile track. Harness racing was introduced there on Labor Day 1962, and I was impressed into duty, adding harness racing to my job description. There would be an occasional return of Thoroughbred racing to nostalgic Washington Park before the aging track, which Marje allowed to deteriorate into a veritable tinder box, burned down to the ground in the fall of 1977. By then, the Everetts were long gone, since 1970, having sold to Gulf + Western.

Washington Park's summer dates had been transferred to Arlington in 1961, the same year Marje Everett formally purchased total control of the two tracks, forming a new corporation known as Chicago Thoroughbred Enterprises. Irreformably ambitious and far-sighted, Marje in 1962 enriched the purse of the combined Arlington–Washington Futurity for 2-year-olds to an unheard of $356,250, making it the richest Thoroughbred race in the world. I called it, of course. Its winner was Candy Spots, owned by Rex C. Ellsworth and trained by Mesh Tenney (they of Swaps fame) and ridden by—guess who?—the indomitable Shoe himself. Arcaro had retired. The king is dead; long live the king!

Shoe had been wonderfully primed to assume the throne. His three major riding indiscretions had served as vital teaching lessons. First, in the 1955 Swaps–Nashua match race at Washington Park, he was out-ridden by Arcaro. Second, in the 1956 Californian, he misjudged the finish, easing up Swaps, dropping an embarrassing decision to Porterhouse. Third was his 1957 Kentucky Derby gaffe astride Gallant Man, when he stood up momentarily and Iron Liege eked out a nose victory.

Like Arcaro before, Shoe was always on the lookout for great mounts, "another Round Table or Swaps" to sweeten the pot. For a year or so, he thought he found his quest in Candy Spots, the latest sensation from Ellsworth and Tenney's Chino, California, empire. Candy Spots was an Ellsworth–Tenney homebred son of the South American sire Nigromante, out of Candy Dish (she by Swaps's sire, Khaled). In winning the world's newest richest race,

Phil Georgeff posing with Miss America of 1962 at a special racetrack appearance at Arlington Park, February 21, 1962.

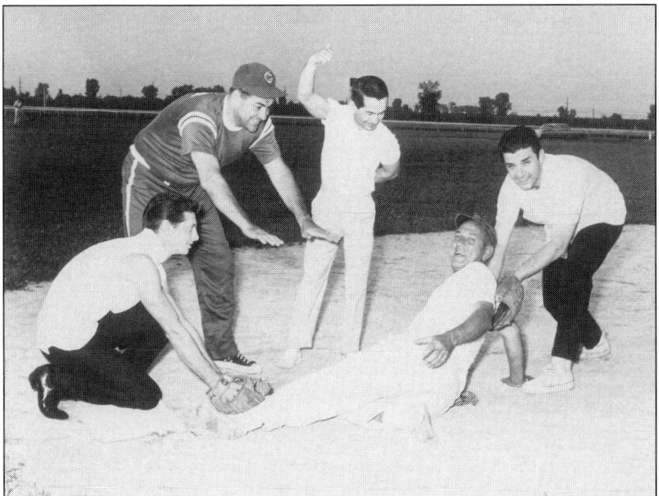

"When thoroughbred racing was also a game." Left to right: a youthful Bill Hartack gets mixed signals—a "he's safe" sign from retired Baseball Hall of Famer Lou Boudreau; diminutive Bill Shoemaker begs to differ with an "an' yer' out!"; on the slide is Thoroughbred owner and breeder, Howard Miller; Georgeff (far right) orchestrates the play at the plate.

"Ah, sweet bird of youth." Thirty-five-year-old announcer Phil Georgeff was only in his sixth year as Arlington race announcer, poised on this day to describe yet another superlative winning performance.

Kelso parades at Keeneland, April 21, 1965. In Georgeff's estimation, the horse rates as one of the greatest Thoroughbreds of all time. *(Courtesy Keeneland Library; J. C. Skeets Meadors photo)*

CHICAGO TRIBUNE, SUNDAY, AUGUST 22, 1965

Tribute to a Big Winner

[TRIBUNE Staff Photo]

Arlington Park's riding corps lines up in backround as Jockey Willie Shoemaker (wearing No. 5) and Phil Georgeff, track publicity director, present award to Johnny Longden, veteran jockey. Longden, 58, has ridden over 6,000 winners in long career.

Arlington Park's riding corps lines up in background as jockey Willie Shoemaker (wearing No. 5) and Phil Georgeff, track publicity director, present an award to Johnny Longden, veteran jockey. August 22, 1965.

Georgeff attending an Illinois Racing Board meeting, 1967.

Mighty Secretariat takes to Arlington Park on June 30 in his first start following his spectacular 1973 Triple Crown triumph. With Georgeff on the call, Secretariat won by 9 lengths. Jockey Ron Turcotte is aboard. *(Courtesy Arlington Park)*

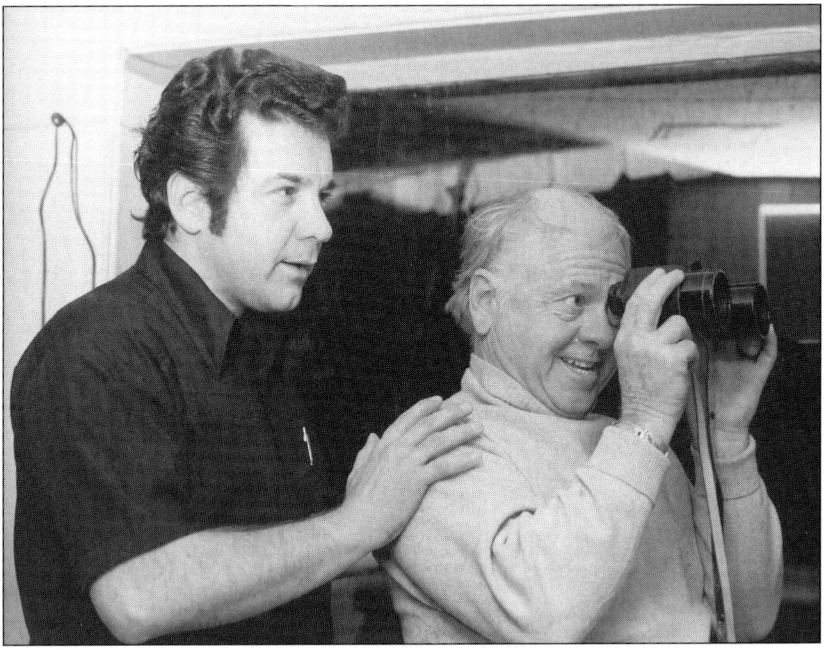

Georgeff giving movie legend Mickey Rooney a few announcing hints at Arlington Park, circa 1975.

Georgeff's off-track exploits included this Chicago Loop scene at the Playboy Mansion with jockey Phil Rubbicco (left) and Playboy Bunny Sharon Gwin.

Georgeff's favorite race call—the 1981 inaugural running of the Arlington Million, Thoroughbred racing's first Million Dollar race. John Henry (outside) noses out The Bart (rail) in a controversial finish heard and seen around the world on NBC.

Fan rebellion following Georgeff's firing in September 1982. Sign "Georgeff is worth a million" greeted the track management the day of Arlington Million II.

Phil Georgeff is honored by Chicago-area racing fans at Hawthorne Race Course in 1982, the year he was fired from Arlington Park for "calling races with too much enthusiasm" by misguided president John Mooney.

October 1982.

Phil throwing out the first pitch at a Chicago White Sox home game in July 1987. *(Courtesy Tony Inzerillo. Copyright © The Sporting News.)*

Georgeff (center), accompanied by his son Scot (left), is honored for his 85,000th race call—a Guinness record—by Hawthorne president Thomas F. Carey. *(Courtesy Luongo Photo. Copyright © 1988.)*

1988.

Phil Teinowitz' Chicago-owned Cryptoclearance is seen winning the prestigious Hawthorne Gold Cup in 1989 for the second straight time. *(Courtesy Luongo Photo.)*

Phil Georgeff and former jockey Gerry Gallitano, co-hosts of *Chicago Racing Report*, a daily racing show covering Thoroughbred and harness racing at all Chicago-area tracks.

Former jockey great Eddie Arcaro (second left) is inducted into Hawthorne Race Course's Racing Hall of Fame on November 10, 1996. America's all-time premier jockey is feted by (left to right): Hawthorne general manager Robert F. Carey; artist Chris Paluso; Hawthorne president Thomas F. Carey; and author-announcer Phil Georgeff. *(Courtesy Four Footed Fotos.)*

Phil (right) signing his book *Thoroughbred* at Hawthorne Race Course in 1996. *(Courtesy Four Footed Fotos.)*

the 7-furlongs Arlington–Washington Futurity, Candy Spots whipped a highly esteemed easterner, Never Bend.

"Candy Spots could be the one," Shoe said to me following the colt's Futurity triumph. "He has a few physical problems, but when feelin' good, he's all runner," Shoe confirmed.

Those "physical problems" allowed Candy Spots only three starts as a juvenile—but he won all three, including his sole meeting with Never Bend. The latter, however, surprisingly was named 2-year-old of 1962.

Shoe's admiration for Candy Spots diminished not one whit as 1963 dawned. As a matter of fact, there was talk of a winter match race between Candy Spots and Never Bend at Hialeah, so torrid had their rivalry become, on paper at least. But like Swaps–Nashua before, Candy Spots sought asylum in California, while Never Bend preferred to hear his hooves rattle in Florida, where he registered a thumping 5-length victory in the Flamingo at Hialeah.

"We stayed in California," Shoe recalled, "and Candy Spots came back running as a 3-year-old. We won our first two, including a weird Santa Anita Derby, which was marred by a spectacular four-horse spill. We just barely escaped with our lives. But Candy Spots was unshaken; he had become quite a mature animal."

Candy Spots—his connections out to prove they ducked no man's horse—flew to Florida, handily capturing the Florida Derby at Gulfstream. Never Bend declined the issue, but the eastern star kept on winning, and winning big, too. Their big rematch inevitably would take place in the Kentucky Derby. It was that kind of virtual annual rivalry that lent drama, intrigue, and expectation to the sport's glory days. Candy Spots vs. Never Bend. Never Bend vs. Candy Spots. Choice of billing belonged to racing's fandom. And there were interlopers, too.

Leave it to an unheralded colt named Chateaugay, owned by the Darby Dan Farm, to spoil the 1963 Kentucky Derby's anticipated duel between Never Bend and Candy Spots. Chateaugay ran down the spirited Never Bend for a going-away 1¼ lengths victory. Candy Spots, victimized by poor racing luck and what I thought a tentative Shoemaker ride, was a neck back in third. Incidentally, Chateaugay was a son of Swaps, bitter irony for the Ellsworth–Tenney team, which had been made famous by the mercurial Swaps only eight years earlier.

"Candy Spots can beat Chateaugay from here to there," Shoe opined angrily, pointing to an auto 20 feet down the stable road. Losing the Derby was an unsavory pill to swallow. Like Arcaro, Shoe considered the Derby "the toughest race in the world to win!"

Candy Spots wreaked sweet revenge in the Preakness, not only humbling Chateaugay with lengths to spare, but relegating Never Bend to third, another 4 lengths back. When Candy Spots tuned up for the Belmont Stakes with a clever victory in the Jersey Derby, everyone including Shoe, figured they had the world-beater they were looking for.

The bubble burst in the Belmont. Candy Spots, again favored, as he was in both the Derby and Preakness, bounced along seemingly effortlessly with a commanding lead turning for home, then came up empty when collared by Derby hero Chateaugay, the latter dashing clear by 2½ lengths at wire's end. The 3-year-old waters were muddier than ever, and they would remain so for the balance of the year. What earlier had been considered a match race with Candy Spots vs. Never Bend now was a three-way skirmish.

Never Bend was the first to run out gas. Speed was his primary stock in trade. As distance became a major denominator among 3-year-olds, Never Bend beat a steady retreat. It was left to Chateaugay and Candy Spots to fight it out for sophomore honors. Chateaugay won the Jerome but settled for third in the time-honored Travers, and fourth in the Lawrence Realization against older stars. I awaited the return of Candy Spots and Shoe to Chicago's summer racing.

Now, Candy Spots never crashed my Top 10 list, but he was a pleasure to call—peppery, handsome, and wonderfully consistent. He loved to compete, and I could always count on him for an honest effort; so could Shoe. Unfortunately, Candy Spots was upset in his summer Arlington debut, the Chicagoan Stakes, won by somewhat of an upstart, B. Major. The latter tried vainly to repeat his Chicagoan win in the American Derby, but a revitalized Candy Spots proved too vindictive.

I remember Candy Spots that day, prancing bumptiously postward, Shoe smiling up at me as if to say, "All's well that ends well!"

Candy Spots left nothing to doubt, scoring well within himself; B. Major was happy to save second money. Had Candy Spots avoided defeat in the Chicagoan, he would have swept what would become Arlington's Mid-America Triple, consisting of the Chicagoan Stakes, the American Derby, and the Arlington Classic. The Classic belied its name from a distance standpoint, having been reduced from $1\frac{1}{4}$ to a flat mile in 1952.

Let you in on a little-known, but suspected, secret: Marje and Webb Everett wore their feelings on their sleeve. They had favorites and often failed to disguise their preferences. Marje often talked horsemen into switching jocks, convincing them of the wisdom to use either Shoe or Hartack as upcoming stakes loomed. Disgruntled horsemen called it "preferred racing," but they tolerated it, realizing the court of last resort was Marje Everett herself.

The Everetts staged a private, by-invitation-only, pre–Arlington Classic victory party for inner sanctum cognoscenti, which curiously included yours truly. I suppose I should have been flattered Marje and Webb were that comfortable to include their caller and publicity man, trusting I'd discreetly not share such secrets with the media. Candy Spots, his owner, his trainer, and all connected with the Ellsworth–Tenney combine were unabashedly toasted at the party, as if the Arlington Classic was in the bag. Now, please, I'm not talking fixed racing, nothing like that. It's just that when Marje Everett exuded such affection and confidence, it was as if she were challenging the gods of luck and fate to dare do otherwise.

Well, Marje was right about the Arlington Classic of 1963. Candy Spots shouldered 126 pounds to a decisive victory in $1{:}35\frac{4}{5}$ over an unsung 3-year-old named Admiral Vic. B. Major this time was shuffled to third. Candy Spots as a 3-year-old in 1963 managed to win more money than either Chateaugay and Never Bend—$600,000 plus—but lost the title in a split decision to Chateaugay. He was robbed!

Admiral Vic, owned by the Sunny Blue Farm, would use his Arlington Classic second to Candy Spots as a springboard to wider fame and fortune. His regular rider, Mickey Solomone, was a good-looking lad from nearby Hinsdale, Illinois. Because of the local connections, as with Armed back in 1947, an Admiral Vic fan club, numbering several hundred strong, was formed. Its membership—flashing banners and T-shirts—grew with each successive victory. Admiral Vic would win three stakes and, with his fans conspicuously boisterous and visible, cap his 1963 season with a whopping triumph over older horses in the rich Hawthorne Gold Cup that fall. Though not yet an official Hawthorne employee, I was hired by managing director Robert F. Carey, with Marje's permission, to call the Gold Cup via tape-delay over the CBS local affiliate, WBBM-TV.

The year 1964 was not mediocre. Shoemaker continued winning stakes that I called, including the Arlington Classic with Powhatan's Stable's remarkable filly Tosmah, and the Futurity with North Forty Stable's Sadair. But 1965 erupted something special for Silent Shoe. With Lucky Debonair, owned by Chicagoans Dan and Ada L. Rice, he won his third of four Kentucky Derbys. The Preakness got away, captured in sensational fashion by a diminutive colt, Powhatan's Stable's energy-endowed Tom Rolfe, ridden by Ron Turcotte, the latter still eight years away from Secretariat fame.

"Man, I love that little colt," Shoe told me later that summer of Tom Rolfe. "I spoke with his trainer, told him if ever that little guy's free, count me in."

Shoe didn't need Marje Everett to go to bat for him, not this time, nor ever for that matter. Tom Rolfe's trainer was Frank Whiteley Jr.; Whiteley and Shoe knew and respected one another. When it seemed Tom Rolfe needed an assist to return to his winning ways, Whiteley called on the man with the velvet touch.

"Tom Rolfe became one of my all-time favorites," Shoe praised him unhesitantly. "That little guy could run all day without needing a second wind. I thought Gallant Man was something, and he was. But Tom Rolfe not only could run all day, but he loved to run all day. He was just getting started at a mile and a quarter."

Whiteley shipped Tom Rolfe for Arlington's Mid-America Triple—the Classic, American Derby, and the Chicagoan. In between, Tom Rolfe treated me to one of two match races I'd call; it was a betless exhibition to crank him up for his Arlington campaign. Little Tom cakewalked. For the record, the other match race

I called was between jockey Jorge Valesquez and Julie Krone at Arlington International in 1989, when the track made its heralded return after the inferno of July 31, 1985. Julie whipped Jorge.

There's a sports truism: A good big man will always beat a small man. Well, Tom Rolfe was the exception to the rule that bigger is better. Because of his size, it often appeared he had to take two strides for every other horse's one. Maybe so, and that would doubtless take its toll—that is, if Tom Rolfe were an ordinary horse. I doubt if his heart was as big physically as either Phar Lap's or Secretariat's. But spiritually, the stuff of which class and heroism is made, there was none bigger.

Tom Rolfe went on a win spree that would make Citation proud. He hammered his opponents in the Citation Handicap, named for his inspiration. Then he uncoiled from dead last to win the Chicagoan. He then clobbered his Arlington Classic field from behind in 1:34⅘, the fastest Classic mile since the race was shortened to one mile in 1952.

But it was the American Derby rout at 1¼ miles that captured the imagination of fans eager to applaud another world-class Thoroughbred of pomp and flair. Shoe never uncocked his whip, circling rivals with a showy display of verve and stamina. What a sight. It took the track outrider a half-mile after the finish to slow down the ebullient Tom Rolfe to a canter, even with Shoemaker tugging at the reins. The colt with the imperious late kick had just set a new track record of 2:00⅗, and he still wasn't satisfied.

"He wanted to go around another time," Shoe grinned. "And he could've, too, and still not blown out a match. He not only had heart, but, obviously, the lungs to match."

Tom Rolfe was unanimously acclaimed 1965 3-year-old champ of the year. From my perch, binoculars in hand, he earned inclusion on my personal all-time Top 10. Actually, I must beg special dispensation—a Top 10 roster is too limiting. Let's see how we stand. My list would include, not necessarily in this order, such stalwarts as Secretariat, Citation, Count Fleet, Whirlaway, Round Table, Nashua, Swaps, John Henry, and Kelso. Now add Tom Rolfe. That's 10 already. To make the list viable, I'm going to expand it to 15. Okay?

I've included primarily horses I've actually seen through my binoculars brightly, which would exclude, somewhat unfairly, the likes of Man o' War and Phar Lap. They rightly belong on anyone's all-time list. So that gives us 12. We need three more. All in good time.

Shoe's relationship continued with trainer Frank Whiteley Jr. They combined with the dashing Chieftain, grabbing top prize in the 1966 Arlington Handicap; in 1967 Shoe and Whiteley joined forces with top-rated Damascus to account for the American Derby. But Shoe loaned his skills to other owners and trainers of note. In 1966, he guided Harvey Peltier's Diplomat Way to victory in the Arlington–Washington Futurity. Finishing second that day was a promising "bug boy," apprentice jockey Earlie Fires, who'd eventually wind up winning more races at Arlington than any jockey, Shoe and Hartack included, and who's still going strong as I write.

Right after Tom Rolfe, two other great 3-year-olds appeared in my binoculars—Buckpasser and Dr. Fager, neither of which benefited from Shoe's expertise, but they didn't have to; they had a cool and accomplished young man from Panama as pilot, Braulio Baeza.

That didn't mean the era of Bill Shoemaker had passed. Sure, he was getting older, and maybe he wasn't winning those Triple Crown events the way he used to, though he did win both the 1967 Preakness and Belmont with Damascus. But new names were exploding on the scene: Laffit Pincay Jr., Earlie Fires, Craig Perret, Carlos Marquez, Eddie Delahoussaye, Ray Sibille, Pat Day, Jerry Bailey, Randy Romero, Sandy Hawley, Jorge Valesquez, Steve Cauthen, and Shane Sellers—and there was room for 'em all in my binoculars.

By the time 1981 rolled around, and Arlington Park conceived Thoroughbred racing's first million-dollar race, the Arlington Million, it was only fitting that I'd be the caller. More importantly, Bill Shoemaker would ride its first winner! Shoe had ridden the winner, Round Table, of my first hundred-grander call, the 1959 Arlington Handicap. Now, here was Shoe again, this time my first million call. John Henry would come boiling down the middle of the track to nip 30-1 longshot The Bart for as controversial a finish as there'd ever be in the sport's long history. The Million

Dollar pot had arrived, and I count myself privileged to be part of Thoroughbred history in the making.

Something occurred the year before that I consider equally as compelling—the appearance at Arlington of Harry, Teresa, and Tom Meyerhoff's spectacular Spectacular Bid, now four, trained superbly by Buddy Delp, and ridden to perfection by Shoe himself. Delp had been castigated by skeptics during Spectacular Bid's 1979 3-year-old campaign for lauding that son of Bold Bidder as the "best racehorse to ever look through a bridle!" Delp meant no harm; he simply loved his colt, and he meant what he said; it came from the heart.

After Spectacular Bid won both the Derby and Preakness with inexperienced Ron Franklin aboard, some were willing to grant Delp status as prophet. His shocking third in the Belmont, after which Delp offered as excuse that his colt had stepped on a safety pin the morning of the race, reduced Spectacular Bid to barroom humor. The 1979 Jockey Club Gold Cup cast serious doubts on Spectacular Bid's claim to greatness. He was beaten less than a length by a then-unbeatable Affirmed, the 1978 Triple Crown champion.

All doubts vanished in 1980. Spectacular Bid emerged as perhaps the greatest 4-year-old colt of all time, crushing foe after foe, winning race after race, including a walkover televised the world over when no rival had the guts to face him. He then came to my hometown, my track, Arlington Park, with an old friend, Bill Shoemaker, sitting pretty on an unbeaten season. Fans turned out en masse for the Bid's appearance in the Washington Park Handicap under 130 pounds.

"The Bid is truly Spectacular today." I said after "spinning 'em out of the turn!" Ears pricking, his stride sure and steady à la Citation, Secretariat, and Kelso before, the Bid galloped home by 10, smashing Round Table's old track mark by a full second, 1:46⅕ for 1⅛ miles. His final time actually wasn't the important thing; the way he did it was! Now I had horse No. 13 in my Top 15 roster.

Shoe continued to ride brilliantly. Six years later, in 1986 at age 54, and riding like the daredevil he was, he became the oldest jockey ever to win the Kentucky Derby. He was astride Ferdinand, trained by another oldster, Charles "the Bald Eagle" Whittingham, and Shoe gave Ferdinand the ride of his life, a broken-field performance that would have made Gale Sayers proud. It was his fourth and final Derby triumph.

Long before that, of course, Shoe had indisputably joined Eddie Arcaro as second of what would be my all-time jockey threesome. All I needed was Bill Hartack.

Chapter Eight

Bill Hartack

One bright summer day in the early 1950s, I lifted my binoculars skyward, and a shiny new comet was streaking across Thoroughbred racing's heavenly realm. He was an impetuous newcomer, a natural southpaw, whose brassy rock-n-roll riding style, a radical contrast to Eddie Arcaro's power and Bill Shoemaker's finesse, uniquely combined elements of both—remarkably recouping a want of symmetry and grace with an eye-popping blend of push, shove, and motion never before seen on American soil.

He was William John Hartack Jr., soon to be known by those who valued their lives simply as Bill Hartack. His independent, fiery, competitive nature precluded precise comparisons with either Shoe or Eddie. He was his own man, and the mark he made on Thoroughbred racing was his alone. Along with Arcaro and Shoemaker, he afforded the sport a remarkably diverse triangle by which all race-riding would forever be defined.

"My name's Bill," he'd command without a smile. Call him "Willie" and he'd probably never speak to you again. I was a track publicity assistant prior to announcing, and I earned what I felt was Hartack's undying respect by changing his first name in the daily program from "William" to "Bill." He barely cracked a smile when I showed him what I had personally convinced the printer to do. There was no "Thanks." Just "That's nice."

Now I knew and loved Eddie Arcaro. And I got to know and admire Bill Shoemaker. I think, however, though he didn't start out as one of my favorites, I got to know Hartack better than I did either the Master or Silent Shoe. In my mind, Hartack deserves the honor to be ranked as "one of the three greatest jockeys" in Thoroughbred history.

First, let's define—be that possible—his personality, not as a rider, but as a flesh-and-blood human. You'd get a different opinion from every individual with whom you spoke, so for the sake of argument, and a semblance of understanding, please accept mine.

Bill Hartack was a loner. He wasn't snooty or arrogantly superior, but rather private, like George "Iceman" Woolf. Hartack would be sometimes distant, occasionally blunt, certainly never flamboyant, but unceremonious to a fault. And he was unwilling to disclose his inner self, at least to casual or business acquaintances or strangers. I don't know if there were exceptions. He may have opened up to his agent Chick Lang, or to his media friend Joe Hirsch, the senior turf columnist and writer in those years for the *Daily Racing Form*. Hirsch's daily columns rarely went to press without some mention of Hartack.

Whether Hartack and Hirsch were truly bosom buddies, or Bill simply the object of Hirsch's ardent sports interest, I have no way of telling. But they were often together, and I'm not talking "boy friends," since Hartack passionately pursued the opposite sex, finding comfort and satisfaction in all of the female conquests he could handle.

Bill visited the Arlington press box almost daily, not only to confer with Hirsch, but because Arlington's 12-inch-with-gloves softball league, which I helped organize in 1953, was so much a part of Bill's racetrack existence. He loved bantering with press box inmates Elmer Polzin, Joe Agrella, Maurice Shevlin, and Dave Feldman. That talk usually focused on upcoming ball games in our weekly competition, and our rival teams, the Jockeys vs. the Chicago Media.

Except on the rarest occasions, Bill preferred talking baseball over horse racing. I genuinely felt he loved baseball more than riding. It may be that he suffered a strange reticence discussing his chosen profession. Throughout Hartack's banner career, and carrying over into retirement and his many years as an Illinois state steward, Thoroughbred racing was among his least favorite conversation pieces. I wonder if Bill ever really understood or appreciated his role in Thoroughbred racing's golden age. He steadfastly refuses media attention to this day; he's more interested in fantasy football, or Hollywood's latest cinema release, than in reminiscing his past turf glories, of which the sport abounds.

When Bill Hartack burst upon the turf scene in the early 1950s, he was described by one observer as "handsome, wavy-haired, blue-eyed, a luminous cynosure, with the looks that neither Arcaro or Shoemaker possessed." Fervently competitive—equally as ball player and rider—he found defeat an impossible pill to swallow. His will to win was so intense, he'd refuse to discuss a losing ride. Win, that's fine. He'd talk a blue streak. Highly articulate, with a fertile brain, he was capable of recalling every nuance, every stratagem, every move he and competing horses made en route to the winner's circle.

During my pre-announcing years, 1953–1958, among my jobs was to collect winner's circle quotes following special events and major stakes. When Bill rode the winner, no problem. We were racetrack friends—especially due to those colorful ball games between the Jockeys and the Chicago Media—and he'd eagerly provide me with descriptive words and phrases to relive the ride and his triumph.

Losing was a different story. We were friends, but not when he lost. He'd stride quickly down the tunnel from the winner's circle to the jockeys' quarters, talking to no one. He made "No comment" a stern-faced retort. Now, I was expected to deliver more than a "no comment" to the waiting press, particularly if Bill's beaten mount was of quality and substance. So I became creative; I discovered a way to circumvent his infamous uncommunicativeness, but I only got away with it because he allowed it.

I had viewed the race through my loyal binoculars in the press box before catching a waiting elevator to ground level and the winner's circle in time to greet both winner and losers. So I had already called the race to myself or to Associated Press or United Press correspondents eager to get a jump on the result thanks to my call, which Arlington gladly supplied as a special fringe benefit for chroniclers of the sport who thought it advantageous.

For example, let's say Bill rode Iron Liege in the Arlington Classic and finished third as beaten favorite (this is a make-believe example for sake of discussion). Clem won the race, let's say, and I'd, of course, interview the winner's owner, trainer, and jockey in great detail. But before that, because the winner would take his sweet time returning to the charmed circle and the crowd's applause, I'd have to discuss Iron Liege's failure with Hartack, he of "no comment" infamy.

"Bill, he got off to a shaky start, didn't he?" I'd proffer. Hartack would nod, disgustedly.

"Didn't Bernburgoo force you wide at half-mile pole?" I would continue, quickening my pace to follow Bill after he had weighed out with the clerk of the scales. Bill would shake his head; that was a "no."

"I saw you get into him in upper stretch," I would comment, "but he just didn't seem to respond." No response from Hartack meant I had observed correctly. "Just wasn't his day, I suppose." Hartack would look agreeably into my eyes. Then we were at the jocks' quarters, and he was gone.

So I would write Hartack's quote: "Iron Liege didn't break too alertly, not like he usually does. But we had no trouble. I got into him real good coming to the eighth pole, but he just didn't respond. Just one of those races we'll have to throw out, and wait until next time."

Not once did Bill ever rebuke me for manufacturing or fabricating such losing comments. He afforded me that latitude, tacitly assessing my observations, barely a word spoken. He knew I had a job to do which I did with his strange blessings.

Bill wasn't always that difficult or impossible following a losing effort. One timely exception was the 1955 Arlington Classic. Belair Stud's rugged Nashua headed an excellent field, which included Traffic Judge, Dedicate, Dogoon, and the speedy but sometimes faint-hearted Impromptu, who had Hartack in the saddle.

During the post parade, *Sun-Times* writer-handicapper Joe Agrella directed my attention to Eddie Arcaro on Nashua, exchanging talk with Hartack on Impromptu. I verified their dialogue via my faithful binocs, but I couldn't read lips, I assured Agrella.

"When you're in the winner's circle after the race," Agrella requested, "ask Hartack what he and Arcaro were talking about, okay?" I agreed, knowing full well that probably Nashua would win, Impromptu would lose, and Hartack would be uncommunicative.

As it happened, Impromptu, skillfully ridden by Hartack, assumed command soon after the start of the 1-mile Classic. Leaving the half-mile marker, he left his field with a flourish, despite Nashua's and Arcaro's impassioned efforts to keep pace. Impromptu lanced to a 4-length bulge, with 3 furlongs to race.

Finally Nashua kicked into high gear and overhauled Impromptu like a shot in upper stretch but then was hard-put to stave off Traffic Judge by a half-length. Impromptu and Hartack faded ever so slightly to third.

Apparently, those were the days before enmity existed between Hartack and Arcaro. After the race, Bill fielded my question without animosity. He obviously had harbored no delusions about whipping Nashua, who, as it turned out, was tuning up for his upcoming match race with arch rival Swaps. Bill actually smiled. "I just told Eddie not to make me look bad, to go easy on me. 'You got it,' Eddie replied. But I think we gave 'em a bit of a scare halfway through the race. For a moment there, I even thought we might have a chance."

Hartack became more intense as the years wore on—more accomplished, too, as he equaled Arcaro's record of five Kentucky Derby winners. Hartack's Derby triumphs were with Iron Liege (1957), Venetian Way (1960), Decidedly (1962), Northern Dancer (1964), and Majestic Prince (1969). He certainly couldn't complain about a lack of celebrity or notability. Three straight years, from 1955 through 1957, he was America's winningest jockey, a wondrous feat for the Pennsylvania native who only a few years earlier had won his first race—in 1952 at Waterford Park in West Virginia. He'd nail down a fourth national title in 1960.

True, he'd never approach his Derby record in either the Preakness or Belmont. And, like Shoe, he'd not win a Triple Crown. But Shoemaker's star took on added sheen, eventually enabling him to surpass Johnny Longden as the world's all-time race-winning jockey. In contrast, Bill's career waned, taking a slow, almost imperceptible downward slide. As weight—the jockey's all-time dread—started to take its toll, he rode with some success in Hong King.

'Twas a shame—the conflict that marred Eddie and Bill's fraternity. But that was their problem, purely personal. It didn't detract from Hartack's immense influence on Thoroughbred racing.

Bill was a natural southpaw, whose powerful left-hand whip earned him my personal nickname as racing's most deadly "left-handed gun." His natural propensity to whip left-handed helped give Bill a decidedly different look in the saddle as horses flashed before the stands. Arcaro didn't exactly pioneer the ace-deuce American riding style—the right stirrup anywhere from 2 to 12 inches shorter (6 inches in Eddie's case) than the left—but he popularized and perfected it. Which meant, as far as spectators were concerned, the rider didn't appear as high in the saddle as the field moved up the backstretch toward the far turn, since the eye focused on the longer left stirrup.

The rider appeared more streamlined once the field straightened out for the sprint home. The eye feasted upon the shorter right stirrup, which helped emphasize the jockey's low profile. Additionally, most riders were whipping right-handed, thus spectators felt comfortable with that sight.

Bill Hartack rarely resorted to a right-handed whip. He also had an individualized lateral-rocking motion, accentuated each time he unhoused his whip left-handed—a whip applied forcefully, emphasizing his body movement all the more. His riding style immediately appeared terribly unorthodox. I didn't care that much for his seat, having been irreconcilably spoiled by Eddie's aerodynamically perfect look. I was also influenced by Shoe's effortless, long-rein perch. Once I got over my biases—that Hartack's style was unconventional and unappetizing—I came to fully appreciate his unique brilliance.

Through my binoculars I've seen thousands of Hartack races since 1953. I've called Hartack races thousands of times from 1959 onward, including his 3,000th victory on Big Steve in 1962. Plus I've seen his every Derby win on TV. Yet I can't recall the last time I saw him whip a horse with his right hand! That's not to even vaguely suggest he never used a right-handed whip. Obviously he had; I just can't recall the occasion. Unfortunately much film footage of Hartack's Chicago campaigns was lost in fires that demolished Arlington, Washington, and Hawthorne racetracks. Washington Park and Hawthorne were destroyed in 1977 and 1978, respectively; Arlington was razed in 1985. But I just took another look at Bill's five Derby triumphs, several of which were achieved in searing finishes. For example, his first Derby win, in 1957, was Iron Liege's disputed nose victory over Gallant Man. Iron Liege clung tenaciously to the rail throughout the final furlong. Gallant Man, ridden by Shoe, was right alongside as they thundered to the wire. Hartack used his whip left-handed several times within the final 100 yards, never the right.

As a sidebar to the 1957 Derby: if Gallant Man had won, as many feel he should, it would have given Bill Shoemaker five Kentucky Derbys instead of four; it would have deprived Hartack of his first of five; the latter would then have been credited with four instead of five Derby scores. Derby history would have been rewritten.

Three years later, under Hartack, Venetian Way won the 1960 Kentucky Derby by an authoritative 3½ lengths over the ill-fated Bally Ache. Bill hardly was required to resort to his whip, but when he did, it was left-handed. Two years later, it was Decidedly, again with Hartack, again no right-handed larruping. In the 1964 Derby, Northern Dancer, under Hartack's vigorous left-handed attack, held off favored Hill Rise and Bill Shoemaker by a desperate neck in 2:00 flat. Throughout Hill Rise's final furlong assault, Hartack never once whipped right-handed. Why should he? He had revolutionized race-riding with a formidable left-sided whip. Obviously, it surprisingly roused his mounts to get the job done, efficiently, and with dispatch.

Hartack was incredibly fearless, also fiercely competitive. He'd rarely get himself blocked or find himself penned in as a result of foolishly racing into a blind switch. Because he required room on his left, or inside, to unhouse and apply his left-handed gun, he was primarily looking to the inside of horses, gaining the reputation as having saved more ground than the Department of Agriculture.

When it came to Triple Crown races, Bill's nine victories ranked him third, tying him with Earl Sande and Pat Day. Arcaro led with 17 victories, and Shoemaker was second with 11. Bill, especially from 1955 through 1960, achieved a deserved reputation as a big-league stakes-winning jockey. In 1957 he became the first jockey to surpass 3 million in earnings—$3,060,501.

I'm sure he took pride in his achievements. Some horsemen and sports scribes, repeatedly scorched by his outspokenness and increasingly uncooperative spirit, opined that Hartack had "an inordinate pride," to the point of "arrogance," and a "personal disregard to give back in kind to the sport that had made him famous." Whether such charges had merit—Bill to this day shuns reporters, and rarely, if ever, participates in affairs calculated to celebrate Thoroughbred racing's rich heritage—he was one great jockey, remembered as intolerant of defeat of any kind, whether in a stakes race, a claiming affair, or a softball game. That I know.

During my years as announcer, I took delight in his daily brilliance as a brusque and bold rider whose sole motivation was to win. He'd excel on the grass, too, as in his 1966 victory astride August Muckler's Climax II in Arlington's Stars and Stripes Handicap. There was also his 1958 winning ride on the great Round Table, when he nipped Clem on the wire in the grassy Laurance Armour 'Cap. I called Bill's second Armour triumph eight years later, when he guided Climax II to a daring come-from-behind tally.

Both Arlington's Classic and American Derby eluded Hartack. However, he won the Arlington Matron for fillies and mares—the 1960 renewal with Royal Native, and the 1963 running astride Russ Reineman's classy Smart Deb, one of Bill's favorite mounts. I called his two Arlington–Washington Lassie wins, aboard Rudoma (1961) and Admiring (1964). Most of all, I remember Bill teaming up with Ridan (the colt I definitively pronounced) when the huge, spirited 2-year-old annexed the 1961 Arlington–Washington Futurity.

Bill didn't ride at Hawthorne as much as I would have liked. He won the 1957 Yo Tambien Handicap with a Chicago favorite, Mrs. Joe Brown's Bornastar. I didn't officially start announcing at Hawthorne until 1969, but I was on hand in 1966 when Hartack won the Illinois Cavalier Stakes, a race for Illinois-breds; Bill was aboard Scottdale Farm's Li'bit Type. I also got to see Hartack ace the 1962 Hawthorne Juvenile on Sky Gem.

What I cherish most, however, is that during the waning years of my announcing career, Bill returned to Chicago, first as an association steward, later as Illinois state steward. He hadn't changed a bit. Maybe he was a little heavier; a bald spot was showing. But he still maintained his implacable austerity.

He'd never win a popularity contest; no, not Bill Hartack. But how that kid could ride!

Chapter Nine

Jockey Shorts

Lest I may have unintentionally misled you, let's set the record straight. Today's star-studded jockey battalion—headed by Jerry Bailey, Pat Day, and Chris McCarron, and including such established cracks as Kent Desormeaux, Jorge Chavez, Mike Smith, Craig Perret, Eddie Delahoussaye, Laffit Pincay Jr., Earlie Fires, Shane Sellers, Jose Santos, Mark Guidry, and Alex Solis, not to forget the enduring Gary Stevens—takes a back seat to none that came before.

True, our golden age retrospective has focused on Eddie Arcaro, Bill Shoemaker, and Bill Hartack as our Big Three, plus their court of resplendent challengers, including Johnny Longden, Earl Sande, George Woolf, Isaac Murphy, Ted Atkinson, Johnny Adams, Conn McCreary, Braulio Baeza, Angel Cordero Jr., Steve Brooks, Walter Blum, Al Snider, Eric Guerin, Ron Turcotte, Steve Cauthen ad infinitum.

It's just that Thoroughbred racing today is in a state of flux. I've heard TV Triple Crown and Breeders' Cup commentators bemoan the fact that after some 20 years they're impatiently awaiting the sport's "next great horse," as if Cigar either never existed or was all too soon forgotten. But there's an element of truth in their despair: too many years have passed since the numerous great ones have come, seen, and conquered. The money's there, to be sure. Yet the lasting quality that made the sport resplendent, back when racing was racing, is overdue for revival—not just an overdue Triple Crown champ, but the ongoing drama and romance of struggle and skirmish. We long for horses with career staying power, for equine superstars worthy of a desperate fandom, not TV debates over odds, favorites, and Budweiser longshots.

I've long insisted that virtually every jockey riding today can be categorized—departmentalized if you please—as one of three types: Arcaro, Shoe, or Hartack. I'm not that sure anymore. Perhaps it's too simplistic, certainly unfair, to file Pat Day and Shane Sellers into a slot called Bill Shoemaker, or to say that Earlie Fires and Jose Santos belong to the Bill Hartack School or that Jerry Bailey, Laffit Pincay Jr., Angel Cordero Jr., and Gary Stevens are graduates of Arcaro University. During this chapter, therefore, I'll try to refrain from assigning labels to current jockey headliners.

This chapter looks at jockeys past and present. We'll address their skills, their feats, and their contributions to racing.

The first time I really became aware of Jerry Bailey's commanding presence was the spring of 1976 at Hawthorne. I was serving as both announcer and advertising-publicity director. All of a sudden, Jerry Bailey was atop the standings. Hawthorne had a split spring–fall season that year, only 23 days in the spring, and Jerry averaged a winner a day to beat such fine veteran riders as Larry Snyder and Jorge Tejeira.

Bailey was only 19 at the time and had been riding for only two years, but the lad from Dallas, Texas, had a special touch, obvious not only to these eyes, but particularly to invading trainers. The latter doubtless convinced him to make New York his eventual summer base, but for the next couple of seasons Chicago was proud to have Bailey as one of its very own. When Arlington threw me an impromptu salute the summer of 1978, Jerry Bailey was in the winner's circle as official representative of the local riding colony. As articulate as he is brainy, Jerry remains a gentleman and one of the game's most respected spokesmen.

I wasn't the least surprised when Jerry Bailey won both the 1991 Preakness and Belmont aboard Hansel. That same year he won the first of many Breeders' Cup Classics on Chicago-owned Black Tie Affair. Trainer Ernie Poulos, who conditioned Jeff Sullivan's vaunted speed merchant Black Tie Affair, had been experimenting with a bevy of top riders. The year before he captured the Hawthorne Gold Cup, with Black Tie Affair leading every step of the way under Juvenal Diaz. In 1991, Ernie treated Shane Sellers to the mount, the pair romping in the Washington Park 'Cap at Arlington. Ernie was upset, however, that Shane used his whip too liberally while scoring with lengths to spare.

"I wanted a jock, strong and eager, but not that eager, one who'd ride patiently," Ernie told me before leaving Chicago for that year's Breeders' Classic, an event that usually crowns the Eclipse Horse of the Year. "I think I got him in Jerry Bailey," he said.

Poulos thought correctly, not that Sellers or Diaz performed shabbily. I thought their rides expertly done. But Bailey benefited from Poulos's obvious confidence; he didn't disappoint. Chicago had another Horse of the Year, and Bailey had new worlds to conquer.

Bailey finally got an overdue Kentucky Derby in 1993 astride Sea Hero. He became a multiple Roses Run hero when he flew like Whirlaway in the straightaway to win the 1996 Derby in the last jump with Grindstone for trainer Wayne Lukas. He was the Eclipse champ jock only the year before, which included a then world record $16,308,230 in purse earnings.

His association with Cigar, who in 1996 tied Citation's modern-day record of 16 straight wins at Arlington, remains a career highlight. Said Jerry: "I've put much thought into how fortunate I've been blessed to have ridden him. I know I'll never ride another horse as good as Cigar."

Even the great Arcaro, who watched Cigar's Arlington triumph on TV, commented: "Bailey's my kind of rider—strong, patient, and smart. He deserves every success he's had. He's the best in the business."

Pat Day rode his first winner in 1973 at Prescott Downs in Arizona. He's been a spectacular winner ever since. Pat's a gentleman on and off the field of battle. He valiantly overcame youthful demons that might have KO'd a less stalwart man. In less than 10 years from that first tally in Arizona, Day in 1982 was America's winningest rider, with 399 scores; two years later he won the first of several Eclipse Awards as the nation's foremost jockey. In 1991 he was voted into racing's Hall of Fame.

Much like Shoe, Day, small and compactly built, exemplifies smoothness. He has a sit-still style and soft but authoritative hands.

A brilliant judge of pace, he is hard as nails when challenged from behind. And don't let his Shoe-like seat fool you. He's a fierce left-handed whipper, à la Bill Hartack.

"Sometimes," he once confided in me and a thousand Arlington Breakfast Club attendees, "I'll use the whip to please the fans, as if to let them know how hard I'm trying to win." No hypocrisy there. He can get the job done almost effortlessly, or so it appears. He realized, however, that fans aren't always that easily satisfied. So he often demonstrates that Pat Day can finish with the best of 'em!

I'm sure you've heard the expression "a Garrison finish." It's part and parcel of racing's exclusive lexicon, a household term used to describe a horse and rider exploding from out of the proverbial blue to snatch victory in the closing stride. The Garrison finish was named for Edward "Snapper" Garrison, whose 19th century exploits have grown beyond legendary proportions.

He really didn't win that many races. He didn't have to. It was the way he won them. In fact, eye-witnesses tell us he was rather tall for a jockey but rode "curled up" tightly, an "extraordinary sight, to say the least." But his finishes delighted racing fans; he happily lent his name to racing's private vocabulary.

Speaking of jockeys and what their names imply, hear me out. Eddie Arcaro ruled as the greatest jockey who ever lived, not only for yours truly, but, and this is true, among his many peers, including a jockey of modest talent named William Carroll. At one point, Carroll was bumped off a potential stakes mount by the horse's trainer, who candidly wanted to turn the reins over to the Master, Arcaro. Eddie agreed, but only when assured by the trainer that Bill Carroll would be restored as rider in the colt's next start. The trainer, who'd do anything to get Arcaro, promised.

Eddie rode as agreed. But when the horse started back two weeks later, lo and behold, Arcaro was again named as jockey. Eddie firmly refused, reminding the trainer of their agreement. Jockey Bill Carroll got his horse back. And he was grateful.

No big deal, you say. It was for Carroll, to say the least. Arcaro's integrity made such a lasting impression that a few years later, when Carroll's wife Barbara presented him with a bouncing baby boy, the rider insisted on naming the newborn Eddie R. Carroll. Go ahead. Let the name—Eddie R. Carroll—roll off your tongue a time or two. See my point?

Every racing fan knows that Laffit Pincay Jr. is the world's winningest jockey, having displaced Bill Shoemaker as the new millennium dawned. But do you know who called Pincay's very first American winner? Okay, I admit it: I did. Pincay was atop Teacher's Art, Fred W. Hooper's 3–5 favorite. The date was July 1, 1966, at Arlington Park. Pincay, if I recall correctly, could barely speak or understand English. He had been brought to this country by Hooper, a close friend of Webb and Marje Everett.

Earlie Fires, who'd win more races at Arlington than any other rider since its 1927 debut, led all jockeys that year, with 90 winners. Pincay, an unknown quality when he notched his first American victory, came back in 1967 with 109 winners to top the standings. The name was pronounced "Pin-*kaye*" in those days. It wasn't until a few years later that he became "Pin-*kie*." I'd call a rider by any name he preferred. About that time, Doug Richard (as in Richard Nixon) started winning a few stakes and personally requested that I call him "Ree-*chard*." I think it improved his riding, too.

Eddie Delahoussaye was noted for his muscular build and powerhouse riding style, much like his contemporary Pincay and much like Snapper Garrison of a century ago and little Conn McCreary of the 1940s. Dellahoussaye wowed Arlington fans in the late 1970s with his affinity for the late run.

Back in 1978, when he topped all jockeys in North America with 384 winners, I reminded Delahoussaye that no Hollywood fictional movie has ever featured a front-runner, that it was the late charge that captivates, lending unmistakable dramatic content. Every movie—including stories starring Wallace Beery, Mickey Rooney, and Elizabeth Taylor—was always climaxed by a runner overcoming all odds by uncoiling from far back to win it all at the shadow of the wire.

"I simply enjoyed mowin' 'em down, you might say," Eddie told me in 1978, after sweeping his second straight Arlington riding title. "I just have this rapport with late finishers, and if it suits the horse, then we make one considerable contender."

Delahoussaye, a Louisiana native born into a family of Thoroughbred owners and trainers, liked racking up back-to-back titles. He won the 1982 Kentucky Derby aboard the late-rushing Gato Del Sol. The following year he won with Sunny's Halo, becoming the fourth rider to capture two straight Derbies.

Speaking of riders of late-run renown, I'd be remiss not to include one of the most underrated of current jockeys—Mark Guidry. If I owned Silky Sullivan, probably the last word among stretch-running Thoroughbreds, I'd look no farther than Guidry, probably Chicago's most dominant rider of the 1990s. When I was still calling 'em, many times I was tempted to say: "And out in the middle of the track, here comes . . . Mark Guidry!" More often than not, he was in the saddle.

Many of the current equine athletes lack the consistency of their predecessors. For a stretch of 21 years, from 1979 through 1999, no favorite won the Kentucky Derby. Then the favorite Fusaichi Pegasus won the 2000 Derby—only to flop spectacularly as odds-on favorite in the Preakness. There has been no Triple Crown winner since 1978. Spectacular Bid, the last favorite to win the Derby, in 1979, went on to win the Preakness but suffered an ignominious Belmont shellacking.

At least the present-day jockey colony remained steadfast. Desormeaux's ride aboard Fusaichi Pegasus as he threaded his way between horses to win the 2000 Derby over 18 rivals was picture perfect. Jerry Bailey's job astride Red Bullet to upset the Derby winner in the shorter (by 120 yards) Preakness was equally superb. As they left the half-mile pole, Bailey was biding his time inside the favorite. Then he out-gunned Desormeaux approaching the head of the stretch—sprinting clear with lengths to spare.

I've never seen a good jockey make a bad horse win, but I've seen a bad horse make a good jockey lose. I've seen a good horse make a bad jockey win, and I've seen a bad jockey make a good horse lose. When you get Desormeaux at his best on Fusaichi Pegasus at his best—or two weeks later, Jerry Bailey at his best on Red Bullet at his best—or three weeks later it's Pat Day at his best on a longshot named Commendable at his best—you have a winner!

Good or great horses make good or great jockeys. It's the dogma expounded by Arcaro himself, and Arcaro tells it best: "The trainer saw me, first fourth at the top of the stretch, then third at the eighth pole, and after we finished third, he asked me pointedly, 'Why didn't you grab the lead and win?' 'What,' I answered, 'and leave the horse?'"

One colt who helped establish at least two riders was Affirmed, acclaimed as the 20th century's last Triple Crown winner. He scored his sweep in 1978, a year following Seattle Slew's sparkling Triple. Affirmed conferred distinction first to youthful Steve "Kid" Cauthen in 1978. The following year it was the turn of veteran reinsman Laffit Pincay Jr. Both jockeys freely called Affirmed the greatest colt they had ever ridden.

I first saw Steve Cauthen, the 17-year-old riding sensation, the summer and fall of 1977, first at Arlington, later at Hawthorne, the same year he set a record of $6 million in purses for an apprentice, amassing an unbelievable 487 wins. When he was 18, aboard Affirmed, Cauthen became the youngest jockey to win the Derby, defeating arch rival Alydar in 1978. Affirmed achieved racing immortality, particularly with his head victory after he and Alydar ding-donged it the length of Belmont Park's long stretch to annex the 1½ miles Belmont Stakes. Alydar set his own record, as the only colt to finish second in all three Triple Crown events.

I was quoted numerous times praising Cauthen's low profile, so reminiscent of Eddie Arcaro, which he admitted imitating. But before long, in the midst of a rare riding slump, he'd eventually lose Affirmed to Pincay. Showing obvious weight gain, Steve voluntarily sought asylum in Europe. By the mid-1980s, no longer a kid,

Cauthen was England's champion jockey, a reign covering 1984, 1985, and 1987. He won no less than nine English classics, including two Epsom Derbies. Upon retirement, Steve was the first jockey to win the Irish, French, and Italian Derbies as well as the Epsom Derby and our own Kentucky Derby.

Man o' War had Upset. Secretariat had Onion and Prove Out. And Citation had Noor. Noor made Citation's comeback life miserable in 1950 with four wins in five clashes, including what many observers still call one of the greatest races of all time—the March 4 San Juan Capistrano at 1¾ miles at Santa Anita. The ageless Johnny Longden to this day ranks Noor "next to Count Fleet" as his all-time favorite mount. Longden will never forget Noor's battles with 5-year-old Cy, the latter returned to the races by trainer Jimmy Jones, who, by his own admission, "foolishly acquiesced" to dying Calumet Farm owner Warren Wright's desire "to make Citation the sport's first Thoroughbred millionaire."

"Even though I always felt Count Fleet was the best colt I ever rode, I had nothing but respect for Citation," Longden told me at Arlington in 1965, a year before he retired as the first jockey to surpass 6,000 winners, "so I took some delight in beating him with Noor, even though I recognized Citation was nothing like his former self."

Citation was good enough to beat Noor—they ran two-three behind Citation's stablemate Ponder in the San Antonio 'Cap on February 11, Citation conceding Noor 16 pounds. Noor beat mighty Cy in the Santa Anita 'Cap on February 25, this time in receipt of 22 pounds. It was the second and last time Arcaro would ride Citation in 1950.

"It broke my heart," Eddie told me. "Cy was just a shadow of his former self. I would stay in New York for the balance of his so-called 'comeback'; I chose to remember the good days we had together when he was greatest 3-year-old ever."

Steve Brooks inherited Citation. He rode him in his first two starts in 1950, including Citation's 16th straight victory on January 11 at Santa Anita. They paired up again for the San Juan Capistrano—their famous clash with Longden and Noor.

Longden recalled: "Noor got in with 117 against Citation under 130. He was still giving us weight. And it was a rip-snorter from the get-go. The fans—and there were some 60,000 there, and on a weekday, too—they loved it. They went crazy. What a race!" Longden said Noor and Citation bided their time early. "At the mile in an easy 1:38, Brooks asked Citation to take command, which he did promptly. I asked Noor to go get 'em, which he did without a fuss."

Citation and Noor left the half-mile pole, locked in deadly combat. "We were head and head, stride for stride, no more than nose or a head separating us the final 3 furlongs. Like I said, the fans went nuts—and Citation and Noor ran their hearts out."

At the wire—$1\frac{3}{4}$ miles in $2{:}52\frac{4}{5}$, a new world record—Noor prevailed by a head. I had a 16mm film of that race, which I kept in my booth and watched often. I died every time I saw Cy drop that photo finish. It was just a head bob, that's all, and he gave Noor 13 pounds. But he did lose fairly on the head bob. Sadly, I lost the film in the fire that razed old Washington Park in 1977.

Johnny Longden continued riding for no fewer than 40 great seasons. For a time there, we thought the Wakefield, England, native would never retire. In 1956, he surpassed England's Gordon Richards as the world's winningest rider. "My greatest thrill, of course," Longden said, "was winning the 1943 Triple Crown with Count Fleet. I never won another Derby, or another Belmont Stakes, for that matter. I'll just settle for the Triple Crown and a colt named Count Fleet." Then he added, and not just as an afterthought, "And Noor, he wasn't hard to take either."

If Johnny Longden were president of what I call the "go to the front and improve your position" club, its vice president would have to be Walter Blum and its secretary R. L. "Bobby" Baird, two riders who'd soar from the starting gate as if shot from a cannon.

Walter Blum is currently south Florida's state steward. I got to know him in the early 1960s. He topped the standings in 1963–1964, not only at both Arlington and Hawthorne but nationally as well. When he retired, he had 4,382 winners from 28,673 mounts and was universally acclaimed as one of the greatest speed jockeys the game has known. A personable guy with high-octane zeal to match his fervor away from the gate, Blum was born September 28, 1934; he accepted his first mount in May 1952, registering his first winner on July 29 of that year, and before not too long he was challenging all others to catch him if they dared.

On TV, I saw one of his finest moments. He had flown from Chicago to ride Gedney Farm's high-powered speedster Gun Bow against mighty Kelso in New York's 1964 Woodward Stakes. The pair battled the length of the stretch, Blum persevering, driving Gun Bow home as victor in a photo finish remindful of Noor's scant win over Citation.

Capturing the 1964 Washington Park 'Cap in Chicago with Gun Bow, as usual in front-running fashion, Blum certified his reputation as an expert with fleet merchants. But he could also come from out of it if the horse's running style so dictated. He did so with the stretch-running Hard Rock Man in the 1963 Stars and Stripes at Arlington, and as I called the daring finish, I couldn't help but admire Blum's versatility as he adapted to the winner's affinity for the late surge.

"Naturally, I liked being in front," Walter told a Chicago audience in October 1999, when inducted into Hawthorne's Jockey Hall of Fame. "It's the safest place to be, out of trouble with nary a fly in your path."

Bobby Baird also "loved the front end of things," he told his audience that same year. "Getting to the front, where I could control things, especially if I had a horse who wasn't faint-hearted, was a lot easier than getting pinched back or having to make your way through and around horses."

Baird won his first race on September 11, 1938. When the 18-year-old Bobby notched victory at old Aqueduct in New York, he launched an extraordinary riding career that would orbit the world of horse racing for 39 years. He returned to earth by retiring in 1982, at age 62.

Bobby's "high-stirrup" saddle perch was a familiar sight wherever he plied his trade. Many horsemen loved his penchant for the front end of things. Before long, he developed a fine reputation as a stakes rider, aboard such stars as Papa Redbird, Star Reward, Stud Poker, and Pintor Lea. Bobby is still a part of the sport he loves. He serves as agent for his exceptional son, E. T. Baird. Like father, like son.

Okay, two trivia questions. First, what did Steve Brooks and Ted Atkinson have in common? Answer: Both were "slashers," heavy whippers, neither of whom believed in sparing the rod.

Second, what did Steve Brooks and Eddie Arcaro have in common? Answer: Both said Citation was the best horse they ever rode.

During Citation's 2-year-old season, Brooks rode Cy only once, for that controversial second to Bewitch in the Washington Park Futurity. They wouldn't be reunited until Cy's 5- and 6-year-old comeback years (1950–1951), and though the horse was a shell of his former self, he still impressed Brooks as the "greatest I've ever seen or ridden." Fine words indeed from a man who had ridden such stars as Two Lea, Round Table, Devil Diver, Bewitch, Coaltown, Ponder, and Bardstown.

When I knew Steve, he was drinking too much, though it never seemed to compromise his riding. Boy, did he know how to apply pressure whip-wise, occasionally incurring horsemen's wrath when they thought he unduly punished his mounts. "I never hurt a horse," Brooks said in defense. "Never left a mark on their hide. Listen, some horses don't give their all unless they're hit, and hit hard. And I was sober every time I rode."

Brooks officially retired several times, only to return to the saddle. Like Citation, he never replicated his former form. He died from injuries incurred in an early morning workout in 1979. The man with the famous whip was only 58.

Ted Atkinson never drank nor cursed that I know of, and to many of his peers he was a highly regarded intellectual. But to most, Ted Atkinson was "the slasher," with a powerful arm out-stretched, poised to descend with impact and regularity to impel his mount onward. A studious gentleman off the track, Ted was a terror in the saddle. Like Steve Brooks, he elicited both praise and criticism because of his dichotomous personality. Critics notwithstanding, Ted was an outstanding jockey. In 1946 he distinguished himself as the first jockey to win more than a million dollars in a single season.

Twice he was America's winningest rider. He won a ton of races and his share of stakes, too, like wins in the 1949 Preakness and Belmont aboard a colt named Capot.

I was an eye-witness to his winning rides on Greentree Stable's Hall of Fame in both the 1951 Arlington Classic and American Derby in Chicago. Two years later, Teddy landed what he called "my greatest mount," the unchained speedster Tom Fool, who as a 4-year-old accomplished a racing rarity, especially for handicap horses—he went unbeaten in 10 starts. Tom Fool captured two crowns that year: Sprint Champion and Horse of the Year.

Often Teddy and I would discuss Tom Fool's greatness. You see, much like Bill Hartack years later, Teddy became my daily companion at all Chicago tracks. His expertise, experience, and judicial temperament earned him the job of Illinois state steward, a job he performed expertly, displaying the same intelligence and racing wisdom applied during his exciting tenure as Hall of Fame jockey. Arcaro once told me: "Ted Atkinson was a race-rider's race-rider. It was a pleasure, and a challenge, riding against him."

I've always had ambivalent feelings about Angel Cordero Jr. I loved his power, drive, courage, and brass when challenged. In those respects he smacked of Eddie Arcaro. Because I was an Arcaro devotee, I was easily smitten by guys like Cordero. Steve Cauthen as an apprentice had Arcaro's low profile; Cordero possessed his fire and punch. So I was ecstatic when Angel was given the mount on Seattle Slew in the latter's historic clash with Affirmed for the September 16, 1978, Marlboro Cup in New York. It was the first time ever that two Triple Crown winners would cross swords. The Slew had humbled all opposition winning his 1977 Triple; Affirmed out-gamed Alydar in all three 1978 races.

I was a Seattle Slew fan and somewhat peeved by Affirmed trimming Alydar, a colt I emotionally backed in his futile efforts to bring the great Affirmed to his knees. Cordero could do nothing but help Seattle Slew's chances. He owned two Kentucky Derby wins—Cannonade, 1947; Bold Forbes, 1976 (and he'd win a third in 1985 on Spend a Buck). I delighted in Angel's strength, verve, and confidence. I exulted beyond words when Seattle Slew decisively trounced Affirmed by three lengths in their ballyhooed encounter. And Cordero's ride was marvelous, too.

I suppose there's a bit of a rogue in every great athlete; Cordero was no exception. He asked for and gave no quarter. Every aspect of life has its scamps and scoundrels. Racing had Don Meade, Manny Ycaza, and at times Angel Cordero Jr. In the 1980 Preakness, he rammed Kentucky Derby victress Genuine Risk inside the quarter pole. Angel claimed that he never touched her, that he simply blew the turn. In my opinion, it was deliberate, and it was flagrantly uncalled for. I enjoyed Angel riding "my horse" in a race, knowing he'd go the extra mile, yet I hated it when he intentionally herded or intimidated another to the point of distraction, often coming dangerously close to being a party to mishap or accident. He never had to resort to such tactics; his skills were all the recommendation he needed.

One of the most talented and clean-riding jockeys I've known is Chris McCarron, a gentleman in every respect. He not only did his best to steer clear of trouble, but he devoted his tactics to keeping fellow reinsmen out "of Harm's Way." Chris escaped by a whisker a tragic spill and pileup in the 1987 Kentucky Derby. The leader in upper stretch, Bet Twice, in rein to Craig Perret, drifted out ever so slightly, causing McCarron's mount, Alysheba, to clip heels and stumble badly. But Alysheba recovered brilliantly under McCarron's confident guidance to win the Run for the Roses in sterling fashion.

"It all happened so quickly, I didn't have time to pause and weigh the possible consequences," McCarron recalled. "All I know is that Alysheba was one sure-footed dude. To recover like he did took courage and class. And he had both."

Alysheba defeated Bet Twice, this time with no miscue, in the 1987 Preakness. In the Belmont, however, Bet Twice gained an early advantage to prevent the Jack Van Berg trainee from becoming racing's 12th Triple Crown hero.

Seven years earlier, in 1980, McCarron came to Hawthorne to ride actor Jack Klugman's Jaklin Klugman to victory in the Hawthorne Derby. Klugman visited me in my booth prior to the race, coyly pleading with me to use all my influence to bring his colt home a winner. Jacklin Klugman and McCarron needed no help from me. They won it in a romp. Incidentally, 1980 also was the year McCarron won his second Eclipse Award as America's Numero Uno Jockey.

Chris was fearless once hoisted aboard 1,000 pounds of horseflesh. He has the distinction of riding two of the world's richest and finest Thoroughbreds of all time—John Henry and Alysheba. The grand gelding John Henry, two-time Horse of the Year, became Thoroughbred racing's first five-million-dollar baby when Chris piloted him home with nearly 2 lengths to spare in the 1984 Arlington Million, yours truly on the call.

Superstar Alysheba broke John Henry's money-winning mark with victory under Chris in the 1988 Breeders' Cup Classic, one of several McCarron Classic scores. In the 1989 Classic, Chris was astride Sunday Silence, who affirmed his superiority over Easy Goer. In 1996 Chris was aboard when upstart Alphabet Soup upset the great Cigar, who already had dethroned Alysheba as money-earner king. It was McCarron again in the saddle when Tiznow took the 2000 Breeders' Cup Classic prize.

McCarron, incidentally, was no late developer. Born in Dorchester, Massachusetts, in 1955, he accepted his first mount in 1974. Before that year was history, Chris scored a world-record 546 wins, more than enough to crown him the Eclipse Apprentice Jockey of the Year.

Barrel-chested Johnny Adams stood four-feet-eight, making Shoemaker a giant. Long retired before the Eclipse Award became vogue in 1971, Adams three times (1937, 1942, and 1943) won more races than any jockey in America. Take it from me, there was no finer grass jockey than Johnny Adams. Any afternoon—at Arlington, Washington, or Hawthorne—so long as the race was on the turf, there was Johnny Adams with that trademark long rein, splitting rivals, then looping his field, boiling imperiously from behind, thrilling his backers with a cavalry charge of his own creation.

In 1955, I was in the winner's circle as track publicist, bestowing proper kudos by way of saluting Adams's 3,000th victory. That summer day, Adams joined Johnny Longden, Ted Atkinson, and Eddie Arcaro as the fourth rider in history to have achieved 3,000 wins.

Earlie Fires has never won a Triple Crown event or a Breeders' Cup. But I'd confidently match him against any rider past or present. You give him the horse, and he'll give you the ride. And what a ride—all movement, all action, whip, hand, and heel. Fires, who hails from a diverse family of Thoroughbred lovers, has been riding steadily and capably since 1964, scoring his first winner on March 6, 1965, at Oaklawn Park in Arkansas. The horse was Carnation Kid. Earlie soon propelled into orbit as the nation's number-one apprentice, with 224 wins. In 1986, astride Camplin at Hawthorne, he registered his 4,000th career win; his 5,000th was recorded at Arlington aboard Tex's Zing on August 19, 1990. A year later he received the George Woolf Memorial Award.

Fires continues to personify perpetual motion in action, a brainy sixth-sense, and a clocklike instinct for pace, as well as heroism under fire no matter the contest—turf or dirt, sprint or distance. I know for a fact he's won more races at Arlington than any other jockey—and I know I called virtually every one of them!

Long before Laffit Pincay Jr. or Braulio Baeza became famous racing names, I was calling them both at Arlington, thanks to Fred W. Hooper, the owner-breeder who was instrumental in bringing Pincay and Baeza to American terra firma. Both Pincay and Baeza were Arlington standouts in the 1960s. And both had interesting secrets I'd like to share with you.

Pincay—I called his first winner in 1966 you may remember—understood English better than he spoke it. That made him an immediate hit with some horsemen, particularly those with a sense of humor.

"Every jock should be like Pincay," opined trainer Joe Pierce Jr., who just happened to top the standings that summer with 52 winners. "He'd listen attentively, and never talk back, never ask questions, or argue or debate instructions. He'd just nod—then go out there and do the job just like you told him to." Then Pierce laughed and added, "We should have more jocks like him who don't know the language." Pincay did know one word very well though: "winner"!

I learned a new word because of Braulio Baeza—the word "stoic." Every reporter from California to Illinois to New York used that adjective—meaning "free from passion, unmoved either by joy or grief"—to describe the lean, tall Panamanian with ice water in his veins. I took notable exception to their use of "stoic," since when it came to horsebacking, Baeza lacked neither passion nor joy. True, he remained unruffled. He could sit and wait with the best of 'em and finish with power and zest when need be.

Baeza topped all American riders for five straight years, 1964 through 1968, and again in 1975, his last full year in the saddle. He was regular rider for Ogden Phipps's sometimes temperamental—"headstrong" was a more accurate tag—remarkable Buckpasser when he emulated Tom Rolfe by sweeping Arlington's Mid-America Triple. Like a colt possessed, Buckpasser zipped the mile in world-record time of 1:32$\frac{3}{5}$ to win the 1966 Arlington Classic.

Two years later, this time astride Tartan Farm's lightning-like Dr. Fager, Baeza again would be the rider of record. Dr. Fager shouldered an imposing 134 pounds, cruising to a ridiculously easy 10-length victory in the 1968 Washington Park Handicap at Arlington in 1:32$\frac{1}{5}$, a new world speed mark—which, if I remember correctly, withstood onslaught for at least 30 years. In 1968, Dr. Fager ruled Thoroughbred racing not only as Horse of the Year, but as Grass kingpin as well.

Now the secret. Yes, Baeza publicly acclaimed Dr. Fager as his fastest, greatest mount of a superlative riding career. Years later, caught in a nostalgic, reflective mood, Baeza recalled an unbeaten, late-developing 2-year-old of 1965 (Buckpasser's juvenile season). The colt was Graustark, owned by Darby Dan Farm and trained by Loyd Gentry.

"We all thought that if he remained sound, Graustark might be the 1966 Triple Crown winner, and one of the Super Horses of all time," Baeza said. "Thinking back to his short but unbeaten season at

2, then as a promising 3-year-old before hobbled by a career-ending injury—I'd be tempted to call him the best I've ever ridden!"

Secrets sometimes are made to be shared.

Jorge Valesquez might not be the most eloquent of Panamanian-born jockeys when it comes to his adopted tongue of English, but he knows the words "apex" and "nadir" and the difference they convey. His nadir occurred in 1978 when, despite his every Herculean effort, he and his favorite mount, Calumet Farm's Alydar, could do no better than second to Affirmed in all three Triple Crown classics, earning a distinction he'd just as soon forget, let alone experience. But Jorge fondly remembers topping all American riders with 438 wins in 1967. And he'll never forget 1985, when he set a single-season record of 57 stakes scores. In between, he won the 1981 Kentucky Derby and Preakness with Pleasant Colony.

Yet Alydar just doesn't seem to want to go away. I interviewed Valesquez several times during our 1989 Saturday morning breakfasts at Arlington in the track's first season as an ultramodern facility following the fire of 1985. He deplored his and Alydar's failure to get the job done in the Belmont.

"I know we were criticized for not being on the proper lead in the final 100 yards," Jorge recalled, "and we were beaten a bare head for all the money. I did my best to get him to change leads. Apparently it just wasn't in the cards."

What was in the cards, however, was a change of riders. Following his historic Triple Crown defeat, Alydar came to Arlington to test his mettle in the 1978 Arlington Classic. Trainer John Veitch replaced Valesquez with Jeff Fell, and without Affirmed to worry about, Alydar proceeded to spread-eagle his field with a 13-length romp. The performance not only enhanced Fell's reputation but underscored Alydar's quality, at the same time attesting to the genuineness of Affirmed's Triple Crown triumph.

During the "swan song" years of my announcing days, a strong young booter from Erath, Louisiana, named Shane Sellers relocated from downstate Illinois to major Chicago racing and proceeded to take Chicago by storm. In 1989, Shane topped all riders at Hawthorne and Sportsman's Park; in 1991, he expanded his riding dominance to include Arlington International, piling up no fewer than 219 wins, shattering the old mark of 181 set by Randy Romero in 1982. Shane continued to scintillate, eventually nailing down titles at Keeneland and Gulfstream Park. In 1996 he was associated with 3-year-old champ Skip Away, including a resounding upset victory over the great Cigar heard around the turf world.

Shane's easy-but-firm riding style fits somewhere between Pat Day and Jerry Bailey. Slowly but surely he's gained the confidence of trainers from Florida to California. Unless a recent injury means the end of his career, I'm betting he remains among the nation's top money-winning jockeys this decade of the new millennium.

I've mentioned Eddie Arcaro's talent for converting bad news into good. Here's a case that affected the industry in general. It was the summer of 1957. I was working track publicity, practicing my announcing while the races were run, then hastily repairing to the winner's circle to collect owner–trainer–jockey quotes following the array of stakes races at Arlington and Washington Parks. One occasion was the Arlington Futurity for 2-year-olds, and Eddie was in town to ride Fred W. Hooper's unbeaten sensation, the fleet-footed Alhambra, who was gunning for his seventh straight victory. He got it, too; well, not really.

You see, trainer Chuck Parke sent the unbeaten Alhambra postward with a green stablemate, Olymar, who really should have stayed in the barn. As was Alhambra's wont, he led from start to finish, winning "eased up" by 5 lengths. But at midstretch—where Alhambra cantered along with an insurmountable 6- or 7-length lead—entrymate Olymar veered in sharply, impeding a colt named Sir Ruler, the latter in rein to Bill Hartack. (Hartack and Arcaro again!) Olymar wound up fourth, Sir Ruler fifth—lengths behind the soaring winner.

Sir Ruler, however, had been legitimately impeded by Olymar, and Hartack, the born competitor he was, immediately lodged an objection against the winning entry of both Alhambra and Olymar.

An antiquated racing rule gave the stewards no discretionary powers. If one part of an entry fouls another horse, neither part of the winning entry was allowed to finish ahead of the victimized animal. Imagine the tumult created by the announcement that a "claim of foul" had been lodged against both halves of the Hooper entry. Alhambra had won in a gallop; now he faced the possibility of having his number taken down.

Arcaro was livid, taking out his disgust, albeit too late, with trainer Chuck Parke. I vividly recall his words. "That'll teach you to run a bum with a champ."

Parke tried to pacify Eddie. "They can't take you down. It wouldn't be fair."

"They can't?" Eddie shot back, removing the saddle from Alhambra's sweaty back. "You know that crazy rule. If Olymar did anything wrong, then we all suffer."

Eddie immediately accosted jockey Doug Dodson, who rode Olymar. Dodson offered this feeble excuse: "Something scared my colt at the eighth pole, and he ducked in. I straightened him out immediately. The judges will see it wasn't my fault, certainly unintentional."

Unintentional or not, the stewards under the rule could exercise no discretion. The rule was established years ago to prevent a trainer from using one part of an entry "to run interference" for the other, purposely impeding a main challenger, thereby setting up his entrymate.

Yes, Olymar did bother Sir Ruler. Not intentionally. Certainly not to improve or enhance Alhambra's chances. The latter was literally "home free" when the violation occurred.

So what if Alhambra's pristine record will be sullied. Hartack fought his case fiercely. So what if the public be penalized by having the odds-on favorite be disqualified for no fault of his own. All Sir Ruler would gain was to be moved up from fifth to third. Leather Button, who finished second but so far removed from Alhambra as if in another race, was moved to first, Rellim S.W. to second, and Sir Ruler to third. Alhambra and Olymar were dropped to fourth and fifth, respectively.

Eddie remained indignant. His justifiable rantings helped fuel a crusade of reform against the controversial rule. Stewards everywhere were in concert, vociferous in their displeasure and helplessness, collectively demanding discretionary powers so that a repeat of "the Alhambra case" should never happen again. Their firm conviction was positively simple: as long as the infraction did not affect the race's outcome, why penalize the public? The stewards should be allowed to judicate matters as if with the wisdom of Solomon.

The rule was soon modified. Too late for Hooper, Arcaro, Parke, Alhambra, or the racing public. But it was a change that helped streamline the court of last resort. Eddie lost 10 percent of a rich winner's purse that day, but the racing public came out a winner.

Sometimes good jockeys, like good people everywhere, die too young. Isaac Murphy, the great black rider, overcame humble beginnings to ascend racing's stratosphere as one of the greatest jockeys of all time. Murphy was the son of a former slave. He achieved lasting renown as one of the sport's true legends, winning easily with better than a third of his mounts year after year. Fact is, his lifetime record of 638 wins in 1,412 races gave Murphy an overall 44 percent winning average, which has never been approached. Yes, Isaac Murphy was unbeatable, except for pneumonia. He was only 36 when he died.

George "Iceman" Woolf gained fame and celebrity riding such fine Thoroughbreds as Seabiscuit—"best horse I ever rode"—Kayak II, Challedon, Bold Venture, Occupy, and Whirlaway. But the Iceman never won the Kentucky Derby. It was his one unfulfilled dream. When he perished in a freak racing mishap in January 1946 at Santa Anita, Woolf was but 36 years old.

In one memorable race, tragedy was averted during as spectacular a spill as racing fans would ever witness without major injury or fatality taking its deadly toll. The year was 1986, the event the Hawthorne Juvenile for 2-year-olds at 1$\frac{1}{16}$ miles. A bright youngster named Momentus, with Alex Solis aboard, approached the eighth pole in midstretch with what I thought an insurmountable 4-length lead.

Suddenly the colt was startled. Some opined he spied the starting gate, which had been pulled clockwise up alongside the outer rail. Momentus swerved crazily to the inside, where he flipped virtually up and over the inner rail, shearing the eighth pole. Horse and rider tumbled heavily into the drainage ditch between the dirt and grass courses.

Lo and behold, both colt and jockey miraculously escaped unscathed. If you ever see on sale a commercial video of *Exciting and Freak Sports Mishaps*, you'll find that incident prominently portrayed, as well it should be. It was one of the most amazing escapes ever captured on film!

Momentus lived to race again. He even started in the 1987 Kentucky Derby. He didn't win, but he lived to tell about it. And Alex Solis, as you know, remains hale and hearty to this day.

Thanks to recent conversations with jockey great Jerry Bailey, I was reminded of a second "happy ending" to what otherwise was a disaster in waiting.

It was in the late 70s—this time at Arlington and again with me at the mike—when a field left the starting gate right before the finish wire on their way to one complete journey around the track's spacious 1⅛ miles dirt oval.

After pulling the starting gate only some 15 feet from the inner rail, the motor of the tractor abruptly quit—leaving only that 15-foot space between gate and rail for horses and jockeys to pass. There was absolutely no room outside the gate and tractor!

Jerry Bailey was one of the dozen riders in the race, none of them aware of what potential danger lurked. From the commotion beneath my booth, I became almost instantly aware of what injury and possible death awaited horse and rider in less than two minutes.

I knew the jocks could hear my call—that is, if they were listening and not totally absorbed in the thrill of action. For sure, I knew Arlington's agile outrider, the late Vince Dimayo, could hear me to the right of the finish wire where he stood for the start.

I beseeched, actually ordered, Vince to head off the field at the top of the stretch, whence he "should alert the jockeys that the starting gate was stalled, and instruct and guide them, to funnel them, single file if possible, through the narrow opening between the rail and the starting gate!"

Vince raced to the top of Arlington's homestretch—I continued warning the riders to follow the outrider's direction—and adroitly guided the field virtually single file but under a full gallop through the narrow channel—and safety!

"I'll never forget that 'ride' to my dying day," Bailey recalls with a deep sigh. "What you and Vince did was amazing. Thanks to you, many of us are still around."

The pleasure was ours, Jerry.

Chapter Ten

The Triple Crown

If the Kentucky Derby is the toughest race in the world to win, then winning the Triple Crown figures to be at least three times as difficult. In fact, the Triple Crown has been won by only 11 colts in American Thoroughbred history—Sir Barton sweeping the first in 1919, Affirmed the last in 1978. In between were Gallant Fox (1930), Omaha (1935), War Admiral (1937), Whirlaway (1941), Count Fleet (1943), Assault (1946), Citation (1948), Secretariat (1973), and Seattle Slew (1977). They all captured the three-ply series which features the Kentucky Derby, the Preakness, and the Belmont Stakes—each race on the dirt at distances of 1¼ miles, 1³⁄₁₆ miles, and 1½ miles, respectively.

The only way to make the Triple Crown more exacting would be to present one of the races on the grass. If that were the case, rather than the agonizing 25-year gap between Citation (1948) and Secretariat (1973) or the 23-year chasm dating from Affirmed (1978), we may never have ourselves another 3-year-old of irrefragable fame and glory. No need to make it any tougher.

A horse gets only one chance to win the Triple Crown—when he or she is a 3-year-old. And you need not have graduated from Thoroughbred U. to know a horse must first win the Kentucky Derby. Win the Derby, fine. Win the Derby and Preakness, good. Win the Derby, Preakness, and Belmont, that's great! But it's easier said than done—just ask Silver Charm (1997), Real Quiet (1998), or Charismatic (1999).

Or ask Pensive (1944), Tim Tam (1958), Carry Back (1961), Northern Dancer (1964), Kauai King (1966), Majestic Prince (1969), Canonero II (1971), Pleasant Colony (1981), Alysheba

(1987), or Sunday Silence (1989). Each won both the Derby and Preakness before suffering lamentable defeat in the Belmont Stakes. Several others, as we'll see, won both the Derby and Belmont, but defeat in the Preakness prevented adding their names to that exclusive Triple Crown roster.

Perhaps, it's true, as some modern-day observers conclude: We just don't breed that kind of extraordinarily great colt anymore. And if we do come up with an exceptional horse, he or she lacks the soundness and durability of past Thoroughbred greats.

A recent example is Fusaichi Pegasus, whose astonishing 2000 Kentucky Derby triumph—over an inconsequential field, we might add—elicited "great horse" claims from a hungry media. But the colt failed dreadfully behind the sparingly raced Red Bullet in the Preakness two weeks later.

The Derby's winner's camp excused Fusaichi Pegasus on the grounds that, to be at his best, he needed more than the two weeks allowed between the Roses Run and Preakness. Then Red Bullet's trainer, Joe Orseno, withdrew the colt from the Belmont with the remark: "We think it's best to give Red Bullet more time in between races right now. If you run in a mile-and-a-half race, that knocks you out three months. It's pointless." It was bad enough that Fusaichi Pegasus's connections decried the two weeks allotted between Derby and Preakness, but here were Red Bullet's people bemoaning the three full weeks between Preakness and Belmont.

The last thing we want is to have a colt injured with strenuous, unnecessary over-racing, but excuse us for saying it again: They just don't make 'em anymore like Secretariat, Citation, Round Table, Kelso, Man o' War, Seabiscuit, Spectacular Bid, and Affirmed. At the risk of having you throw a horseshoe my way, allow me one more testimony to Citation's greatness.

Citation had already made six starts—winning five—before annexing the April 27 Derby Trial only four days before the May 1, 1948, Kentucky Derby, which of course he won in a gallop. Two weeks later (May 15) he won the Preakness; two weeks later (May 29), the Jersey Stakes; two weeks later (June 12), the Belmont; three weeks later (July 5), he whipped older horses in the Stars and Stripes—six major stakes in less than 2½ months! Citation would start and win eight more times that year—a total of 20 starts as a 3-year-old in seven different states at nine different tracks.

We admit to the countless unforeseen mishaps and circumstances that can befall a racehorse. Meadowlake, Graustark, and Hoist the Flag—each of whom we felt epitomized potential Thoroughbred greatness—had their careers cut short by injury. But for each of them, there has been a long list of durable glory days champions: Secretariat, Citation, Round Table, Kelso, Man o' War, Seabiscuit, Spectacular Bid, Affirmed, Native Dancer, Armed, Tom Fool, Whirlaway, Assualt, Seattle Slew, Hill Prince, Nashua, Swaps, Forego, Bold Ruler, Swoon's Son, Damascus, Tom Rolfe, Dr. Fager, and John Henry. They raced brilliantly over long periods, and with durability and distinction to make their breed proud.

Yes, we've had the wonderful Cigar, Skip Away, Touch Gold, Victory Gallop, and Silver Charm in the final decade of the 20th century. And to each we tip our hats. We just need more, that's all.

But let's return to the Triple Crown, particularly its first leg, the celebrated Kentucky Derby, arguably the most exciting two minutes in all of sports. The annual Run for the Roses is a happening, it's a destination, it's a fever every true sports fan wants to catch.

Rightly called the world's most popular horse race, the Derby is a spark in the air, like an electrical arc, a mood, bustling and crackling, a swirl of fancy so breathtaking as to be almost fictional, a writer's conception of what the world's greatest horse race should be.

No wonder every owner, trainer, and jockey dreams of winning the Kentucky Derby. A jockey could win multiple races daily, week after week, but all that pales on Derby Day. "There's a something special in the air when they play 'My Old Kentucky Home,'" confessed Jerry Bailey, a two-time Derby winner.

"I suppose the only thing equaling it," said jockey Gary Stevens, who also won three Derbies, "is to win the Triple Crown, and I should know. I came awfully close, you know." Stevens won both the Derby and Preakness on Silver Charm in 1997, then lost the Belmont in a scorcher to Touch Gold. Incidentally, Stevens came back the following year aboard Victory Gallop to spoil jockey Kent Desormeaux's Triple Crown quest on Real Quiet, nailing the latter by a scant whisker in the Belmont Stakes.

Racing's middle jewel, the Preakness, finds special consequence in that it either affirms or repudiates the Derby winner's majesty, often only temporarily, sometimes setting up a rubber match for the final jewel, the Belmont Stakes. The Belmont is called "the test of champions," not only as the final leg of the Triple Crown, but at the most demanding of distances, 1½ miles, once around Belmont Park's sprawling dirt oval. Many pretenders to Triple Crown immortality lose the Belmont simply because they're not great horses. I've learned the truly great ones win the races that count, like the Belmont, the 1½ miles notwithstanding.

History confirms that the Kentucky Derby took its sweet time becoming legendary. It started inauspiciously in 1875 when the Louisville Jockey Club presented a 1½ miles affair for 15 starters. Aristides won the inaugural, enriching his owner's coffers with a modest $2,850 purse, and history was made. I'm certain turf historians would have a lot to say about the Derby's early years, horses like Hindoo and Ben Ali and Donerail, also the great jockey Isaac Murphy. But the sport's first Triple Crown winner, Sir Barton, awaited 1919 for his triumph. Gallant Fox collected his Triple Crown in 1930; his son Omaha duplicated the feat in 1935. War Admiral, Man o' War's greatest son, captured racing's Big Three in 1937, a year before he'd lose his famous match race against Seabiscuit.

Since my story of racing's glory days starts with 1941 and Whirlaway's Triple Crown conquest, let's concentrate on the Triple Crown classics since that time, until 1984 when the Breeders' Cup made its appearance. We've devoted enough space to Whirlaway. Suffice to say, his Derby winning margin of 8 lengths, equaled by Assault in 1946, remains the biggest in Derby history. And his Preakness score was a wonder to behold. I remember it on *RKO Pathe News*. Dead last going into the first turn, he and Eddie Arcaro maneuvered artfully inside, between, and outside horses for a picture-perfect last-to-first Preakness victory. Mr. Longtail's front-stepping tally against only three Belmont Stakes opponents also was one for the book.

Greentree Stable's Shut Out, who became jockey Wayne D. Wright's mount when Arcaro selected entrymate Devil Diver, won the 1942 Derby going away, dropped the Preakness to Chicago-owned Cinderella colt Alsab, then walloped his Belmont foes in typical come-from-behind fashion.

We talked about Count Fleet's 1943 Triple, also Pensive's 1944 wins in both the Derby and Preakness before his Belmont upset by Bounding Home. Hoop Jr., the first horse ever owned by Fred W. Hooper, gave Arcaro his third Derby win in 1945, a flashy 6-length victory in the slop. He finished a good second to Polynesian in the Preakness despite a career-ending injury. That year's Belmont was won by Pavot, a pickup mount for Arcaro. Pavot the year before was one of the last fine stakes colts to be ridden by Georgie Woolf.

Incidentally, it was in 1945—I was 14 at the time—that I saw two fine 3-year-olds both beaten by Hoop Jr. in that year's Derby. One was Pot o' Luck, owned by Calumet Farm and ridden by Doug Dodson; the other was Murlogg Farm's Fighting Step, Georgie South up. Pot o' Luck was second to Hoop Jr. in the Derby; Fighting Step was unplaced, the only time he would be out of the money in 15 starts that year.

My father and I zigged when we should have zagged that summer at Washington Park. We loved Fighting Step in the Arlington Classic—Arlington raced the war years of 1943–1945 at Washington Park—but he settled for third behind Pot o' Luck. A month later, won over by Pot o' Luck's late kick, we picked him to win the American Derby. This time he finished third behind Fighting Step. No wonder horse players go broke.

Assault was unbeatable in the 1946 Triple Crown. Jet Pilot held on to beat Phalanx in the 1947 Derby; Faultless topped Jet Pilot to win the Preakness, the race that announcer Clem McCarthy miscalled; Phalanx beat his rivals to win both the Belmont and the 1947 3-year-old title.

Citation rewrote racing history in 1948, winning 19 of 20, including not only the easiest Triple Crown ever but 7 wins over older horses. Calumet Farm was on an unprecedented roll, topping the owner's list in seven of nine years during the fabulous 1940s. Their Ponder won the 1949 Derby just as his daddy Pensive did in 1944. If anything, Ponder dwarfed his sire as a stretch-rusher. Last early, Ponder was still 12th as the Derby field swung around the final elbow. But he powered to 6 with a quarter-mile to go, then uncorked a final burst that carried him 3 lengths before Capot and Palestinian.

I was in the stands at Arlington—now back in business following the war—when Ponder stormed from last to first to win the 1949 Arlington Classic, in which he humbled Belmont Stakes winner Capot. He did his Whirlaway impression to win the American Derby at Washington Park. I was there in the stands. I've seen a lot of great-finishing horses, including Whirlaway. When right and in the mood, Ponder was in a class by himself. Later, jockey Steve Brooks, who rode Ponder for Calumet Farm, confirmed my opinion. "I've ridden a lot of fine horses for Calumet and other stables," Brooks told me. "Citation was far and away the best, Coaltown the fastest, but Ponder was the most exciting stretch-runner I've ever ridden."

Hill Gail's 1952 Kentucky Derby victory was Arcaro's fifth; it was also the first Derby televised to a major market. Its viewer acceptance monumental, TV decided to televise the entire 1953 Triple Crown, a decision that made Alfred G. Vanderbilt's Native Dancer an equine matinee idol. At the same time, it helped shove jockey Eric Guerin into racing's dog house. Guerin handled the Dancer so tentatively, losing out to Dark Star in an historic Derby photo finish, one spectator observed: "Guerin took Native Dancer everywhere on the track except the ladies' room." Poor Eric. I met him at Arlington the summer of 1953 when he flew in to ride Native Dancer to a 9-length victory in the 1-mile Classic. "Don't—don't ever ask me about the Derby, okay?" Guerin all but pleaded, desperately hiding his anger and shame. "Ask me anything else but that!"

By 1954, Johnny Adams was still making big news with Hasty House Farms' Hasty Road. They lost the Derby to Determine but reversed that decision in the Preakness. High Gun won the Belmont for Eric Guerin. The latter was riding high again, but his gaffe astride Native Dancer in the 1953 Derby haunted him until his last day on earth.

The 1955 season belonged to Nashua and Swaps; to owners William Woodward Jr. and Rex C. Ellsworth; to trainers Sunny Jim Fitzsimmons and Mesh Tenney; and to jockeys Eddie Arcaro and Bill Shoemaker. It was a very good year, to say the least. The $100,000 Swaps–Nashua winner-take-all match race is covered more fully in Chapter Twelve.

If there was any doubt how Needles would dispatch his 16 rivals in the 1956 Derby, all one had to do was look at his pedigree. He was a son of Ponder. At the Derby, 16th and some 16 lengths off the leader at the half-mile pole, Needles exploded from out of the proverbial blue to collar Fabius by less than a length at wire's end.

Fabius, a stouthearted son of Citation, upended Needles in the Preakness, but the latter came back with his usual stretch verve to account for the Belmont. The Triple Crown eluded Needles; so did Chicago's American Derby on the grass, where Eddie Arcaro provided the magic on front-running Swoon's Son. Jockey Dave Erb, regular rider for both Swoon's Son and Needles, had felt compelled to select Needles, lest trainer Hugh Fontaine throw a fit similar to that when he heard Erb call Swoon's Son "the best 3-year-old I've ridden this year, bar none," after Swooney had just scored a decisive victory over Fabius in the Arlington Classic.

I got Erb's quote in the winner's circle following Swoon's Son's Classic verdict, the jockey obviously not factoring in Fontaine's temper tantrum. Later, as a trainer, Erb compared his favorite mounts—Swaps, Needles, and Swoon's Son: "They were all special in their own way. I have to give Swaps the nod as the greatest I ever rode. He was a magnificent athlete. Needles was tireless, just like his sire, and with a little luck he could have won the Triple Crown. Swoon's Son next to Swaps was the fastest thing on four legs. He'll always be my favorite mount."

What can we say about the 1957 3-year-old crop that hasn't been said before. Iron Liege edged Gallant Man in the Derby, Bold Ruler annihilated Iron Liege in the Preakness, and Gallant Man murdered 'em all in the Belmont. Meanwhile, Round Table went on a winning spree second only to Citation's and Cigar's 16 straight—11 in a row, including 3 on the grass, eventually ruling the grass as its first three-time champion (1957–1959). There was sufficient glory for all.

I never saw Tim Tam in person. What I did see on TV as he coveted the 1958 Triple Crown convinced me he would have won it were it not for a career-ending injury in the Belmont. He might have been one of the all-time greats of racing's glory days. Tim Tam surely was bred in the purple, a bay colt by Horse of the Year Tom Fool, out of one of Calumet Farm's great mares, Two Lea. A late bloomer, in early 1958 Tim Tam played the role of Coaltown to Citation of 1948, figuring as backup to Kentucky Pride, another Calumet blueblood. Kentucky Pride was a full brother to Real Delight, the latter praised by Arcaro as the finest filly or mare he ever saw (1952–1953).

Kentucky Pride fizzled, succumbing to a host of physical problems, yet managed to sprint with the best of 'em. Tim Tam, however, started flashing promise as early as February 5, finishing a strong third behind Olymar and entrymate Kentucky Pride in the 7-furlongs Bahamas in Florida. "Looks like we got our Derby horse," trainer Jimmy Jones said that day.

Jimmy was absolutely right. Tim Tam would never lose again, not until breaking a bone while finishing second on three legs in the Belmont Stakes. He pulverized his foes in the Everglades, belying his sire's famed speed with a late kick of his own creation. He won the Flamingo via disqualification from the well-regarded Jewel's Reward, and he annexed the Fountain of Youth, again on the heels of a powerhouse late surge. Then Tim Tam gave the Chicago-based speedster Lincoln Road a 6-length lead going into the far turn of the Florida Derby, rallying for a going-away, albeit narrow, score.

It was on to Kentucky for Tim Tam. We Chicagoans figured the Derby was shaping up as a veritable match between Lincoln Road's speed and Tim Tam's late punch. Tim Tam won two more, including the Derby Trail. His new rider, Ismael Valenzuela, who had replaced Bill Hartack, freely predicted "it will take a wonder horse to beat Tim Tam in the Kentucky Derby." Even as Arcaro was being considered as jockey for Jewel's Reward in the Derby, my heart belonged to Tim Tam. What I had read and had seen on TV suggested he could be "one of the ones" who'd punctuate racing's golden age with wonderful regularity.

Lincoln Road loved the muddy track Derby Day and went about his business as spirited front-stepper. Passing the quarter pole, Lincoln Road was a good 5 or 6 lengths in front of Tim Tam, but the latter was sizzling, gobbling up the mud as if it were chocolate cake, surging in the final yards to win it clearly by a half-length.

Now this was also Silky Sullivan's Derby, a fiasco by any yardstick. True, Silky had given stretch-running a new term, "a Silky Sullivan!" His exploits out West, including a smashing victory in the Santa Anita Derby, constituted "impossible" late-running at its best. But Silky was a godsend freak who simply lacked genuine class. Oh, he'd pull it off against mediocre company—I still have a film in which he charged from 40 or 50 lengths off the leader in a race's final half mile. And now he had Shoemaker as pilot. Together they were the 1958 Derby cynosure. Network TV gave Silky split-screen coverage throughout the 1¼ miles. But he couldn't uncork his brand of unbelievable late run against the likes of Tim Tam or Lincoln Road or Jewel's Reward.

Arcaro told me prior to the Derby: "Silky can beat those horses a rung or two below the top at any distance, 6 furlongs to 1⅛ miles. Shoe tells me he's the most amazing stretch-runner he's ever been around. But even Shoe doubts if he can uncork 'the big one' against top colts."

Shoe and Eddie were right. Silky trailed throughout. He tried to rally leaving the half-mile pole but finished a disappointing 12th in the 14-horse field. He flopped again in the Preakness. The Silky phenomenon was finis. Although he won again back in California, the old magic was gone. But not forgotten. Silky Sullivan made a lasting impression during the glory days.

Tim Tam extended his 1958 win steak to eight straight with a patented come-from-behind Preakness victory, again at the direct expense of sprightly Lincoln Road, this time striding clear by 1½ lengths. "He's the real thing," I bragged. "We've got ourselves an overdue Triple Crown champ!" And I was talking 10 years since Citation, not realizing it would take another 15 years to fulfill my prophecy.

Tim Tam surrendered meekly, but in obvious pain, as a horse named Cavan stormed into command after the mile in the Belmont, winning handily by 6. It was at that moment, with a half-mile to travel, that Tim Tam fractured a sesamoid bone in his right foreleg, courageously racing the final half-mile on only three good legs, still saving second. He never raced again. His dream of greatness, mine, too, was over.

In 1959, I started my career as a race caller. As I mentioned, the winner of my second call, the second half of the Daily Double, May 18, 1959, was Venetian Way, who wound up winner of the 1960 Kentucky Derby. Johnny Longden flew in from California to win the feature of my opening-day program at Washington Park, and from that time forward I'd be more than just an interested witness to racing history in the making. From that day forward, almost every horse, owner, trainer, and jockey would have to pass personal inspection by my trusty binoculars from my announcing perch high atop the stands.

Since 1941, I had seen the best in Thoroughbred racing. Yet, in many ways, now as track announcer, the best was yet to come. In the 1960s, some of racing's true elite would cavort at Arlington, Washington, and Hawthorne. True, I'd not preview the likes of Carry Back, Decidedly, and Chateaugay, but back home in Chicago we'd be prepping racing fans with such future stars as Ridan, Candy Spots, and Golden Ruler; such outstanding 3-year-olds as T.V. Lark and Kelso; such older stars as Admiral Vic, Beau Purple, Crimson Satan, and Chief of Chiefs. The sport remained vibrant and healthy.

Northern Dancer gave Hartack his fourth Derby winner in 1964, and his second of three Preakness wins. We all hoped that Northern Dancer, who wasn't the soundest of colts, would win the Triple Crown. But High Gun, giving Eric Guerin his second straight Belmont, captured the third jewel.

The drought was just starting. Yet, at the same time, we were being exposed to some of the finest performers the sport had ever seen. But, whatever the reason, it had ostensibly become one Herculean task to come up with another Triple Crown winner.

Northern Dancer, of course, retired early, only to become one of the great sires of all time, more than reproducing himself at stud.

For every top equine hanging up his racing shoes, there was another new name emerging gloriously. The diminutive Roman Brother, owned by Harbor View, won the 1964 American Derby in handy fashion; Harbor View dominated Arlington stakes that year, sending out Master Dennis to annex the Arlington Handicap.

It was also a banner year for fillies and mares. Briardale Farm's sophomore sensation Tosmah ran off and hid from the boys in the mile Arlington Classic. She then showed disdain for older members of her sex by winning the 1⅛ miles Arlington Matron. I got to meet her eastern rider, Sammy Boulmetis, following her Matron score. They also teamed up in the Classic. She made her sex proud.

Shoemaker was still winning added money features with eclat. He won that year's Futurity with North Forty Stable's Sadair. Some felt the latter would prove a strong contender for the 1965 Triple Crown. It wasn't in the cards, but the Chicago-owned Lucky Debonair, who gave Shoe his third of four wins in the race, copped the Louisville classic.

Among older cracks, we got a close-up look at the sensational 4-year-old Gun Bow, who ran in the 1964 Washington Park Handicap. His pilot was an Arlington regular, the speed-minded Walter Blum. "Gun Bow's all heart," Walter told me the day of his Washington Park Handicap attempt. "I like to ride up front, and he loves it, too. And he becomes a tiger if someone tries to pass him."

Gun Bow made me a believer. I called him "home free" in the Washington Park. The nifty little 4-year-old with the big heart later out-fought mighty Kelso for a big win in New York's 1964 Woodward Stakes. With Walter Blum again aboard, Gun Bow gained a nose triumph over five-time Horse of the Year Kelso. Their rivalry helped make 1964 a year to be remembered.

Mrs. Ada L. Rice's Chicago-owned Lucky Debonair won the 1965 Kentucky Derby; Tom Rolfe annexed the Preakness as a forerunner to his Chicago summer successes; and Hail to All captured the Belmont. By early summer, the nation's 3-year-old title had seemed anybody's race. That's when diminutive Tom Rolfe caught his second wind. The nation's eyes were on Chicago, and I was privileged to call all of Tom Rolfe's victories, including the Mid-America Triple.

As I said before, I loved that little colt. When right, which he was all summer long, the son of Ribot belonged in that upper echelon that included Round Table, Nashua, and Swaps, perhaps a short step behind Citation, Secretariat, and Kelso. That mighty little mite belonged to the club of equine greats. And he'd prove himself as a sire, too.

Speaking of extraordinary Thoroughbreds, 1965 was the year that Darby Dan Farm's Graustark launched an all too brief racing career. When I was track publicity director, Arlington clocker Jim Milner told me about the mysterious 2-year-old colt, that his workouts, which trainer Loyd Gentry tried to hide, were "nothing short of sensational." Milner said if he put down the true times, like 6 furlongs in 1:09⅘, nobody would believe it. I passed on the info to sports columnist Dave Condon of the *Chicago Tribune*, who did a full report on the unraced juvenile. Graustark won as predicted and was undefeated that season, including the Arch Ward Stakes in 1:09—⅕ for 6 panels—incredible time for a juvenile eased-up at the wire.

I not only had Tom Rolfe dear to my heart, but now Graustark as well, and for the future. As the racing enthusiast I was, in 1965 I proclaimed: "If Graustark doesn't win next year's Triple Crown, then I'm a monkey's uncle!" Well, I was swinging on a vine of my own creation come the first Saturday in May 1966. Graustark, hailed not only by me but by the media and racing community as well, was injured irreparably prior to the Derby and immediately retired. Racing and its public were denied the opportunity to see a certifiable champion do his thing.

A curious phenomenon was developing in the 1960s, set in motion in 1960 when Kelso became the first 3-year-old to be voted Horse of the Year without having won one of the Triple Crown classics. Before then, it was unheard of to have a 3-year-old crowned as year's best without having won either the Derby or Preakness or Belmont.

Ogden Phipps's eccentric but absolutely amazing Buckpasser followed suit in 1966. Not as screwy as Nashua or Bold Ruler, but equally fast and erratic was Buckpasser. His trainer, Eddie Neloy, insisted that Buckpasser "had a mind of his own."

His jockey was the Panamanian Braulio Baeza, fresh off undeniable disappointment over Graustark's demise as a 3-year-old of note. "Buckpasser wanted to win, yes, but only on his terms," said Baeza. "He waited for opponents, as if it didn't count unless he could beat 'em eye to eye. And why beat 'em by big margins? Just beat 'em, that's all, whether a neck or a length—so what!"

The first time I saw Buckpasser was on TV; he was a fledgling 2-year-old; the occasion was the 1965 Sapling Stakes at Monmouth Park. He was taking on a good field, headed by the juvenile leader pro tem, Our Michael. Buckpasser walked out of the gate and was dead last before the first three jumps. Halfway up the backside, Baeza, seemingly unconcerned, asked the son of Tom Fool to move. Buckpasser exploded, splitting horses, charging into third behind Our Michael. The big colt then snuggled in behind the two leaders, Our Michael and Kinta, until well within the Monmouth stretch. Guided three-deep approaching the eight pole, Buckpasser collared Our Michael with a flourish, then deliberately maintained a half-length margin to the wire.

"He just hated to pass horses," Baeza afterward explained. "He enjoyed the competition, that's for sure, but he had no desire to leave 'em once he caught 'em."

The nation's 2-year-old champion won 9 of 11 starts, including the rich Arlington–Washington Futurity. I was set for the call, prepared for the colt's well-publicized antics.

Bill Winfrey—of Native Dancer fame—was Buckpasser's trainer when the colt was just 2; Neloy would take over the following year, 1966. Winfrey freely called Buckpasser the "best 2-year-old" since Native Dancer, predicting he'd win the Futurity "unless he got up on the wrong side of the bed that morning."

Well, bullheaded or not, Buckpasser decided to run on Futurity Day. Even though his winning time of 1:23 for 7 furlongs failed to excite, his manner of triumph was doubly impressive. Yes, he took his time. By then, Baeza refused to be rattled by his mount's lack of zeal early. When Buckpasser overhauled the leaders in mid-stretch, Baeza just shook his stick alongside his colt's face, just in case he might choose to relax or wait for challengers.

Once again, even with Graustark's defection, I had myself a new Triple Crown pick. I was convinced there wasn't a 3-year-old around who could touch Buckpasser at 1 mile or over. I was right, too. The only trouble was that Buckpasser would suffer a quarter crack, bypassing the spring classics. But, like Kelso six years earlier, he'd subsequently scintillate, eventually to be crowned 1966 Horse of the Year. However, before he incurred the injury that would force him to bypass the 1966 Triple Crown, a curious thing happened that winter at Hialeah—the "chicken" Flamingo.

The "chicken" Flamingo, which I watched on TV, was so-called because an alarmed track management, intimidated by the aura of invincibility created by Buckpasser, cowardly chose to all but curtail wagering on the stakes, despite the good field marshalled to face the colt, including the rapidly improving Illinois-bred sensation Abe's Hope. Bill Shoemaker was selected to ride Buckpasser on this occasion. Abe's Hope had the services of Chicago's own Earlie Fires. Later that summer, when reconnected with both Shoe and Earlie, I discussed at great length what happened in that Flamingo.

Here's how it worked out. Not that familiar with Buckpasser's eccentricities, Shoe allowed the big colt to forge an easy, earlier-than-usual lead turning for home. "He simply relaxed on me," Shoe recalled, "just like he had run out of gas. Suddenly, Abe's Hope is not only on us, but he passes us effortlessly."

Fires, aboard Abe's Hope, agreed: "We moved three or four deep in upper stretch—I couldn't believe how easily we were picking up the leaders. Inside the eighth pole, we go right by Buckpasser, opening up at least 2 lengths with maybe a hundred yards to go."

Bewildered by Buckpasser's nonchalance when collared, Shoe wisely surmised "my colt really didn't see Abe's Hope go by, he was that far outside us, so I roused him the best I could."

Now Buckpasser really didn't care if his rider was concerned or not; he spied Abe's Hope himself. And what he did was astounding. The Phipps colorbearer reaccelerated like a fresh horse. Going at twice the speed of Abe's Hope, flying through along the rail, he nailed his rival for an incredible going-away nose victory on the wire!

"I wasn't loafing on Abe's Hope," Fires confirmed. "What Buckpasser did was unbelievable. I've never seen anything like it before!"

And stranger things started to happen. Buckpasser, heavy favorite for the Triple Crown, suffered a serious hoof injury. Shoe was left without a Derby mount, so he chose Abe's Hope, who had all but upset Buckpasser in the Flamingo and later won the Florida Derby only to be disqualified.

I thought that Abe's Hope owners, Chicagoans Joe Bartell and Bob Byfield, were chickens themselves for dumping Fires for Shoe. Such is the allure of fame and glory, although as justice would have it, Baeza got Buckpasser back for a sparkling Arlington summer campaign, and Fires was returned atop Abe's Hope after the latter's abortive try in the Derby.

Meanwhile, I was taking on more weight—in the form of extra jobs—than Kelso and Tom Fool combined. While still serving as both announcer and director of advertising and publicity at Arlington, I was made part-time executive secretary for the Illinois Thoroughbred Breeders Foundation (ITBF), also weekly Illinois-breeding columnist for the *Daily Racing Form*, also editor of *The Winner's Circle*, a pretty classy new monthly publication by the ITBF on Thoroughbred racing, with an emphasis, of course, on horses bred or foaled in the state of Illinois. Illinois breeding, just like the state's racing, was at its apex again, and local products like Abe's Hope and contemporary Better Sea combined to give the Prairie State legitimate bragging rights all through 1966.

Illinois was proud to have Abe's Hope parade postward on Kentucky Derby Day as favorite. Under the title "Give Abe's Hope an 'A' for Effort," I described the occasion in the May edition of *The Winner's Circle:*

> *The doughty Illinois-bred, carrying the hopes of Illinois breeders and all segments of local racing, gave it the old college try on Saturday,*

May 7, before settling for a close-up fifth in the most ballyhooed of all horse races, the coveted Kentucky Derby at Churchill Downs.

It was the event, and occasion, all Illinois awaited, the first time an Illinois-bred loomed a solid contender in America's greatest horse race. . . .

Abe's Hope, despite his outside post, had run his heart out, merely coming up a little short. . . .

As the great Bill shoemaker, who chose Abe's Hope for his Derby mount following injury to Buckpasser, said afterward: "The race went as we planned, but he just couldn't do it in the final quarter mile." . . .

Racing along in 10th in the opening quarter, Abe's Hope saved valuable ground, cut inside several horses as they settled up the backstretch, then swung to the middle of the track for the final quarter-mile surge.

Kauai King, meanwhile, was cutting out his kind of pace, the Maryland-bred son of Native Dancer throwing in perfect fractions, given a breather by jockey Don Brumfield at the half-mile pole.

As they passed the quarter pole in upper stretch, Kauai King shook off Mrs. Ada L. Rice's Advocator, with Abe's Hope charging out in the middle of the track . . . even at mid-stretch our pride-n-joy was still in the hunt. . . . Shoe switched sticks, though the chunky Illinois-bred appeared to drift wide as if feeling the effects of his supreme effort. . . .

Abe's Hope comported himself admirably . . . and the season's still young!

I always like Abe's Hope. I suppose he was my favorite Illinois-bred, and that includes the 1970 Kentucky Derby hero, Dust Commander. But Abe's Hope boasted a special charisma; every time he raced, he carried the hopes of Chicago racing fans. Later that summer, when he won the $50,000 added Assault Handicap at Arlington, without Buckpasser of course, he did so in patented come-from-behind fashion—and, yes, with Earlie Fires back in the saddle.

Kauai King, incidentally, who won the 1966 Derby impressively, passed before my eyes the summer before at Arlington as an unsung 2-year-old. Except for running down his connections to correctly pronounce his name, I had no idea that he had the right stuff to capture America's most popular race. How good was Kauai King? Good enough to come back and win the Preakness—although a colt named Amberoid won the Belmont that spring.

Kauai King was also good enough to rate highly against a stellar field that summer against Buckpasser and Creme Dela Creme in the $100,000 added Arlington Classic, which lived up to its billing, and then some, as "the race of the year!"

It was the first time Kauai King, Creme Dela Creme, and Buckpasser would cross swords in the same arena, and some 30,000 fans were lured to Chicago's northwest suburban plant. They expected that the 1966 Classic winner would come from the nation's Big Three, but they never expected the winner to whistle the mile in 1:32⅗, breaking the old mile world mark of 1:33⅕ held jointly by Swaps, Intentionally, and Pia Star—Chicago regulars all.

Those of us close admirers of Buckpasser did expect a monumental effort, especially when informed that trainer Eddie Neloy was employing stablemate Impressive as "rabbit," to ensure an honest pace, to make sure Kauai King knew he was in a horse race. Jockey Kenny Knapp, who rode Impressive, admitted: "Listen, I had a job to do, and did it the way I was told," which included incredible fractions. Impressive ran 22⅕ for the quarter, the half in 43⅗, and 6 furlongs in an unheard of 1:06⅘. I was even breathless at that juncture.

Buckpasser uncoiled from seventh in the field of eight, ran down Impressive just outside the 16th pole, then defeated Bwamazon Farm's Creme Dela Creme by 2 lengths. A sad note was sounded when the recently syndicated Kauai King took a bad step leaving the mile chute. He managed to finish fifth in the power-packed field but pulled up sore, never to race again. He was retired to stud. Thus, I called Kauai King's first and last races of a brief but brilliant career.

Buckpasser was hardly finished, emulating Tom Rolfe of just the year before, becoming the second and last winner of Chicago's Mid-America Triple—the Chicagoan, Arlington Classic, and American Derby—en route to official crowning as 1966 Horse of the Year. After leaving Arlington at summer's end, he completed a royal season with an authoritative decision in the 2-mile Jockey Gold Cup, run that season at Aqueduct, his 13th win in 14 starts as a sophomore. Buckpasser deservedly became one of my 15 all-time favorites.

Damascus very easily could have edged his way into my all-time roster of personal greats. He was that brilliant. Proud Clarion, however, won the 1967 Kentucky Derby, Damascus throwing in a clinker, choosing Derby Day of all days to leave his best at home. Shoe told me that when right, and in the mood, and especially if the moon were full, Damascus "is capable of beating any man's horse." He made Shoe a prophet when he accounted for both the Preakness and Belmont in festive style. Then he journeyed to Arlington Park, where, under trainer Frank Whiteley's expert tutelage, he ran off with the American Derby in 1:46⅘ for 1⅛ miles, staking a valid claim not only to the 1967 3-year-old title, but Horse of the Year as well.

Having called Damascus an Arlington winner, I took exceptional interest in his subsequent start, the 1¼ miles Woodward in New York, in which he met a dispirited, older Buckpasser, who was making his final career outing. He also met a new sensation, the 3-year-old Dr. Fager, whose speed was fast becoming legendary. Damascus routed his opponents to cement Horse of the Year honors.

By then, I already knew how fast Dr. Fager was, but not how fast he'd eventually become. The speedster earlier had taken the measure of Damascus in New York's Gotham, and his performance within range of my binoculars in 1967 and 1968 in Chicago was the stuff of which memories are made. Tartan Farm's Dr. Fager was just another fleet merchant, or so I thought, when he won the 1967 Arlington Classic in 1:36 for the mile. Yes, he performed superbly, but his time, to which I should have naturally not given undue attention, was so-so. Plus, he toted only 120 pounds, 5 pounds less than Buckpasser carried only the year before when he hung up his 1:32⅗ world record. But Dr. Fager, who like Buckpasser also belonged to jockey Braulio Baeza, was just learning to run. "He was a good 3-year-old," Baeza volunteered, "but a great 4-year-old, one of the very best."

It all came together for 4-year-old Dr. Fager on August 24, 1968, in the 1-mile Washington Park Handicap at Arlington Park. His feats already noteworthy, he eagerly accepted top weight of 134 pounds, including a confident Braulio Baeza. We all ceded the Doctor victory in the event, despite the crushing impost. What we didn't figure on was the manner in which he'd humble his field. There were some imposing contenders in the race, including the speedy Racing Room and fast-finishing Out the Window, the latter hoping the former and Dr. Fager might get caught up in a suicidal early speed duel.

There was speed aplenty, to be sure. But it all belonged to Dr. Fager, who cruised to the lead turning for home, astonishingly dashing clear in the final 100 yards to a startling 10-length victory in 1:32⅕, a new world record, one which would defy onslaught for some 30 years. Every once in a while, I replay that race on tape. We didn't have fractional times posted then; I had to await the finish for the final running time. Now preserved on tape, after I announced the 10-length margin and order of finish, acknowledging the time as a new world record for the mile, all I whispered was "Wow!"

A weird year for the Triple Crown and its participants was 1968. Dancer's Image, a colt I loved, won the Kentucky Derby over Forward Pass, the latter latest in a string of Calumet Farm stalwarts. Forward Pass went on to annex the Preakness, but the 1968 Belmont went to Stage Door Johnny. Neither of these colts was able to withstand Dr. Fager's genuine claim to Horse of the Year. The good doctor was also honored as Grass Horse of the Year. Let's back track, however, to that Derby win by Dancer's Image, which in my opinion was achieved fair and square.

Dancer's Image's Derby score, accomplished in eye-catching come-from-behind fashion, was tarnished by what seemed an interminable debate over the use of the drug phenylbutazone, a pain-killing analgesic, whose usage is now commonplace as a Thoroughbred training aid. Even though declared the Derby's official winner—all bets were paid—Dancer's Image was disqualified years later (1973), and first place purse money was awarded to Forward Pass. The latter, incidentally, invaded Chicago in 1968 to win the American Derby, a race I called as another coup for that waning dynasty known as fabled Calumet Farm.

I have two major regrets about 1969. One is not having a chance to call all of the 1969 spring–summer season at Arlington. I was forced to resign over an internal ethical debate with Marje

Everett that ultimately culminated in the sad imprisonment of former Illinois Governor Otto Kerner, a bona fide political travesty. I called the first 30 days of Balmoral's spring meeting at Arlington before stepping down. But I'd be back at the mike in 1970, smarter, braver than ever—I'll explain why in my chapter on race calling.

My other major regret of 1969? Marvelous Majestic Prince failed to win the Triple Crown. Majestic Prince enabled Bill Hartack to equal Eddie Arcaro's record of five winning Derby rides. But then, Majestic Prince's owner forced trainer Johnny Longden to start the colt in the Belmont despite obvious soreness. The result was premature retirement. The Belmont was his sole defeat in 10 lifetime starts, which included his smashing wins in both the Derby and Preakness.

With Majestic Prince's Belmont failure, racing all but gave up on gaining its ninth Triple Crown hero—after all, 21 years had passed, and all too quickly, since mighty Citation in 1948. I felt I had possibly seen the 1970 champion as the 1969 2-year-old leader, Silent Screen, made a brilliant Chicago invasion expressly for the Arlington–Washington Futurity. A fine field assembled for the 7-furlongs sprint, including local star Insubordination.

Silent Screen was owned by Sonny Werblin, the man who 13 years later would fire me for nearly one full season as Arlington announcer (we'll cover that scenario in our next chapter). Trained by J. Bowes Bond and ridden by the sport's newest discovery, Johnny Rotz, Silent Screen certified his standing as 1970 Derby winter-book favorite with a rousing 8-length victory in Chicago's rich Futurity dash. He also captured the Champagne and Cowdin Stakes as America's latest 2-year-old sensation.

Through no fault of his own—his class and stamina were unquestioned—Silent Screen flopped in the 1970 Derby, leading the field of 17 into the stretch before faltering, obviously in pain, and finishing fifth to Illinois-bred Dust Commander. He was smarting from a sore ankle and probably should have been laid up even then. Major calcium deposits in his right foreankle had taken their toll, and though he tried mightily in the Preakness, finishing third behind Personality and My Dad George, Silent Screen's career for all intents and purposes was finis. Johnny Rotz moved over to High Echelon to win the 1970 Belmont.

Upstart Canonero II won both the 1971 Derby and Preakness but hardly anything else. Pass Catcher precluded a Triple Crown win by taking the Belmont. Once again—à la Kelso, Buckpasser, and Dr. Fager—Horse of the Year went to a colt who failed to win at least one of the Triple Crown events: Cain Hoy Stable's Ack Ack, who two years earlier (1969), used the Arlington Classic as a springboard to national recognition.

Thanks to Majestic Prince and Canonero II, racing turned the corner into the 1970s under a full head of steam, allaying the fears of some observers that the sport's golden age was coming to a close. Its glory days, however, seemingly sputtered amid questions of discontent. Would we ever again have a Whirlaway, Count Fleet, Assault, Citation, or even a Nashua, Swaps, Native Dancer, Tom Fool, Tom Rolfe, or Kelso?

Riva Ridge, much like Majestic Prince, came close in 1972. With Ron Turcotte riding, the colt aced the Derby and the Belmont. The Preakness, however, went to Bee Bee Bee.

The scene was set for Riva Ridge's stablemate Secretariat! Actually, he set the scene all by himself in 1972, when as a 2-year-old he gleaned unprecedented glory as Horse of the Year, as if expert observers were daring the radiant chestnut son of Bold Ruler to fulfill their high expectations once he launched his 1973 3-year-old campaign. Secretariat would disappoint no one. Not *Daily Racing Farm* columnist Charlie Hatton. Not millions of starved racing fans. Certainly not yours truly. He was a sight and experience for sore, aging, desperate eyes. He breathed new life into a struggling sport, and for the next decade we rode his shiny coattails into an era approaching that of the glorious 1940s.

Secretariat precipitated racing's renaissance, a decade which would also include the grand but ill-fated filly Ruffian; the rugged gelding Forego; back-to-back Triple Crown kings Seattle Slew and Affirmed; and the equally formidable Spectacular Bid, who really delayed achieving greatness until his 4-year-old campaign of 1980. But it was Secretariat who dazzled the world of Thoroughbred racing.

Personable, charismatic, the epitome of excellence, the strapping copper-colored chestnut had three white feet and a white star that announced undeniable nobility among his breed. With the media somewhat discounting the likes of Kelso, Nashua, Swaps, Tom Rolfe, Round Table, Buckpasser, and Dr. Fager simply because none won the Triple Crown, the industry canonized Secretariat as the long-awaited cure for racing's blues and the 25-year vacancy since Citation.

Secretariat's racing presence was massive, his impact incredible. The sports world came alive; especially were racing pundits elated. The colt was acclaimed as not only the first Triple Crown champion in a quarter-century, but perhaps the finest Thoroughbred who ever lived.

His aura of invincibility was temporarily shattered by unexpected defeat prior to his Kentucky Derby conquest. That also was the year the great speedster Shecky Greene discovered he'd best restrict his talents to sprints—he led the Derby field turning for home before succumbing to Sham; then really had his heart broken when Secretariat unleashed his thunderous bid from last.

Secretariat ran the fastest Derby on record—1:59$\frac{2}{5}$—and observers, particularly those obsessed with time, showered him with effusive accolades. He dutifully won the Preakness, again with a last-to-first effort, this time more spectacularly as he powered into command before the field settled for their run up the backside. Again, he whipped Sham, again in sensational time. When he sauntered as none before to win the grueling 1$\frac{1}{2}$ miles Belmont Stakes by an astounding 31 lengths, Secretariat was deified as "the second coming of mighty Pegasus." His fame spread abroad; every sports fan, thanks to TV, applauded the game's first Triple Crown winner in 25 years. To many, he was worth the long wait.

He was America's Super Horse, and when his connections chose Chicago's Arlington Park for his first outing after sweeping the Triple Crown, midwestern racing went ecstatically hysterical. Secretariat was tonic to what ailed the sport. His picture was everywhere, on every magazine cover. Fact is, racing's media coverage once again approached that given the sport during its golden age. Unfortunately, Secretariant was retired at the close of his 3-year-old season. The wonderful hullabaloo that catapulted Thoroughbred racing again into America's sports spotlight was short-lived. Racing's modern-day Big Red was an impossible act to follow.

Little Current's scores in the 1974 Preakness and Belmont—Cannonade won the Derby—were almost anti-climactic. Besides, Chicagoans were still gloating that Secretariat chose Arlington to make his first start following his spectacular Belmont, making him the fourth of the sport's last five Triple Crown champs to start back at Arlington—Whirlaway (1941), Assault (1946), and Citation (1948)—another coup for midwestern racing. Only Count Fleet (1943) missed out.

Three different colts won the 1975 Triple events—Foolish Pleasure, Master Derby, and Avatar—but nobody seem to care. The sport had its long overdue star in Secretariat and was satisfied to revel awhile in that triumph. Besides, a 3-year-old filly named Ruffian was making waves; there were those who felt she could have trimmed the boys in the spring classics had her connections desired.

Ruffian was a marvelous creation, undefeated, a dark bay filly by Reviewer. Owned by Mr. and Mrs. Stuart S. Janney, she was trained by taciturn Frank Whiteley Jr., of Tom Rolfe and Damascus fame. Foolish Pleasure, who unleashed a mighty surge to win the Derby, then settled for a closing second to Master Derby and Avatar in both the Preakness and Belmont, generally was considered America's pro tem 3-year-old leader. Jacinto Vasquez was regular rider for both Foolish Pleasure and Ruffian. He'd choose Ruffian for their July 6, 1975, match race in New York, an event we'll discuss later in a chapter devoted exclusively to match racing.

Incidentally, I thought I had a lock on the 1976 Derby, maybe the whole Triple Crown, with a colt named Honest Pleasure, who wound up America's number-one 2-year-old of 1975. Owned by Mrs. Bertram Firestone, the nimble son of What a Pleasure was trained by Leroy Jolley, son of Moody Jolley, the latter of Ridan fame.

I got my first look at Honest Pleasure when he was shipped from New York for the Arlington–Washington Futurity. He was preceded by his press clippings; he was everything they said he was; he won galloping. He was my sure-fire 1976 Derby horse. There was a major concern, however. Much like Bold Ruler before, Honest Pleasure was an equine swashbuckler, blessed with raw, incomparable, unbridled speed. If left alone, he was capable of subduing any field; if left alone, he might also fritter away a race with too much too soon.

His rider was the accomplished Braulio Baeza, whose experience with the erratic Buckpasser and the speed-minded Dr. Fager suited him perfectly for Honest Pleasure's modus operandi. Unfortunately, whenever Jolley and Baeza tried to halter the colt's speed, he'd resist and fight back.

Honest Pleasure's victory in the sprinting Futurity as a juvenile was a no brainer. No colt alive could match his quick feet. But he'd have to go 1¼ miles in the Derby, 1½ miles in the Belmont. This called for restraint, something he couldn't endure. As a result, Jolley's orders to rate Honest Pleasure in the Derby backfired. Another almost equally as fast, Bold Forbes, took advantage of Honest Pleasure's newly enforced tactics, blasting to an open-lengths lead at the start. Honest Pleasure, struggling against a ton of restraint imposed by Baeza, fell a length shy of running down Bold Forbes after a demanding 1¼ miles effort.

Tactics again dealt Honest Pleasure a paralyzing blow in the Preakness. This time, Jolley and Baeza refused to play the waiting game. Their colt grabbed Bold Forbes by the throatlatch at the start, the pair hammering away at each other without concern for a breather. But the Preakness was no match race. Capitalizing on their suicidal duel was Chicago-raced Elocutionist—I called him a winner, the year before in the Hawthorne Juvenile—who roared from far back, collaring the leaders in midstretch. Bold Forbes tired to finish third; Honest Pleasure was an exhausted fifth.

The bubble had burst. Honest Pleasure skipped the Belmont; Bold Forbes won it with uncontested speed. Rested, Honest Pleasure made a comeback of sorts that fall, only to have the misfortune of bumping heads with a fearsome gelding named Forego. Oh well.

The final three years of the 1970s were wondrous. Seattle Slew and Affirmed registered back-to-back Triple Crowns (1977–1978), and Spectacular Bid, who appeared a cinch to cop the 1979 Triple. I have already numbered Spectacular Bid among my Top 15 picks. If I must select my final choice to round out the list, let it be Seattle

Slew. Bypassing Affirmed might upset a few, and I respect their opinion—objections so noted. He definitely would be on my list of those worthy of honorable mention.

Here's my complete Top 15—my personal picks for Thoroughbred racing's greats:

1. Citation
2. Secretariat
3. Man o' War
4. Kelso
5. Count Fleet
6. Nashua
7. Swaps
8. Round Table
9. Phar Lap
10. Spectacular Bid
11. Whirlaway
12. Tom Rolfe
13. John Henry
14. Seattle Slew
15. Buckpasser

Of the above, I called or saw all but Man 'o War, Count Fleet, and Phar Lap. If forced to omit those three, I'd replace them with my top honorable mentions: Native Dancer, Bold Ruler, and Affirmed. Four others in my honorable mention category would be Forego, Graustark, Swoon's Son, and my top filly of all time, Real Delight. I select the latter with apologies to Ruffian, Personal Ensign, Regret, and Twilight Tear.

I was totally impressed with the manner in which Seattle Slew devastated his 1977 Triple Crown foes, emerging with lofty distinction as the only unbeaten American Triple Crown colt in Thoroughbred history. His daddy was Bold Reasoning. He was owned by Tayhill Stable, trained during his Triple Crown days by Billy Turner (later Doug Peterson), and ridden by Jean Cruguet (later by Angel Cordero).

I watched in amazement as Seattle Slew continued unbeaten through the Belmont Stakes, the rarest of rare achievements, a colt whose every effort announced perfection. He knew not the meaning of defeat; finishing second found no place in his vocabulary. The Slew took on all opponents, ducked no issue, avoided no track, argued not with conditions or how the race was run. He could sprint or go 1½ miles. Seattle Slew was invincible. I was convinced that as long as he stayed sound, no horse in the world could match his speed or class.

That was until early July 1977. Cockily wearing his Triple Crown symbol of unmistakable sovereignty, he flew to Hollywood Park, sights affixed on the $300,000 Swaps Stakes. A controversy continues to this day whether it was Slew's trainer, Billy Turner, or his primary owners, Karen and Mickey Taylor, who insisted on the California foray. My understanding was that Turner was against the trip, though other accounts suggest the Taylors resisted the temptation. The truth has been lost in the debate melee over the years. At any rate, Slew threw in a lackluster effort, finishing fourth, 16 lengths behind the victorious J.O. Tobin—England's 1976 2-year-old champ, who earlier ate Slew's dust in the Belmont Stakes.

J.O. Tobin loved the hard Hollywood strip; Slew obviously did not. Whether weakened by the long journey or his arduous 3-year-old campaign, Slew simply did not run his race. The defeat resonated loudly among the colt's people. Controversy erupted into acrimony, and Billy Turner and the Taylors parted company. It was a black eye for racing, what with accusations of greed hurled back and forth.

Through it all, Seattle Slew remained proud and stately, and when the following year he and 1978 Triple Crown champ Affirmed met up in the Marlboro Cup—the first clash ever between Triple Crown winners—the Slew emerged with a resounding 3-length victory to certify his greatness. Yes, the 1970s continued aglow; in 1978 Affirmed and Alydar spotlighted their searing rivalry, finishing 1-2 in a glorious Triple Crown renewal.

In an earlier chapter we talked about the game of musical chairs that jockeys often play, sometimes through no fault of their own. Owners and trainers naturally are always searching for the perfect combination to guarantee victory. Jean Cruguet and Seattle Slew seemed a perfect marriage, especially with trainer Billy Turner at the helm. After Turner split with Slew's owners, jockey Cruguet and the colt's trainer, Doug Peterson, had public differences. So Peterson fired Cruguet, selecting the fiery Angel Cordero for Slew's heralded confrontation with Affirmed in the 1978 Marlboro Cup.

Saddened by Cruguet's loss, I nevertheless found solace in Cordero as replacement.

I admired Cauthen's ascendancy as riding cynosure during Affirmed's explosive winning bouts over Alydar, though my heart belonged to the latter. I've always believed Alydar superior to Affirmed; it was hard admitting he fell short no matter how scant the margin of defeat.

Seattle Slew's victory over Affirmed remains one of my most satisfying moments. I never got to call either Seattle Slew or Affirmed, but I enjoyed the next best thing when Alydar, fresh off becoming the only colt to finish second in all three Triple Crown races, invaded Chicago for the Arlington Classic.

Chicago fans, whose roots unashamedly stretched back through Calumet Farm's long reign at Arlington and Washington Parks, hailed Alydar as if he had actually conquered Affirmed. Fact is, Alydar's trainer John Veitch had replaced Jorge Valesaquez with Jeff Fell for the Classic, and the pair literally romped, making a shambles of the Classic field, bounding home by 13 lengths. As far as I was concerned, Alydar had gained revenge, at least in part, for his Triple Crown disappointment.

Wow! Two straight Triple Crown heroes: Seattle Slew in 1977 and Affirmed in 1978. Suddenly, the world of Thoroughbred racing was big news everywhere. Better still, the game's potential third straight Triple Crown champ was in the batter's box—Spectacular Bid.

Under the inexperienced Ron Franklin, Spectacular Bid handily won the 1979 Derby and Preakness, only to meet well-chronicled defeat in the Belmont. As with Seattle Slew and Affirmed before, a jockey change was in order. Seattle Slew got Angel Cordero; Affirmed as a 4-year-old was taken away from a slumping Steve Cauthen and given to Laffit Pincay; and Spectacular Bid's reins were handed over to Bill Shoemaker. The genuine excellence of the three colts gave the 1970s a unique sparkle. Until Fusaichi Pegasus's victory in the 2000 Kentucky Derby, Spectacular Bid was the last favorite to win the Run for the Roses. And Eclipse Award–winning 2-year-olds since the advent of the Breeders' Cup in 1984 haven't done any better.

Among Triple Crown performers during the 1980s, I was most impressed with 1981 Derby–Preakness winner Pleasant Colony. His powerhouse late kick dominated the first two legs of the Triple; he was, in my opinion, a one-run colt, simply unable to sustain his punch and class over the 1½ miles of the Belmont. No one colt stood out in 1982–1983, though Belmont winner Conquistador Cielo was named 1982 Horse of the Year. John Henry, unknown at 3, was acclaimed Horse of the Year in 1981 and 1984 (ages 6 and 9); in both years, he won the Arlington Million. In 1984, I tagged the fleet 2-year-old Spend a Buck "a galloping winner" the first time the Arlington–Washington Futurity was lengthened to 1 mile. Provincial as I am, Spend a Buck was my 1985 Kentucky Derby pick. He won, too, in a gallop, from start to finish.

A good year for me was 1986. I called Alysheba's maiden effort, also Bet Twice's Arlington Futurity win, both during Arlington's abbreviated 13-day festival under makeshift tents following its fire of 1985. Alysheba and Bet Twice would dominate racing in 1987, particularly the Triple Crown. They performed their Affirmed–Alydar impersonation perfectly in the Derby and Preakness, finishing 1-2, respectively.

Alysheba, trained by Hall of Famer Jack Van Berg, pardonably loomed a solid Belmont favorite; it seemed the farther he went, the stronger he got. But Bet Twice, whom jockey Craig Perret had unsuccessfully tried to rate in the sport's first two jewels, was allowed to run free in the longer Belmont, spurting to an easy, early lead. Catching Alysheba totally off guard, Bet Twice rolled to a ridiculously handy triumph, setting an example Easy Goer would copy two years later (1989).

Before that, however, Winning Colors, trained by Wayne Lukas, in 1988 became only the third filly—after Regret in 1915 and Genuine Risk in 1980—to capture the Kentucky Derby. A bona fide filly threat always added spice to the Derby. To have both Genuine Risk and Winning Colors in the same decade was exceptional indeed.

Sunday Silence, à la Alysheba, won both the 1989 Derby and Preakness over favored Easy Goer, the latter prematurely acclaimed by many as worthy successor to Secretariat, Seattle Slew, Affirmed, and Spectacular Bid. Easy Goer, given free rein by jockey Pat Day in the Belmont, spoiled Sunday Silence's quest for Triple Crown glory with an unequivocal score. Soundly whipping Sunday Silence, however, wasn't good enough for Easy Goer to achieve titular recognition. Curiously, both Alysheba and Sunday Silence went on to garner Horse of the Year titles. Victories by each in the Breeders' Cup Classic saw to that.

Before my retirement in 1992, I'd call such 3-year-old cracks as Summer Squall, Hansel, and Unbridled, all genuine articles. Although Black Tie Affair did not compete in the Triple, he'd ultimately wind up 1991 Horse of the Year—and I was at the mike for his every start at Arlington, including a thumping score in the Washington Park 'Cap and his flagfall-to-flagfall victory in the 1¼ miles Hawthorne Gold Cup.

Those were the years, my friends. Even by then, however, Thoroughbred racing was struggling against the proliferation of casino gambling on land and sea. Despite splendid efforts, Silver Charm, Real Quiet, and Charismatic failed valiantly in successive quests (1997–1999) to become the first Triple champ since Affirmed. In 2000, Fusaichi Pegasus succumbed to Red Bullet in the Preakness. Injury to the former and reluctance on the part of the latter kept both out of the Belmont, which fell prey to an unheralded colt oddly named Commendable, whose only other win was a maiden score. Racing's efforts to achieve "paradise restored" had been unequivocally frustrated; worse, denied.

Chapter Eleven

The Art of Race Calling

I'm sure my Thoroughbred announcing style matured and evolved during a 34-year race-calling career spanning a world-record 96,131 races from May 18, 1959, through December 31, 1992. I'm equally sure that my personal announcing philosophy remained unchanged from the moment I handled my first microphone:

First, I would call every race the way I'd personally like to hear it called for me.

Second, I would call every race as if it were the Kentucky Derby.

Third, I would call every race as if I bet on the winner.

I'm flattered so many fans say they enjoyed the accuracy, drama, and excitement with which I imbued each race, be it the Arlington Million, or the Hawthorne Gold Cup, or the first half of the daily double. Chicago sports columnist Jim O'Donnell tagged my style with the label "theatricality." I assure you, whatever theatricality was involved was neither forced nor manufactured. It was simply me, totally natural, the way I felt every time two or more horses arrived at the starting gate.

Unlike most race callers I've known past or present who feel compelled to rise to the occasion of a major stakes, even the day's featured event, I'd often have to apply the brakes to come down from the natural high I experienced every time horses and jockeys paraded under colors on the track before spectators, betting or not. I didn't have to wager at all to enjoy the thrill of horse racing. But I sincerely believe—and I say this with utmost modesty—that every race I called—Thoroughbred, Standardbred, Quarterhorse, Arabian, dogs, turtles, pigs, or ducks—hopefully succeeded in exciting, entertaining, and informing every listener right down to his or her very being.

I confess the following with an amalgam of pride and one iota of regret: because I was conceived, foaled, and educated in Chicago, complete with a degree from the Medill School of Journalism at Northwestern University's Evanston campus, I never coveted racing elsewhere. My parents were Bulgarian immigrants, my father a Chicago cab driver. Both parents were solid citizens, and ultra conservative, having survived the Great Depression. I was an only child. I married my childhood sweetheart, Roberta Arnold, after a three-year courtship—she was 15 when we first met in 1950—and we lived our first married eight years together in a second-floor apartment in the small home my parents owned on the 4600 block of Monroe St. on Chicago's west side. Our only child, Scot, was born June 29, 1961, three months before we purchased a new home in Villa Park, a suburb directly west of Chicago proper.

I had been introduced to Thoroughbred racing in 1941. For a spell, I believed that Chicago's Arlington, Washington, Hawthorne, and Sportsman's racetracks constituted the major hub of American racing. In those days all of what I believed was indeed true. To work at Chicago tracks, to call first at Arlington and Washington, later at Hawthorne and Sportsman's, then also harness racing at Maywood and Balmoral Parks was a dream fulfilled.

Chicago racing took a back seat to none anywhere from the 1940s through the 1970s. I lacked both the ambition and the drive—also some foresight—to uproot or seek employment outside of Chicago. I had the opportunity once or twice, particularly in 1969 when Arlington and I briefly parted company; I refused job offers at Florida's Hialeah, Arkansas's Oaklawn, Kentucky's Churchill Downs, and the circuit in New Jersey. I chose rather to stay in Chicago, acceding to offers from Hawthorne, Sportsman's, and Maywood. I had a family, home, and deep roots. An announcer's per diem pay wouldn't support having two homes.

I stayed put. I chose the security of Chicago and the joy of family over career. I'm sure I blew a few chances to call elsewhere. *Que sera, sera.* I really have no complaints.

As race caller, I lived by this motto: "Some people are enthusiastic for 30 seconds; some for 30 minutes; it's the man who's enthusiastic for 30 years who makes a success of his life." I never had to fabricate that enthusiasm. It was unvarnished, mine naturally, particularly for Thoroughbred racing and what I consider the sport's next best thing—the race call itself.

From my earliest moments in the 1940s at Washington, Arlington, and Hawthorne, I was intrigued by the role the track announcer played. The actual date escapes me, also the track, although I'd bet it was at now defunct Washington Park—but Air Risk won the first, Joe Burger the second, and the daily double paid a whopping $13.20, which I shared with my father. I had to run from the bathroom for the second race, and while running through the lower-level crowd, I was forced to listen to Frank Ashley's call from the start to the top of the stretch.

Ashley, a native of Arkansas, replete with a heavy Southern drawl, was the very first race caller I heard. To me, despite a sameness of tone, an occasional word slur, and some pregnant pauses, he sounded like Sir Laurence Olivier himself.

The only time race calling took a back seat among my dearest fancies was when I was enthralled with becoming a jockey as the sport's next Eddie Arcaro. That dream evaporated by the winter of 1948, and though I redirected my energies to journalism and writing, race calling remained a spellbinding facet of my psyche. I purchased a horse-racing game named "Suffolk Downs," which had six horses moved manually after a toss of dice. I broke the race into quarters, renamed each horse, then audibly called the race as it developed. And I played that game virtually every afternoon after school, until I nearly drove my mother nuts. "Can't you call it to yourself?" she begged. I complied by learning to whisper loudly to myself.

As I was exposed to more racing, also to other announcers, locally as well as out-of-state on radio, I discovered a spate of new, smoother styles. Those with sing-song patterns I dismissed. Locally, Frank Ashley's calls were rarely carried on radio, but often heard were Jack Drees and Dave Feldman, the latter a turf writer for the *Chicago Herald-American* who went by the name of Dave King for his radio broadcasts. Feldman also served as track announcer for the half-miler Sportsman's Park for some 25 years until 1971. Drees chiefly worked in public relations for Arlington and Washington Parks's Ben Lindheimer. Ashley was track caller. Fred Caposella was New York's regular announcer; Morris Tobe and Ray Haight called in New Jersey; Joe Hernandez manned the mikes in California. Each differed in their approach, style, and vocal dynamics.

Jack Drees was my favorite. He was smooth, conversational for the most part, yet would heighten enthusiasm once the horses entered the home lane. He also used the expression "Here they come" as they curved out of the final turn into the homestretch. I liked that transition. You rarely know where the horses were with the others. An announcer might say "they turn for home," call a horse or two, then suddenly shock you with "they've got a hundred yards to come!" You wondered how much of the action and changing positions you missed.

Not with Drees. He'd bring 'em into the stretch, tell you they're approaching the eighth pole, call 'em at the 16th pole, then name the 1-2-3 finishers as they hurtled under the wire. The last part was done for radio only. Over the track public address system, poor Frank Ashley was obliged to stop inside the 16th pole.

But I must confess, my real idol was Clem McCarthy, who some turf veterans recall for his throaty, heel-and-spur descriptions of America's outstanding races. I'm not sure, but I believe Clem was the first to broadcast a race live over a national network. I vowed if ever I got to call Thoroughbred racing, I'd do it with a combination style—one eye on McCarthy, the other on Drees—to which I'd add my own brand of spirit and zeal.

If I were captivated by race calling by the time I landed a summer job in 1953 at Arlington and Washington, I was totally intoxicated when I started working full-time at the tracks in 1955. A caller from California, Hal Moore, had replaced Ashley; by the mid-1950s, Harry Henson, from Seattle, Washington, became regular announcer. Moore did little to impress me, but Henson was outstanding. I loved his gravelly voice, also his stressing of margins separating horses as he ran down the field.

Most announcers rarely ran down a field of 12 going 6 furlongs. Following a race, many a disgruntled fan despaired: "My horse was so bad, he never even got a call." Which meant his horse was so badly outrun, the announcer had no chance of mentioning his name because he did not run down the field. I was determined to give every horse a call, no matter how big the field.

I discussed the "art of race calling" many times with both Drees and Henson. I'd give each horse a call, replete with position—"so-and-so is fourth . . . then a gap of two . . . so-and-so is fifth"—while running down all 12, always counting 'em down, too, 9th, 10th, and so on. I never just spouted names without positions as most callers do today. If the race was 7 furlongs, or a mile, or longer, then I'd run down the field as many times as possible before they hit the far turn.

From the half-mile marker at the far turn, the race caller should then concentrate on the contenders. Pick up moving horses back to sixth or seventh, but don't abandon the action changing up front by making another unnecessary attempt to run down the field. Only the race caller able to stick with movement up front—which normally accelerated as the field turned for home—only he was worth his salt. My opinion anyway.

Without exception, from June 1953, I practiced calling races to myself, sometimes within earshot of other press box habitues, often for reporters anxious to follow a race's outcome. I gave my binoculars a real workout those early years. Jerry Liska and Chuck Chamberlain of Associated Press, Ed Sainsbury of United Press, and Bob Glass of United Press International wanted a jump on the chart of a major race from the local *Daily Racing Form* crew. My boss, director of publicity Harry Sheer, acceded to their requests that I call the race live while Bob Glass took it down.

It wasn't a sophisticated or polished call compared with the full *Daily Racing Form* chart. It went like this, using the 1955 Arlington Classic as an example. Glass already marked his paper with Start, Backstretch, Halfway backstretch, Far turn, Halfway far turn, Top-stretch, Eighth pole, Sixteenth pole, and Finish.

"And they're off, Bob," I'd begin. "That's Dogoon going to the lead, followed by Munchausen, Nashua, Dedicate, and Impromptu . . . coming out of the mile chute, there goes Impromptu along the rail . . . it's Impromptu by a length, Dogoon between horses second by a neck, Dedicate is three-wide third . . . then a gap of a length and Nashua's moving between horses fourth, then a gap of three and Traffic Judge . . .

"Around the far turn, Impromptu opens up 3 lengths . . . Dogoon is second by a neck . . . there's goes Nashua—and he's under urging—charging second . . . they turn for home, Impromptu has opened up a 4 lengths lead . . . Nashua is under a heavy drive second . . . Dogoon is dropping back third . . . and Traffic Judge is flying to the extreme outside . . .

"Here they come, into the stretch, and here comes Nashua, and he's flying . . . Impromptu is dropping back second . . . and here comes Traffic Judge . . . he's on the far outside, and he's charging . . . it's Nashua in front by a length, but here comes Traffic Judge . . . and nearing the wire, Nashua in front by a length, but here comes Traffic Judge . . . and at the wire, Nashua wins it by a half-length . . . Traffic Judge is second by 2 . . . and Impromptu is third."

Glass would have made several carbon copies—no photocopy machines in those days. He'd distribute them to the others, and they were ready to dictate or write their account of the 1955 Arlington Classic without undue delay. They appreciated my efforts; I loved doing it!

Also in 1955 was the memorable $100,000 Swaps–Nashua winner-take-all match race on August 31. Allow me a moment to recall that event from a race-calling standpoint. Washington Park had added 125 additional media accommodations, extending the rooftop press box by some 150 feet. One of my jobs was to cover the Nashua camp for news. Dan Desmond, who also did publicity for the Chicago Bears football team, was hired to cover the opposing Swaps team.

My other job on match race day was to call my own chart of the race for Bob Glass, who took my call on mimeograph stencil, off which sufficient copies were provided for all media—as if they needed help in covering a two-horse race. Still, we provided them with furlong-by-furlong description. The only trouble—although certainly not for me—was that Nashua led at every pole. His margin at various stages of the race was my primary challenge and contribution. But I learned quite a bit that day about announcing—

lessons that would stand me in good stead for when I had the mike myself.

The track didn't use the same announcer for TV and track. Drees did the TV call for CBS; Henson called over the track PA system. I naturally heard neither call, concentrating rather on my assignment of calling the chart for visiting press. Strangely, both Drees and Henson were noticeably crestfallen later that day and evening during sundry moments of what should have been lively celebration and rehashing of the race itself. Later I learned that both announcers unwittingly chose the match race for major blunders that would haunt them for years to come. You've heard the old chestnut about "the guy who'd screw up a one-car funeral"? Drees and Henson had screwed up a two-horse race. I could only imagine how many sleepless nights they suffered in the months and years to come. In all fairness, both gaffes were minor. But they served as major reminders to me during the 34 seasons I'd call races of all shapes and sizes. And that day was far from being just around the corner.

Jack Drees was a sportscaster who always wore his feelings on his sleeve. As much as he tried, he could rarely hide his partiality. But then all racetrackers—and Drees truly loved the game—have that problem. It is a game of opinion, to be sure. He was the radio announcer of record back in 1947 who, while calling the Futurity at Washington Park, opined winner Bewitch "could have won by 15 lengths had her jockey wanted," even though she appeared all out after staving off her stablemate Citation by a dwindling length. Drees was a Bewitch fan, no doubt about it, and allowed his love for the filly to color his call.

Like so many others the day of the match race, and particularly because he was a longtime employee and friend of Ben Lindheimer and daughter Marje Everett, who were unabashed Swaps lovers themselves, Drees was convinced Swaps couldn't lose. So when Nashua started to sprint clear instead of capitulating in upper stretch, Drees' disappointment was evident in the spiritless manner in which he brought Nashua home in his final 100-yard romp to glory.

Add to that his impromptu commercial remark following the race. As reported by Chicago freelance reporter Jeff Davis in a December 1999 issue of *Chicago Magazine*—in an article in which I offered Davis my match race remembrances—Drees commented: "That's why I always carry a handy roll of Tums in my pocket, now that the race is over and Swaps has regained his winning ways." I'm sure Nashua glowered at the remark. Seconds later Drees realized his slip and sheepishly corrected the gaffe, which was no more than a trifle. But my hero Jack Drees had committed the unforgivable, showing and verifying his partiality. From that moment on I vowed I'd call every race as if I bet on the winner, whether I liked the outcome or not.

Harry Henson's announcing flub was twofold; however, he was more embarrassed over the second rather than the first mistake. I repeatedly talked the race over with him, not to add to his shame but to comfort him. In retrospect, I'm sure my lack of age and experience offered him little solace; even then, I came to realize the insufferable pain and mortification error could cause.

I still have the actual tape of the match race and Henson's call over the track PA system. Harry was calling a near-perfect race until the field turned for home. Washington Park in those days was home of America's longest homestretch, 1,531 feet, well over a full quarter mile. Over the PA came Harry's call: "Heading into the stretch, it's Nashua with Eddie Arcaro in front by almost a length . . . and right behind him . . . Nashua is second."

Henson had tears in his eyes when he talked about it later. "Could you believe it? I had *two* Nashuas in the race. I miscalled a two-horse race."

Harry realized his faux pas at once, wondering whether it was smart to instantly correct the mistake. He chose not to, continuing his call as if the flub had never been made. "I was doing all right, too, until Nashua started to draw clear inside the 16th pole," Harry recalled. "Suddenly I was overcome with shame. It was as if the bottom dropped out!"

One mistake Henson rarely made was to miscall the final winning margin. I think he took greater umbrage over blowing Nashua's winning margin at the wire than calling two Nashuas in upper stretch. "And Nashua's the winner by almost 5 lengths,"

Henson said. Then, after a pregnant pause, he mentally collapsed with "And . . . that's it!" Like "who cares . . . it's over!" Nashua's margin was 6½ lengths.

If you don't think I learned from Drees and Henson, then go directly to jail, and no bail. I saw the drama, the fun, and the celebrity of the race call. More importantly, I learned, should I ever get the chance to be a race caller, I'd have to stay on my toes—from start to finish!

Henson's problems were apparent only to the 32,000 on hand that day at Washington Park, if they really listened that closely. We had no TV monitors for fans at the track, no tape, so no replay. When a 15-minute color film short of the Swaps–Nashua match race was produced for general distribution, Drees did the voice-over. So very few of us were privy to Henson's flub. But he knew. And, as he often said, "that's one person too many."

On the 15-minute feature, Drees changed his call from the top of the stretch home—not to make it more exciting, but to offer the excuse that during the course of the race "Swaps had injured his foot, and had cause for hurting." Jack couldn't accept the fact that Nashua had wreaked sweet vengeance for his beating by Swaps months earlier in the Kentucky Derby.

Speaking of announcing mistakes—and all race announcers past and present make them—the most monumental of all came, not in the Kentucky Derby, but in the 1947 Preakness with Clem McCarthy at the mike. Maine Chance Farm's Kentucky Derby winner Jet Pilot was seeking to add the Preakness to his laurels and had assumed his usual role as pacemaker. McCarthy later explained that Jet Pilot's cerise colors were similar to the red of Calumet Farm's Faultless. When Faultless swept into the lead circling the far turn—and a broadcast truck parked in the field might have obstructed the view around the final bend—Clem failed to visually grasp the change in leadership, continuing to call Jet Pilot in front right down to the wire.

Realizing his error as Faultless hit the wire with top prize, Clem proceeded to apologize profusely to his listeners—we had no TV coverage in those days. He bemoaned his mistake over and over again. Unfortunately, his color associate Bill Stern, infamous for his own radio sports inaccuracy, relentlessly chided Clem on air about the miscall.

Now, during radio broadcasts of football games, Stern was known for occasionally having the wrong player toting a football into the endzone. He'd compensate with the excuse that a player had "lateraled the ball to so-and-so," thereby covering his error. Provoked by Stern's continued on-air ribbing following the Preakness, Clem McCarthy retorted smartly: "Bill, in horse racing, we can't lateral a horse."

Years later, in the 1970s, Chic Anderson miscalled the Derby winner the length of the stretch, managing to catch his blunder at the wire, causing waves throughout the television industry. Colossal flubs like the above are the bane of race callers. But gaffes are just waiting to happen.

Through my first 80,000 races I prided myself that on only a few occasions (fewer than 10) did I ever miscall the horse in front in midstretch—and when I did, I made sure to acknowledge it publicly over the PA system. "Sorry, ladies and gentlemen, my brain got in the way of my tongue," I'd say, or often when the horses would reach the post for the next race: "They're entering their stalls . . . and I'll try to get it straight this time." Usually the fans below chuckled, even applauded. We're all imperfect, let's face it. But a race caller must face his imperfections as often as 9 or 10 times a day. And always within earshot of others.

I've always boasted that if the announcer faithfully does his homework—that is, memorizes and diligently practices associating colors with their horses—there's no reason he'd make a mistake. But there are extenuating circumstances: bad weather, poor visibility, slop or mud obscuring the jockeys' silks. My bugaboo was an unexpected memory lapse. Call it overconfidence. I'd handle hundreds of races flawlessly, never a pause, not a slur. Suddenly, from out of the blue, a mental lapse—in my case, not really listening to what I was saying, not making sure I had the right horse. The only major event I miscalled was the 1961 Arlington Classic. Globemaster and Editorialist slugged it out the length of the stretch to the wire. Unconsciously I said, "Editorialist wins it!" I knew better. Globemaster got the nod. As they passed the wire, I corrected my call and apologized: "Sorry, I should've known better."

As a race caller, I have witnessed racing greatness, a golden age packed with elegance, excitement, intrigue, romance, and incomparable drama far beyond what any Hollywood scriptwriter could imagine. I missed nary a moment. Nor was the action always confined to the field.

The first of three major career crossroads occurred for me in 1957. I was completing my third year as a full-time Arlington–Washington publicity assistant. Actually, we were now a coordinated 97-day spring–summer season, having acquired Balmoral Jockey Club (formerly known as Lincoln Fields) in 1955. We'd race from mid-May through Labor Day. Marje Everett was becoming increasingly prominent as her aging father's right-hand person. It was leaked to me that she wanted to scale me back to a seasonal employee following the 1957 season. I was now married, and as much as I loved the racetrack, I was floored by Marje's cold inconsiderateness. My boss, Harry Sheer, to his credit, felt I was dealt a dirty deal, and he told me so.

I learned that *Daily Racing Form* editor Mel Schreier was looking to expand his staff. He created a position as assistant editor, which I took without batting an eye in the spring of 1958. Harry Sheer was left without major assistance but blamed me not a whit for jumping ship. By mid-May, believe it or not, Marje admitted her mistake, apologized to me personally, and allowed Sheer to use me every Wednesday, my *Daily Racing Form* off-day, to write publicity features and columns, as I had done the past three years.

I was at the *Form* almost a year when, in the spring of 1959, announcer Harry Henson and Marje Everett came to a parting of ways. He resigned before he could be fired—and the announcing job at Balmoral–Arlington–Washington was up for grabs. Harry Sheer and administrative manager Peter Brandsness recalled my avowed love for race calling, and Marje Everett allowed me to audition with seven others. Six were established race callers; the seventh, like myself, was an unproven amateur.

To my surprise, both Marje and her father liked my sound. They preferred me over the others not because I called a better race, but because of my voice, which at the time I feared was too young, too high, and too inexperienced. But that's what they really wanted: a clear, incisive sound, one easily heard and understood over what most track PA systems at that time were—outdated and clogged. The "talky" or "wordy" or "smoothly conversational" callers we have today would have been lost in a sea of garble and distortion. In fact, I invented and adapted my personal style to overcome existing inferior systems long before good PA came into demand. For the record, Tom Durkin is absolute tops among announcers today.

Before taking a chance on a neophyte, however, no matter how much they admired his sound, Ben Lindheimer and Marje Everett demanded outside confirmation from a reliable expert not in their employ. Jack Drees by that time had gone on to bigger and better things. He was a full-fledged ABC sportscaster, but he remained an Arlington consultant, and he knew of my dream of becoming a race caller. When told they were considering me as Harry Henson's replacement, Drees replied unhesitantly: "Ben, Marje, Phil's your man, and he'll do great by you, too." And that's how I was launched on my world-record run.

I was always a "power" speaker; that is, I held nothing back. I punched my words and phrases, harking back most likely to guys like Clem McCarthy and track caller Harry Henson. I admired Jack Drees's smoothness but soon realized that his fluidity of speech would be lost over a typical track PA system. Besides, my job was not only to inform, and to inform accurately, but to excite and entertain. I could do none of the above, however, unless I could be heard clearly. So I developed a cadence, a rhythmic, somewhat staccato manner of presentation. I admired Frank Sinatra, especially his lyric-phrasing, the way he clipped certain words, allowing nearly imperceptible pauses between words and phrases.

For example: "They settle up the backstretch (pause) . . . there goes (smaller pause) On-and-On (pause) . . . he takes command (pause) . . . that's On-and-On (smaller pause) sprinting clear (pause) . . . Heroshogala takes up the chase second (pause) . . . but there goes Kelso on the move third (pause) . . . they turn for home (pause) . . . On-and-On has it by 2 lengths (pause) . . . but here comes Kelso (pause) . . . and he's under a full head of steam (pause) now second (smaller pause) . . . and he means business! (pause)"

Now the pauses were short breath-takes, just enough to prevent the words running together and stepping over one another as they resonated over the PA system. I created what I hoped were exciting visual pictures without excessive verbiage. I'd rely upon a natural exuberance—something I never had to fabricate—using intonation to excite and inform rather than descriptive verbal phrasing. I considered my call something akin to "vocal interpretative reporting," conveying information by voice rhythm and tone rather than by a mere recitation of words.

As far as my "young" voice was concerned, I'll never forget Drees's explanation by way of encouragement: "Phil, a sharp, young, incisive voice carries far better over public address systems than one deep in pitch. Plus, a tenor voice can more readily soar in the heat of excitement. It can explode with clarity, like reaching for those high C's. The baritone voice rarely dazzles when at the top. Besides, your voice will mellow and mature with years. As long as you're not shrill, let 'er rip—there's no need for you to spare the horses."

Drees was right. Evidently, I had the voice; also other essentials: a knowledge of the sport, the love to entertain, a good memory, and most important, the courage of my convictions. The latter, I felt, was my ace in the hole.

The bane of any race caller is fear of making a mistake, miscalling a horse, particularly a horse making a bold move once the field leaves the half-mile pole. The caller is obliged to call all the action, especially horses mounting challenges. That requires what I've already alluded to as "interpretative announcing." Such vocal editorializing takes courage, also confidence in your skills and trust in your mental deductions as to which horse is fading and which are on the move.

All announcers make mistakes. As a result, too many become gun shy. They'll commit themselves to a moving horse, only to be embarrassed if the horse fails to follow through. Or the caller is scared he might misidentify the horse. This makes him even more tentative, allowing doubts to suppress both his spirit and delivery.

I had one other special announcing conviction that I possessed the courage to implement—calling 'em right down to the wire! No announcer at any major track in those days dared for fear of incurring the stewards' wrath. Well, I did it before my first week in May 1959 was over. Yes, I drew the stewards' immediate ire. I also drew Marje Everett's approval. She in turn convinced Ben Lindheimer that its time had come.

Therefore, to my way of thinking, in 1959 race calling attained new freedom. Announcers now had greater latitude, which most initially did not copy. At least I'd be able to entertain as well as inform, but never at the expense of accuracy.

Over the years I enjoyed sharing my booth with guest announcers, many of whom were movie, TV, and sports celebrities who sportingly welcomed and enjoyed the challenge. My first guest caller was comedian Myron Cohen, whose convivial Jewish accent delighted fans. As always, I would whisper horses' names and positions into his ear whenever he'd hesitate or lose concentration, which was often and always.

One of my favorites was Don Knotts, whose charming real-life nervousness equaled that of his movie and TV persona. Muhammad Ali was rendered virtually speechless. News anchor Bill Kurtis, whose investigative reports are a staple on the A&E cable TV station, gave it a try, as did football great-turned-sportscaster Johnny Morris. They screwed up delightfully; the fans loved it. Mickey Rooney was a track regular but never took a chance before the mike. Nor did TV's Ben Casey, racetrack regular Vince Edwards; he admitted to poor eyesight. Desi Arnaz and Jimmy Durante considered giving race calling a chance; when push came to shove they refused with a smile. Even baseball legend Harry Caray declined, graciously ceding horse racing as "the toughest sport of all to call."

One of my most unusual experiences came when Chicago's biggest Polish newspaper, the *Daily Polish Zagoda*, sponsored a night at the races in the 1970s for a rare Arlington Park harness meeting. As part of the promotion an amateur caller was selected, who did the entire race in Polish. He good-naturedly concluded his call: "That announcer certainly sounded like a Polack to me!" We could hear the enthusiastic crowd acceptance.

I adopted my trademark "Here they come, spinning out the turn!" for two reasons. One, to add color and excitement with a personal, special cachet; two, to provide a transitional hook for film or video-tape coverage. For example, prior to my calls, whenever the day's feature was shown by, say, WGN-TV, the announcer would lead into the race thusly: "And today's big race at Hawthorne was the Sun Beau Handicap . . . 12 grass runners faced the starter . . . here with the stretch call is 'so-and-so.'" Often, the film would catch the announcer between words and horses. With my call, technicians knew there was that slight pause before I'd utter, "Here they come . . ." This made the presentation and the transition from TV commentator to race call smoother and cleaner.

Because I also doubled as publicist and announcer, especially in the 1960s at Arlington and Washington, I actually saw through my binoculars a great deal more than your average announcer. My mornings were spent on the backside, also the racing secretary's office, gleaning track information via interviews and personal contact with owners, trainers, jockeys, and their agents. Calling them in action each afternoon, therefore, was actually frosting on the cake. And it was delicious fare upon which I feasted.

In 1969, however, I suffered by second career crossroads when my relationship with Marje Everett came to an abrupt end. It was more political than personal. But I was devastated.

Some background info is necessary. Marje's longtime confidant and personal racing guru was a slick, smooth politician, William S. Miller, an Illinois owner and breeder who also served a long term as Illinois racing board member, and later as chairman of the board. No one was surprised to hear that Miller was stepping down as racing board commissioner to assume one-third private ownership of entities belonging to Chicago Thoroughbred Enterprises, Inc., of course with Marje's blessings. Miller took over the Balmoral Jockey Club, which raced its annual 30-day spring meeting at Arlington, and Chicago Harness Racing, a winter–spring segment each year at still-existing Washington Park on Chicago's south side.

Naturally, I was loaned to Miller for his meetings, which on surface remained as they had existed as part of Marje's empire.

Changes, however, were happening fast and furious. Marje sold out to Gulf + Western, mistakingly assuming she was still boss and in command because the huge conglomerate retained her as president.

Meanwhile, Illinois was facing a political wildfire that ultimately resulted in the felony conviction of former Governor Otto Kerner. Headline-making charges and counter-charges involved the Everett–Miller alliance, which not so shockingly broke ranks. Their split was rancorous, irreparable, and to many, totally unexpected. And I was caught in the middle. The tug-of-war between two implacable powers tore at my innards. I decided to go with Miller—a decision that sent Marje Everett ballistic.

I skipped the balance of the 1969 coordinated Balmoral–Arlington–Washington meet after Balmoral's 30-day session at Arlington. I was stricken to my very marrow. Miller hired me as a year-round employee, but things would never be the same. Once again I could have pulled up stakes and sought greener pastures out-of-state. Rather, I decided to stay put; I loved Chicago, and now I was free to work other local tracks seasonally.

When Hawthorne opened up in 1969, I was hired as both announcer and publicity director. I stayed on in both capacities for Egyptian Downs, a harness tenant at Washington Park, and Maywood Park offered me the harness announcer's job. A couple of years later I'd hire on as Thoroughbred announcer for Sportsman's Park, replacing Dave Feldman. But just months after Marje and I went our separate ways, she was fired by Gulf + Western, and I returned as track announcer in 1970 for the coordinated Balmoral–Arlington–Washington meeting at Arlington.

My problem now was that I had too much work. I was calling virtually every day of every month of every year. And except for Sportsman's summer harness season, I was at the mike for every day or night of Chicago's Standardbred sport. For the next 13 years I'd call some 3,700 races yearly, including doubles—Thoroughbred in the day, harness at night—some eight months of the year. For my first 31 years announcing, I missed only three programs: May 2, 1960, struck down by a flu virus, and two days in 1978 following my mother's death in Florida. I don't know whether to be proud or ashamed of establishing such a dubious, although incredible, record. I did it out of pure, unadulterated love for the sport—but I wouldn't ever do it again!

In 1971 I called the nation's first major commercially sponsored stakes—the Pontiac Grand Prix, formerly the Arlington Classic. We did it on CBS as a regional telecast. The winner was Calumet Farm's Son Ange, and the day of commercial involvement in racing began. By then, track public address systems had improved perceptibly. I was able to increase my delivery speed and add words, even phrases. But I avoided outright editorializing. I never wanted to insult an owner or trainer by knocking a horse's performance. "Hold Your Peace is beaten," was as far as I dared go during the running of 1971 Pontiac Grand Prix at Arlington when it became obvious in midstretch that Maribel Blum's 3–5 favorite had tossed in the towel.

Long before peerless Tom Durkin popularized his exciting verbal announcing technique starting with the Breeders' Cup Inaugural TV presentation in 1984, I bravely tested the waters of impromptu PA calling with new expressions. "He's for real, the real McCoy," I complimented a popular stakes winner.

When two equally highly rated 3-year-olds clashed in a major event, I contributed: "Here's the race we waited for—the clash of the titans!" I believe I stole that from a movie title.

When Secretariat galloped in his Arlington debut following his 1973 Triple Crown conquest, I saluted him generously: "Here he is, America's Super Horse, Ron Turcotte up, drawing clear by 7, now 8 . . ."

"Let's hear it for Alydar!" I shouted. "Alydar's back on the winning path," as he rolled to a sparkling 13-length victory in the 1978 Arlington Classic. Nothing ingenious or innovative.

My favorite was the 1984 Million, prior to Durkin's Breeders' Cup telecast: "Here he is . . . John Henry . . . a living legend . . . it's John Henry by 2 . . . and the beat goes on . . . Thoroughbred racing's first five-million-dollar baby."

I might've done more, but I was committed to voice and vocal intonation in describing races. Others did it with words; I chose to do it with sound. If I was thrilled, my listener had to be thrilled also—that's how I felt.

During the 1970s I was invited to team up with the late Bruce Roberts, CBS sportscaster for Chicago affiliate WBBM-TV, for weekly Saturday telecasts, which began with the 1971 Pontiac Grand Prix. Roberts was a true racing aficionado, a gentleman, a class act, and a pleasure to work with. A genuine professional, he prepared assiduously for each Arlington telecast. He taught me immensely; his death shocked my soul.

Things seemed to move smoothly, especially at Hawthorne where the Carey family touch guaranteed a genial, kindly work environment. Backbiting and hostility found no home at Hawthorne. The Arlington empire, however, was undergoing monumental changes. Ownership was purchased by Madison Square Garden. A power-happy Jack Loome had replaced Marje Everett, but his reign was short-lived. When the gregarious, thoughtful, and inventive Joe Joyce ascended the throne, among his first concepts was creation of the Arlington Million, Thoroughbred racing's very first $1,000,000 race. And I called it! John Henry nailed The Bart for a controversial nose win heard around the Turf globe. I was never happier. It was a Cloud Nine experience I foolishly thought unending.

Then the despotic John J. Mooney replaced Joyce as Arlington president. Inconsiderate and authoritarian, he ruled Arlington without regard for individual feeling or freedom of expression. Moreover, he hated me. It wasn't personal, he insisted. "As an announcer who infuses every race with excitement and enthusiasm, you are without equal," he told me candidly. "But out east, tracks are considered betting factories. I don't want our patrons entertained. I want a dull, monotone call. Oh, maybe once a day, or when there's a stakes race on the docket, you can spark it up. And no more calling 'em to the wire. That's out. So is spinning out of the turn. It's my way, or no way." He decked me for the count!

CBS sportscaster Johnny Morris and *Herald* sports-media critic Jim O'Donnell became acutely aware, as did myriads of racing fans, that my announcing style had changed. They wanted to know why. I told them. Gary Deeb, the entertainment-media critic for the *Chicago Sun-Times*, wrote a column trashing Mooney for interfering with my style. Mooney went bonkers. Two days later I was fired by

Mooney—with Madison Square Garden president Sonny Werblin's blessing. It was one week before the 1982 Million II. I would miss Arlington's final seven weeks of 1982.

Not only was I favorably surprised by fan response, I was elated, and deeply touched. I loved my Chicago fans. There's nothing worse than unrequited love, but they loved in return. Enraged by Mooney's action, they rose in protest with banners, signs, bumper stickers, phone calls, catcalls, and a public boycott. Lest I appear immodest, I must confess that I was overwhelmed by the wonderfully loud but peaceful mob action taken by Chicago fans. I was on radio and TV about 21 times during the week following my firing. Wherever I went, fans told me: "Don't worry, Phil, we'll get you back!"

Within a year Richard L. Duchossois, Sheldon Robbins, Ralph Ross, and my former boss, Joe Joyce, had purchased Arlington Park. Their first act was to fire John Mooney. Their second, which thrilled me equally, was to bring me back. The day following the Million III, I was flown by helicopter to Arlington's winner's circle to return to my job as race announcer. Safe to say, Chicago's fans, who are second to none, afforded me rare and priceless job security for my final nine years, though retirement at that time was the farthest thing from my mind.

Also in the early 1980s, I was hired to announce two 13-week half-hour TV segments of a worldwide Thoroughbred racing show, *Let's Go to the Races!* The show was commercially sponsored, and free promotional tickets were handed out at shopping outlets such as Osco or Walgreen Drugs, and Jewel and Kroger food stores. Each week, the program offered the post parade and race of five separate events, all recently filmed at Gulfstream Park in Hallandale, Florida. I did all the audio, including the saddling in the paddock and the post parade introductions—all climaxed, of course, by the race's actual running, start to finish, called by both number and actual name, with a slow-motion replay of late stretch action where needed. Free rub-off cards had numbers for the five races, and the fifth race offered the richest viewer prize, $1,000 cash. A big hit, the shows aired in major markets in the United States, England, and South America. I know folks who saw the game advertised in Barbados.

Producing a new series of races became prohibitive as tracks recognized and demanded costlier rights. I was asked to recall the entire 1960s *Let's Go to the Races!* series that had been originally called by Jack Drees, who by then was residing in Mobile, Alabama. I was flattered that my sound would be used for wider distribution of the earlier shows. The onset of computer and video games and the spiraling costs of buying a half-hour's time on even a small local station were the show's undoing. But I did the call for 48 of those races for a Parker Brothers' video game, which sold some 350,000 units, unimpressive against the advent of computer video games with their "virtual reality" appeal to younger folk. However, in 1997, I called a 4,000-race CD-ROM game that featured animated races, with the 1-2-3 finishers randomly selected by computer. The experience provided gratifying affirmation of my race-calling style.

By the mid-1980s, thanks to Spectacular Bid and John Henry, also the birth of the Arlington Million and the burgeoning concept of the Breeders' Cup as the World Series of Thoroughbred racing, the sport enjoyed a brief but satisfying renaissance. Television finally came to be appreciated. In Chicago we had daily, also weekly, Thoroughbred and harness shows, co-hosted by myself and the courageous producer, former jockey Gerland "Gerry" Gallitano, who prematurely retired from riding to concentrate on daily TV as a service to fans. Confidently, and foolishly, he relied on financial support from the tracks to keep the show afloat. No such continued support materialized, except from Hawthorne.

Politics, personal enmity, and envy over dates permeated Illinois racing, accelerating noticeably after Arlington's tragic blaze of 1985. I must clarify, however, that Hawthorne's reputation for decency and fairness was so well-known as to be considered somewhat archaic by those pseudo-sophisticates among Chicago's racing hierarchy who held no such scruples. I was one of the few employees allowed to work all three Thoroughbred tracks—Arlington, Hawthorne, and Sportsman's—with dignity and impunity. The proven loyalty of Chicago fans had afforded me that luxury.

I was "the voice of Chicago racing," a badge I cherished and wore proudly. My reputation endeared me with such institutions as the *Chicago Sun-Times*, the Let-Us-Entertain-You Restaurant chain, the Chicago White Sox, and Pizza Hut, for whom I cut several TV commercials. At the time, horse racing rated par with football, baseball, basketball, and hockey. I was elated when the Chicago Bulls hired me to do their nightly "dot races," a nightly animated racing feature presented between the third and fourth quarters at every Bulls home game. Twice since retirement at the end of 1992, I've been called back by the Bulls management—including Michael Jordan's championship years—to update those nightly races, which, I must admit, Chicago hoop fans applaud unreservedly.

It's a treat to hear my name still announced at the Bulls stadium as "the voice of Chicago racing!"

Chapter Twelve

Match Race

I not only see visions; I dream dreams. Sweet dreams. Joe Louis vs. Muhammad Ali. Jack Nicklaus vs. Tiger Woods. Babe Ruth vs. Barry Bonds. Johnny Weissmuller vs. Mark Spitz. Citation vs. Secretariat.

Impossible, right? And yet, although the above sports icons competed in different eras and under dissimilar conditions, any one of the above imagined encounters immediately stirs the soul and challenges the imagination. Each of them, in effect, would constitute a match race.

Match races once were an integral part of American Thoroughbred racing. Sadly, whatever the reason—the sport's year-round growth, teeming with rich opportunities for stakes stars, or perhaps the bad taste left by Ruffian's fatal injury, sustained in her New York match race against Foolish Pleasure that fateful July 6, 1975—yes, whatever the reason, match racing is no longer a viable component of the game.

Among racetrackers today, match racing is rarely discussed; its scheduling is as unlikely as a July snowstorm in Florida. Relegated to a footnote in racing history, the match race is a relic of the past. I appreciate that racing's future is *now,* that making new fans is a frenzied priority. Track ads, particularly TV spots produced by NTRA, are pop-culture oriented. Everything's *today,* not yesterday. At the risk of really sounding like an old incurable curmudgeon, however, I must confess I'm deeply troubled by one pervasive development. Once the Thoroughbred industry loses interest in its past, the emphasis inevitably seems to shift almost entirely to numbers, luck, and the seductive lure of pure gambling. If that becomes the sport's primary concern we're forced to accept a frightening truism: the action's surely a lot faster, more furious, and certainly more daring at the gaming casinos. You can bet on that.

We have so much Thoroughbred racing these days—even as some tracks suffer serious declines without the aid of slots and sundry other alluring gaming devices—that the match race has lost both its appeal and practicality. For example, in 1973, Secretariat and Sham needed no match race to decide who was champ. They launched a sizzling rivalry in both the Derby and Preakness; their duel lent zest to the Belmont Stakes, in which Secretariat hammered home spectacularly in world-record time by 31 lengths. Sham, obviously not at his best that day, broke down midway through the race to finish a pulled-up last. He never raced again.

Affirmed's historic Triple Crown conquest of the equally gifted Alydar in 1978 required no climactic match race to crown the superior colt. And their Belmont was a humdinger. For Silver Charm and Touch Gold of more modern vintage, and even more recently Real Quiet and Victory Gallop, there were ample opportunities in the spring and fall classics to test their competitive mettle.

Conditions and circumstances—yesterday and today—must be perfect for the match race to exist. Year-round racing virtually precludes that chance. Nonetheless, the match race remains a magnificent racing history lesson, a peerless crowd pleaser, an irresistible media magnet, doubtless the most fascinating way to settle an issue. But the match race, despite its honored place in Thoroughbred lore, may never happen again.

Without resorting to inexhaustible research, I respectfully submit that the first of racing's great match races took place in 1920 when Man o' War mercilessly annihilated 1919 Triple Crown champion Sir Barton at Kenilworth Park, Canada. Some historians forget, however, that although the Man o' War vs. Sir Barton clash was popularly and accurately billed as a match race, Man o' War had also faced and defeated but one single challenger in five previous races, his swelling fame pardonably scaring off all opposition.

The last of the great match races—with apologies to the 1974 Chris Evert vs. Miss Musket event at Hollywood Park—occurred on Wednesday, August 31, 1955, at now defunct Washington Park on Chicago's great south side. It was the $100,000 winner-take-all Swaps–Nashua affair, ambitiously billed, and not too incorrectly, as "The Match Race of the Century!"

In between these two great events were a number of noteworthy match races. At Pimlico in November 1938, iron horse Seabiscuit, teaming up with Georgie Woolf, took on 1937 Triple Crown hero War Admiral, under Charlie Kurtsinger, at equal weights of 120 pounds over $1\frac{3}{16}$ miles. The Biscuit, honed perfectly by training wizard "Silent Tom" Smith, beat the Admiral at his own game—pure, unadulterated speed—leading every step of the way for a thumping 4-length triumph!

In 1942, Cinderella horse Alsab had the gall to challenge the charismatic Whirlaway, a Triple Crown winner, on September 19 at Narragansett Park, also at $1\frac{3}{16}$ miles. Alsab's "rags-to-riches" status started when he was purchased for a paltry $700 as a yearling at the 1940 Saratoga Sales by Chicago attorney Al Sabath—thus the name Alsab, a contraction of his new owner's name. His Cinderella fame took hold with his triumph in the 1942 Preakness and was indelibly certified by his electrifying nose victory over Whirlaway on Match Race Day.

Whirlaway was a seasoned 4-year-old when he dropped that squeaker to 3-year-old Alsab, the latter carrying 119 to Mr. Longtail's 126. Carroll Bierman rode Alsab; Georgie Woolf was astride Whirlaway, who quickly shook off the defeat to nail down his second straight Horse of the Year crown.

Here's some little-known match race trivia: both Alsab and Seabiscuit, just like Man o' War himself, had experienced one-on-one bouts before. Neither were strangers to match racing. Seabiscuit only three months earlier tuned up for his tally over War Admiral by whipping Bing Crosby's Ligaroti at California's Del Mar by a scant nose in a special $1\frac{1}{8}$ miles match race on August 12, 1938. Little Alsab was a budding 2-year-old on October 23, 1941, when he trimmed another his age named Requested by $3\frac{1}{2}$ lengths in a $6\frac{1}{2}$-furlongs match sprint at Belmont. The purse that day was $10,000. Almost exactly one year later, Alsab bested Whirlaway for a $25,000 pot.

Calumet Farm's amazing gelding Armed—the former stable pony, remember?—pulverized King Ranch's Assault by 8 lengths in a race that should never have been run. Assault, the 1946 Triple Crown king, wasn't exactly lame but had tailed off noticeably and was somewhat sore from a splint. He should have stayed in his stall that September 27, 1947, at Belmont Park rather than suffer the shellacking of a grueling 1¼ miles. Both combatants were under equal weight of 126 pounds. Doug Dodson stood tall in Armed's saddle that afternoon. Eddie Arcaro compassionately eased Assault in upper stretch when he realized what distress his mount was suffering.

Capot's 12-length victory over Coaltown at Pimlico in 1949 was a hollow result that barely justified expectations. Coaltown, erratic and unpedicatable, was eased long before the finish when his rider, Steve Brooks, sensed all was not well with Citation's lesser stablemate. Capot had already earned his title as 1949 Horse of the Year.

Most fans would sooner forget Ruffian's heartrending 1975 tragic mishap against Foolish Pleasure. After dashing the first quarter in :22⅖—and in front, as was her marvelous wont—the august, undefeated filly snapped an ankle and, refusing to stop, proceeded to smash the bone into splinters. Ruffian was performing as the 5–2 favorite before a national TV audience when tragedy struck, a sight I'll never forget—nor ever want to see again. With Ruffian staggering helplessly on a smashed ankle, her rider, Jacinto Vasquez, bawled shamelessly at her side.

Of course it wasn't only in match races that two equine champions would directly challenge each other. The separate Triple Crown events were ample stage for such drama. The first Kentucky Derby ever televised to a major market was Hill Gail's front-stepping 2-length victory over Sub Fleet in 1952. The first complete Triple Crown telecast took place the next year (1953), keyed by Dark Star's whopping upset of Native Dancer in the Derby, followed by the Dancer's narrow tallies over upstart Jamie K. in both the Preakness and Belmont.

Only two years later (1955), the sports world in general, racing in particular, was aglow with a vibrant spirit of adventure created by two of finest 3-year-olds of all time, Nashua and Swaps. The former had been narrowly crowned 1954's 2-year-old champ over the highly regarded Summer Tan. Swaps, on the other hand, as a 2-year-old was a virtual unknown. In fact, Swaps wasn't all that visible during the early stages of his and Nashua's 1955 3-year-old campaign, though he did annex the Santa Anita Derby in so-so fashion, failing to impress observers. Just another California speedball, they figured.

By early spring, the Kentucky Derby loomed a veritable duel between Nashua and his eastern arch rival Summer Tan. Nashua's reputation as a brilliant but screwball son of Nasrullah was widespread. Said his jockey Eddie Arcaro: "He'll scare the hell out of you during a race. You just never knew what to expect. But he's got real talent, as good, if not great, as any when he's in the mood."

Swaps, meanwhile, was a virtual stable pet of partners Rex C. Ellsworth and Meshach "Mesh" Tenney. Docile as a lamb Swaps was more like an oversized chestnut-colored Doberman pinscher—minus the attitude, of course. He minded not a bit that co-owner Mesh Tenney, who also doubled as trainer, slept with him in his stall during their Churchill Downs stay. As a Thoroughbred, Swaps was a rare bird.

Arcaro would be the first to admit he and Nashua trainer Sunny Jim Fitzsimmons underestimated Swap's quality and class. "I knew he was fast," the Master shook his head, "but his Santa Anita Derby, in which he just did hold on for a half-length win after turning for home 3 or 4 lengths to the good, wasn't all that great. Sunny Jim and I figured all we had to do was beat Summer Tan and the Derby was ours."

Bill Shoemaker, aboard Swaps, capitalized on Arcaro's error. He flawlessly rated Swaps, waiting up front with the patience of Job, while Arcaro glided along confidently in third moving up the Churchill Downs backstretch. Arcaro had his eyes glued on Summer Tan in fourth.

"By the time we hit the far turn," Eddie recalled, "I was convinced we had Summer Tan beat. Then, it struck me. There was Swaps just waltzing along on a leisurely lead. He hadn't taken even a deep breath. That's when I got a little weak-kneed. But I still felt I had the best colt—so I asked Nashua to go get 'em."

Nashua picked up Swaps with a flourish and was only a half-length back in midstretch when the unbelievable happened. Swaps kicked free! He actually drew clear to win decisively by just over a length. Eddie took the blame, but he never acknowledged his miscue as monumental until years later. "Had I not allowed Swaps that easy, early lead, I might have gotten not only my sixth Derby, but a third Triple Crown as well. But, then, that's horse racing."

Swaps did not thereafter intentionally duck Nashua, what with the Preakness and Belmont Stakes on deck, but Ellsworth and Tenney stuck by a previous commitment to return to California after the Derby, win or lose. Swaps proceeded to burn up the west coast, going undefeated, as if to prove his Derby score no fluke. Nashua also bounced back with his usual verve, handily winning both Preakness and Belmont, thereby in many minds all but expiating his Derby debacle. But the awakened specter of Swaps wouldn't go away. Too many unanswered questions had been raised.

Swaps was for real—a star was born! He certified his ranking as a world-class colt, crushing everything in sight in California, including an eye-popping victory over older steeds in the 1$\frac{1}{16}$ miles Californian Stakes in world-record time. Nor did Nashua rest upon his Preakness and Belmont Stakes laurels. He continued to conquer all he surveyed, winning the Dwyer in New York authoritatively. Fact is, both Nashua and Swaps had Chicago on their summer calendar of engagements; unfortunately, not at the same time.

Belair Stud's Nashua drew bead on Arlington's 1-mile Classic in July, which we described in some detail earlier. He won as expected, but not in the fashion expected. Eddie had flown in a few days before the race to publicly work Nashua 5 furlongs in :58 and change, a morning drill that attracted exceptional media attention. Everybody on hand, including trainer Sunny Jim, marveled at Nashua's time, particularly his apparent ease in ripping off early fractions. He pulled up 6 furlongs in 1:12 flat.

Arcaro, however, confided in me on the condition his thoughts be kept private. "Phil, he went fast and all that, but something's missing. He seemed a bit listless, as if his spirit was sagging. But that's between us, okay? Sunny Jim thinks he's perfect for Saturday's Classic." I had gotten to know Eddie. Even though I was now a full-time track publicist, Eddie knew he could trust me with off-the-record comments. I told no one. Besides, I was a Nashua devotee; I wanted to believe he was the best thing since Citation.

As you know, Nashua did win the 1-mile Classic. He was under brisk pressure leaving the half-mile pole to run down the sprightly Impromptu, then was hard-put to stave off Traffic Judge by a dwindling half-length in so-so time of 1:35⅕.

After calling the chart for the press box boys, I took the elevator to the ground level. Eddie, while unsaddling, winked at me. "I told you the other day he's not himself." I nodded, then sought a quote for publication. Eddie was candid. "He won all right, did everything right, too, but he just wasn't his old self. Why he can beat that other colt from here to paddock any day of the week. But he did win, and that's what we get paid for doing." Eddie could fairly gauge the comparative skills of Nashua and Traffic Judge because he often rode Traffic Judge in eastern stakes whenever he wasn't committed to Nashua.

Despite the disappointing showing, at least Nashua, just like Swaps, had kept on winning. Talk about a possible match race surfaced. Many others, of course, were hoping they'd simply square off in a major scheduled stakes, like the upcoming American Derby in mid-August at Washington Park, for which Swaps would be shipping in soon. Nashua's people declined the issue, however, because the time-honored event was slated to be run on grass for the first time in history. Sunny Jim wasn't sold on the game's newest, most fascinating medium.

Swaps took Chicago by storm, his victory in the grassy 1³⁄₁₆ miles American Derby a work of art. Flashing his vanted speed, Swaps effortlessly toted Shoemaker right to the front, where they stayed, pursued early by Parader and jockey Bill Hartack and by Summer Solstice with Johnny Adams aboard. Shaking them off with nary a deep breath, Swaps turned for home with an authoritative 4-length lead. Nashua's old nemesis Traffic Judge, this time with Pete Anderson up, uncorked his usual late spurt, gamely whittling away at Swaps's easy lead, ultimately falling three-parts of a length short. Shoe never unhoused his whip, though he kept craning over his right shoulder, saving Swaps, as it were, for things to come. As it was, Swaps spun the $1\frac{3}{16}$ miles in $1{:}54\frac{3}{5}$, a new American record on the turf.

The cry of "Match Race!" now really stirred the nation. Remember, in those days there was no Breeders' Cup to help crown divisional champions. Nashua, following his Classic win, repaired to his New York haunts, and Swaps would be returning to the west coast around Labor Day. So if East is East and West is West, the only way the twain could ever meet was over a neutral battleground—Chicago and Washington Park—sites of Nashua's and Swaps's most recent scores. Clamor for the race surpassed drumroll proportions that weekend, and the man who helped put it all together was actor Don Ameche. Ameche truly loved the sport and the national spotlight it commanded. He talked to both camps, and the race was on!

There were no lawyers, no agents, no merchandising experts, certainly no NTRA. Just friendly conversation, agreement in principle, and handshakes all around. It was a $100,000 winner-take-all event; the winning jockey would get 10 percent of the pot; the loser would receive $35, the traditional riding fee of the day. No ifs and buts. The Nashua–Swaps match race was a done deal.

CBS hesitated not a second grabbing up the event, although one proviso was not entirely to their liking. Ben Lindheimer, beneficent despot of Arlington–Washington in those days, forsook the usual Saturday setting, choosing rather to present the match race in mid-week—Wednesday, August 31, 1955, a date which would live famously in American racing. New York's Win Elliot would serve as TV host, Chicago favorite Jack Drees was hired to do the TV call and track announcer Harry Henson would call it over the track PA system.

American Thoroughbred racing came alive! Once again, Chicago stepped front and center. You'd think we were staging the Kentucky Derby all over again. The whole sports world was captivated. Plus, now we had national TV, a medium unavailable in Citation's and Man o' War's heyday. Anyone who was anyone among America's news media converged on Washington Park. The track was spruced up and 125 new media accommodations were added to its press box. All this was accomplished in just the 11 days allotted between Swaps's American Derby victory and Match Race Day.

I don't think I slept more than three hours any one night. I flew higher than the newest plane. Chicago was abuzz, bursting with energy and excitement. What a coup Don Ameche helped orchestrate—Swaps vs. Nashua for the first time since their heralded Derby encounter. If this wasn't a match race made in heaven, then there just ain't no such animal. East vs. West. Swaps, a flaming chestnut blessed with catlike speed and western aplomb; Nashua, rugged, aloof, the epitome of eastern snobbery. Both had remained unbeaten. It would be the classic 1¼ miles again, with equal weights, plus Arcaro and Shoe, the two greatest jockeys of all time!

Racing's glory days had scaled yet another incredible summit. Virtually every TV station, every major, even minor, newspaper, and every radio news and sports reporter the country over were mesmerized. Like everyone else, I had strong feelings about the race. I couldn't ignore the doubtless fact that Swaps was America's horse, and Shoe, the young American riding phenom, added incalculably to Swaps's growing mystique and appeal. Nashua, on the other hand, was owned by wealthy socialite William Woodward Jr. and, in keeping with his eastern heritage, to many appeared smug, haughty.

If a canvass were taken, as far as racing fans were concerned, Swaps would win, and in a landslide! Swaps had trimmed Nashua in their only meeting, the Kentucky Derby. Why not again? Speed's the name of the game, right? Nashua would have to chase Swaps again. Why should the outcome not be the same?

I was collecting news and views, facts and anecdotes, chiefly from Nashua's camp by way of publicity updates. I also had some dealings with Swaps's people. Remember during Derby week in Louisville when Tenny slept with Swaps in the latter's stall? I have an even stranger tale.

True, Ellsworth and Tenney treated Swaps no differently than any other Thoroughbred, or Quarterhorse, or stable pony in their barn. Many Thoroughbred devotees were horrified that they treated Swaps as just another outdoor, four-legged animal in their care. He was an equine star and hero; he should be accorded treatment commensurate with his stature and dignity, many felt.

Three mornings prior to the big race, I escorted sportscaster Johnny Erp and his NBC film crew to Washington Park's racing secretary's office to run down trainer Mesh Tenney. Erp wanted a filmed interview involving both Tenney and his famous charge, Swaps. As always, Tenney was available and cooperative. Racing secretary Pat Farrell told me Tenney knew we were looking for him and was on his way.

In those days, tracks like Washington Park were located outside city limits. They were invitingly rustic, usually nestled among trees and greenery. The racing secretary's office, where all horsemen and their grandees congregated daily in the mornings, was located on the lip of the backstretch area, in this case a good half-mile from the track proper. A busy, easy world all its own.

Erp and I opened the side door, much like cowboys opening a door at the town's friendly saloon. Fact is, two hitching posts were standing a few feet from that very door. Here comes Mesh Tenney galloping up to the office. He dismounts and loops the reins of his mount over a hitching bar just like in those Gene Autry movies.

I introduced Tenney to Erp. "Mesh, Johnny would like to do a special interview with you and Swaps. Is this a good time?"

"Good as any," Tenney drawled, smiling at Erp, who was short and would have made an excellent jock if he could lose 50 pounds or so. But he was one heckuva sports reporter.

"Okay," I agreed, "as soon as Swaps is available."

"Right now's fine," Mesh said and pointed. "That's him over there."

Yep, Tenney had ridden Swaps over from his stall right to the racing secretary's office, as if Swaps were just another stable pony, not one of the greatest Thoroughbreds of all time.

If that didn't take the cake, every afternoon between races during the week before the match, Tenney would pony Swaps in front of the stands, coax him gently to the rail, and allow railbirds that once-in-a-lifetime opportunity to reach out and pet a colt they've come to idolize. The kids went wild every time. It personified Thoroughbred racing's age of innocence. Sure, Nashua and his people would never deign to such shenanigans. But horses like Swaps, and guys like Ellsworth and Tenney, graced the sport with an aura no money could buy, or restore.

Regardless, my heart belonged to Nashua. Sure, his eastern connections—owner Woodward and trainer Sunny Jim Fitzsimmons—gave his camp the feel of lofty high-mindedness. He had Arcaro, too, which was more than enough to make me a Nashua fan. Besides, I felt the Nashua camp had served Swaps the Derby on a platter with their miscalculations.

In fact, it was Arcaro, pleading with Sunny Jim in those days prior to the big match, who masterfully switched tactics as August 31 loomed. I'll never forget Eddie's reasoning: "No horse—I don't care who or how good he is—likes going head to head, eyeball to eyeball, with another. That kind of competition can gall the spirit, rub the horse the wrong way. You've got to attack early, gun 'em right from the start. One or the other—maybe both—will crack. Swaps is a great one, proved that in the Derby. Hell, he can run all day. But can he run all day with Nashua eyeball to eyeball?"

I thought his thinking ingenious. Part of my job as publicist was to research prior match races. I didn't have to be Einstein to see that Seabiscuit vanquished War Admiral with speed; same for Alsab over Whirlaway; ditto with Armed over Assault; not to forget Capot over Coaltown. Except for Alsab nipping Whirlaway, each of those front-stepping winners scored imperiously, with lengths to spare. Besides, Nashua appeared reinvigorated, smartly freshened up following his mediocre Arlington Classic score; he had put on a few pounds, seemed vigorous again, robust and hearty as the morning dew.

Racing's pulse rate spiraled upward with a big, warm, enthusiastic welcome Match Race Day. The mid-week date no deterrent, over 32,000 spectators jammed Washington Park despite the local telecast, which was the one thing CBS insisted upon. It had rained Monday and Tuesday, but a bright sun greeted fans Wednesday, and by race time, the day's seventh event, the track was officially listed as "good," though a few paths on the track were drier than others.

Now if CBS's claims are true that 35 million American homes had TV sets in 1955, and, projecting three viewers per set, that gave approximately 100 million viewers—and if, according to A. C. Nielsen, half of the sets were tuned to the race for a phenomenal 50 rating—then the "Match Race of the Century" had more than lived up to its name! For Arcaro it was even bigger. Had Nashua won the Derby, Eddie would have had six, not five, Derbies, and three Triple Crowns. This one race, therefore, figured as his supreme effort.

What a sight leading up to the race itself! The two wonder colts were saddled in the infield, on the grass. Nashua's corner seemed subdued, hardly ostentatious as Woodward, Sunny Jim, and Arcaro conferred quietly.

Swaps's corner of the world, by contrast, bustled with activity, teeming with energy and spirit. Ellsworth and Tenney appeared lighthearted, professional to be sure, but with a cool that bordered on nonchalance. You'd think they did things like this every day. And "Silent Shoe" lived up to his name, too. The Shoemaker poker face defied the tension that had to swirl inexorably. This great young jockey was prepared for the race of his life.

Nashua had drawn the No. 1 post. An empty stall separated him from Swaps. Most experts felt the post position draw of little importance, what with a grueling 1¼ miles of tiring terrain to travel. Both colts would have ample time and room to jockey for position. How wrong they were!

The gate was sprung instantly, the throng emitting a simultaneous roar. And from that second on, the unexpected became the order of the day. Arcaro and Nashua came out swinging, fists and hooves flailing, Eddie screaming like a banshee, slapping Nashua right-handed, the pair exploding as if shot from a cannon. Thus, the first surprise: Nashua, not noted for quickness of foot, had actually outbroken his avowedly swifter foe. As a by-product of that maneuver, for the first time in his life Swaps would have to play catch-up.

The second surprise also served to shake Swaps's confidence: Eddie chose one of the several drier paths about 15 feet off the rail and, realizing Swaps and Shoe would try to compensate their tardy start by closing the gap as soon as possible, carried the Ellsworth–

Tenney colt wide, thereby forcing him to lose more ground in the run to and around the first turn.

Eddie and Nashua had wrestled control of the pace and the race. Swaps never recovered from Nashua's one-two punch. He continued to race outside the leader, where the going was slower and softer—a deeper, more tiring surface. For all practical purposes, the match race was over!

Shoe, to his credit, never gave up, nor did Swaps. They bravely kept up the chase. Twice, thrice, maybe four times, Swaps was spurred by Shoe to collar Nashua. Twice Swaps moved nearly right alongside Nashua, maybe a neck or so back. Each time, Arcaro sharply roused his comrade, calling for greater acceleration, confidently tapping his wallet of reserve. And each time, Nashua delivered.

No trotting race this! Despite the deep going, Nashua led at every marker, the opening quarter in :23, the half in :46, 6 furlongs in 1:10⅖—fast fractions to be sure. But at the mile in an exhausting 1:37⅗, Swaps finally threw in the towel. Not that Nashua was rolling up the score on a beaten rival, but approaching the furlong marker in midstretch, Eddie craned over his right and then his left shoulder to assess damage done to Swaps. The latter was drifting wearily to the rail, but Eddie took no chances, applying the stick, just light taps, to seal the unconditional surrender—6½ lengths at wire's end.

There were excuses from Swaps's dazed entourage, who said that Swaps had reinjured a hoof only the day before the race, that he was allowed to start against better judgment, only to satisfy the madding crowd, thereby avoiding the appearance of being bad scouts. To be fair, I'm not totally convinced that some of what they said wasn't true. But I do know that Swaps on that day was grand enough to match Nashua stride-for-stride, virtually eyeball-to-eyeball, for as far as he could—a full, excruciating mile—before giving it up. It was a devastating defeat for some really fine people, and mostly, of course, a valiant Thoroughbred.

Nashua went back to New York, later to score a powerhouse victory in the 2-mile Jockey Club Gold Cup, thereby winning unanimous selection as 1955 Horse of the Year. Swaps returned to California, where he rested up to await an even more brilliant 4-year-old season.

Both Nashua and Swaps scintillated as 4-year-olds. Nashua won the 1956 Jockey Club Gold Cup for a second straight time. But Swaps's sparkle had a special glow, and ultimately he was crowned 1956 Horse of the Year. Both were amazing champions. However, their paths would never cross again. Let the record stand: Swaps soundly whipped Nashua in their very first clash, the Kentucky Derby. Nashua turned the tables with a resounding triumph four months later in Chicago. Each encounter was a Thoroughbred moment to remember. Their memorable clash of August 31, 1955, at Washington Park, the last of the truly great match races, is an unforgettable reminder of Thoroughbred racing's glory days.

Time for a little secret. I've never revealed this before, so the conversation I had with Eddie Arcaro the summer of 1997, just months before his death, constitutes what I treasure as an intimate insight into what once truly was an integral part of Thoroughbred racing—the match race. I asked Eddie if it were possible for him to compare Citation's greatness with that of Secretariat. Arcaro was Citation's regular rider during the colt's phenomenal 1948 season, and he worked as network TV color-commentator during Secretariat's heyday in 1973.

"I would have loved to ride Secretariat," Eddie admitted. "He was the fastest colt I've ever seen. He was, I believe, what some horsemen call a freak, in a good way of course, a one-in-a-million."

Eddie hesitated momentarily. "But I've had many years to ponder that question. My only problem with Secretariat is that he lost those two races to Onion and Prove Out following his Triple Crown, races he should have won. Both defeats were unexplainable. Even mystifying.

"Now Citation as a 3-year-old, the times I rode him, including the Triple Crown, and all those races against older horses, I never really let him run. Jimmy Jones didn't want him hurt, so we'd win by 2 or 10, whatever. We'd just win 'em, that's all. And he still equaled or set some track records. He beat every good horse there was, but the fans in 1948 never saw him full-out doing anything.

Even then, he was the greatest I ever rode or saw. I wonder how much greater he might've been had we let him really run."

I asked Eddie about match racing, about Nashua and Swaps. Then I put the big question to him: How would you ride Citation against Secretariat in a match race—were such a dream possible—with both colts at their absolute best?

Eddie heaved a long sigh. "I thought of that, too. One thing's certain, I'd not bust Cy out of the gate like I did with Nashua against Swaps. That's a great tactic to gain the advantage, but I'd try to handle Secretariat a different way."

He said he'd utilize Citation's two invincible traits. One, he could catch any horse in the world he could see, and his eyesight was perfect; and two, he was never caught from behind once he wrested command in a meaningful manner.

"Don't get me wrong. I'd never underestimate Secretariat. He was truly one of the greats of all time. And I couldn't read Turcotte's mind, assuming all was well with Ron, and he was able to ride Secretariat. I doubt if he'd try to fire from the word go," Eddie said.

"I would allow Turcotte and Secretariat the first shot," Eddie continued. "I wouldn't try to outrun 'em, unless they, of course, tried to pull a stall like those jocks did in Whirlaway's Belmont. If that happened, I'd just take control with Cy.

"But the Citation I knew could do anything, and do it right. He could lead, like he did in the 1½ miles Belmont and in the 2-miles Jockey Club Gold Cup. Or he could come from out of it like he did in the Stars and Stripes, or the Sysonby Mile.

"I'd not stalk Secretariat, like a length or so back, unless forced to. But I'd ask Cy to run as slow or as fast as Secretariat at any or all stages, preferably right alongside, at his neck or flank. None of that 'see who cracks first' stuff. That wouldn't work.

"Please, don't take this as brag, but no matter how fast Secretariat went, Cy would stay with him. I'd ask Cy to take the lead in upper stretch. And if he did, and I believe he could, there's no horse living or dead who could ever catch Citation from behind.

"It'd be one helluva race, win or lose. But the Citation I knew and rode would lose to no man's horse."

I asked Eddie to predict the winning margin.

"Let's call it 'a long neck.' Secretariat was great enough to make it that close."

"But with Citation, a neck's as good as a mile," I suggested.

Eddie winked, smiled that smile. "Heck, I'd give up retirement this very minute to ride that race!"

Me, too, dear Master, just to see you and Citation together one last time.

Chapter Thirteen

Of Tracks, Trainers, and Things

Ageless Saratoga, beloved Churchill Downs, mercurial Arlington, historic Hawthorne, magnificent Belmont, charming Santa Anita, fabled Washington Park, showy Del Mar, and legendary Pimlico are part and parcel of a storied history of "when racing was racing!" Add Hollywood, Monmouth, Delaware, Hialeah, Gulfstream, Fair Grounds, Jamaica, and Golden Gate—tracks also steeped in rich tradition. All of them stood proud and tall, especially since 1941, when racing's glory days shot like a bullet from the game's newfangled starting gate. Although I worked Chicago racing exclusively, I was keenly aware, by way of personal visits, television and simulcasting, and regular newspaper and radio reports, of the above tracks' significant involvement as the sport's golden age climbed its peak.

Arlington, which was born in 1927, then razed by fire in 1985, only to reappear in 1989 as the world's newest and finest facility of its kind, at this writing remains one of the most provocative sports anomalies of the new millennium. Having been associated with Arlington either as a fan or employee since 1941, I must confess to one remarkable truism: the palatial northwest suburban track boasts almost as many lives as the proverbial cat. The grand lady of Chicago racing returned again in 2000 after a self-imposed two-year hiatus, doing so with her usual sparkle and finery, reprising an enduring but checkered reign as queen of midwestern racing. And to nobody's real surprise either. Even the most jaundiced observer was overheard to remark: "See, I told you so—she'd be back!"

If Arlington's now-fabled indestructibility were put to music, the original libretto would be credited to masterful maestro Ben

Lindheimer and his equally clever daughter, Marje Everett, with a rousing, innovative new score by the enigmatic Richard L. Duchossois. Amazingly, the opera endures, words and music compelling as ever, brimming with more plot twists than a tortuous Sherlock Holmes novel.

Especially during the last 15 years of the 20th century, Arlington took the world of Thoroughbred racing on a wild roller-coaster ride over mountain and meadow, an incredible journey set in motion by the catastrophic towering inferno of July 31, 1985, which left her a heap of smouldering rubble. And the ride's hardly over. I'm no longer a passenger. Even the new millennium is powerless to inhibit sassy Arlington from sashaying about like the fickle and beautiful dame she is. Just when you think you've figured her out, she lets you down, or picks you up, depending, of course, on your point of view.

Arlington kept its post-inferno comeback dream alive for five years from 1985 to 1989, Duchossois forging an uneasy alliance with Tom Carey's Hawthorne Race Course. The latter, a unique family-owned-and-operated track, rescued Arlington right from the start and would continue in its role as lifeguard through 1989. That fact was not always fully appreciated by Arlington, and certainly less prized by a weirdly inimical, at times inscrutable, Illinois racing board. Suffering a short-term memory loss, the board failed to express the faintest appreciation for Hawthorne's efforts to safety-net the real danger of a Thorough-bred freefall caused by Arlington electing not to race in 1998–1999. It's this kind of inexplicable, behind-the-scenes, cryptic administrative maneuvering that I miss least of all since voluntarily fleeing the jungle of racing politics at the end of 1992.

Arlington's sister track, Washington Park, which burned down in 1977, was never rebuilt. Buried within her ashes is the memory of some of Chicago's finest racing, not the least of which was the 1955 Swaps–Nashua match race. Original Washington Park had its beginning in 1884; yes, on Chicago's south side, but north of its later Homewood, Illinois, site. It featured a 1⅛ miles track, reputedly comparable to anything the east had to offer. Its first president was none other than Civil War hero Phil Sheridan, and its best race, the American Derby, was inaugurated in 1884 amid fanfare befitting a national holiday. It more than doubled the Kentucky Derby in value. In 1893, the year of the World's Fair, the American Derby ruled as America's richest race.

Sportsman's Park, once known as racing's most exciting and dangerous half-miler, is a fading memory, having been dismantled and transformed chiefly as a motor speedway. Hawthorne remains stalwart as ever, as befits Chicago's oldest racing establishment, begun in 1891.

Arlington, Washington, and Hawthorne played a major role during the sport's glory days, as did old Lincoln Fields, which was purchased by the Arlington–Washington combine in 1955 and renamed Balmoral Jockey Club. Balmoral today caters only to Standardbreds.

At those tracks, not only the game's best horses and jockeys, but also it finest trainers plied their trade before my eager binoculars from 1941 onward. Trainers Wayne Lukas, Bob Baffert, Neil Drysdale, Bill Mott, Ron McAnally, Bobby Frankel, and Nick Zito occupy the nation's spotlight these days, particularly Lukas and Baffert, each a training conglomerate, sufficiently big and mighty to dominate the nation's blue-ribbon classics, especially the annual Triple Crown and Breeders' Cup. They've surely rewritten racing history, often flooding major stakes with multiple entries. Lukas and Baffert are the sport's Tiger Woods—dominant, preeminent, occasionally a tad boring what with a field of also-rans often reeling in their wake. They've had the racing world on a string, no doubt about it.

But I like to remember Ben and Jimmy Jones, Sunny Jim Fitzsimmons, Bill Molter, Hirsch Jacobs, Max Hirsch, Elliott Burch, Jack Van Berg, Frank Whiteley Jr., John Gaver, Charles Whittingham, William Hal Bishop, Allen Jerkens, Frank Martin, Harry Trotsek, Richard Hazelton, Arnold Winick, Buddy Delp, Joe Bollero, Bert Sonnier, Carl Nafzgar, Gerry McGrath, Harvey Vanier, Noel Hickey, Steve Ippolito, William J. Schmidt, Lou Goldfine, J. R. Smith Sr., Frank Brothers, Joe Pierce Jr., Loyd Gentry, Del Carroll, Jack Hodgins, Woody Stephens, Smiley Adams, Phil Johnson, Eddie Neloy, Bill Winfrey, Moody Jolley, Mesh Tenney, Lex Wilson, Jim Levitch, Eddie Poulos, Marion H.

Van Berg, Wayne Catalano, Bobby Voelkner, Tom Tomillo, Gene Cilio, Rickey Harris, Charlie Vinci, and Lucien Laurin. For those trainers I missed or overlooked—please forgive me.

A stable is like a sports team. The breeders and owners are the stable's athletic department. They plan and scheme behind the scenes to scare up athletic talent. Some breed all their own; others rely on sales, purchasing yearlings they think were "bred in the purple." They hitch their star to a sire, stallion, or broodmare for a spate of well-bred yearlings or a crop of sprightly 2-year-olds. But they need a knowledgeable coach for all this equine talent. It's the trainer who molds and shapes them into winners.

Concomitant with Whirlaway's 1941 Triple Crown sweep, Ben Jones became the first of the great trainers I'd become aware of, eventually meet, and eternally respect. Curiously, many trainers in those early days had interesting nicknames. Jones was "Plain Ben." James Fitzsimmons, the man who saddled two Triple Crown winners in Gallant Fox (1930) and Omaha (1935), was known everywhere as "Sunny Jim," the "Sunny" a tribute to his cheery disposition. King Ranch mentor Max Hirsch was nicknamed "Canny" because of his cozy yet sagacious dealings with jockeys, agents, and other horsemen. "Silent" Tom Smith, W. E. "Smiley" Adams, and Harold "Baldy" Tinker were some of the other descriptively monickered trainers. But is was "Plain" Ben Jones who intrigued me most.

Actually there was nothing "plain" about Benjamin Allyn Jones, except maybe his outward appearance. In 1953, my first year as track publicist, Ben was 71 years old and had already smoothly transferred most of Calumet Farm's training reins to his son Horace A. "Jimmy" Jones. I wrote a thumbnail sketch about the man everyone called the "greatest trainer of 'em all."

According to Webster's, "plain" denotes a person or thing that is ordinary, without pretense, lacking superiority, or physically unattractive or undistinguished. Maybe Ben was all that. But he also embodied other traits the word "plain" suggested—clear, distinct, decisive, free from ambiguity or evasion, simple, and forthright.

That was the "Plain" Ben Jones I got to know. I saw him countless times in his second home, the Chicago's winner's circle, starting with Whirlaway's appearances in 1941. I still vividly recall his stern, no-nonsense manner, his white floppy hat, and his look—yes, that look he gave every one of his horses, whether in the paddock while saddling up, or greeting them minutes later in the charmed circle following what appeared to be consistent victory. He didn't smile much, and he rarely let out anything resembling a belly laugh. He just looked right through every horse he trained, right through to their heart and soul.

It may seem a bit presumptuous to judge the relative merits of Calumet and Ben Jones, but if anybody made anybody, it was Ben Jones who made Calumet Farm, not the other way around. Sure, owner Warren Wright, heir to the Calumet Baking Powder Company and fortune, possessed both the money and smarts to launch his breeding-racing empire. That occurred in 1932, long after Jones had already made his mark as a trainer and horseman of the first water.

Plain Ben saddled his first winner in 1909; less than three years later he'd own his own breeding establishment. For 10 years, 1922 through 1931, he ranked among America's Top 10 leading breeders and horsemen. In 1932, Ben Jones was head trainer for Woolford Farm stable; six years later, in 1938, he saddled his first Kentucky Derby winner, a Woolford colt named Lawrin, ridden by a fiery, big-nosed, 22-year-old saddlemite named Eddie Arcaro. Their association augured well for future greatness.

Wright right then wanted Ben Jones for Calumet. The feeling was mutual. Thus the dynasty known as Calumet Farm was born, and by 1941 Thoroughbred racing had swung into its most magnificent orbit. Plain Ben was complemented shortly thereafter by his son Jimmy, and the Jones boys enabled Calumet Farm to dominate racing with unprecedented glory and authority. They'd win a total of eight Kentucky Derbys, seven for Calumet, topped off by two Triple Crown winners, Whirlaway and Citation.

Ben Jones for the most part appeared phlegmatic; his preoccupation was with horseflesh, not people. Horses never talked back; they discouraged conversation. So Ben placidly studied their body language. He looked them over with quiet, patient diligence. He got to know each of his horses personally. He lived and loved his job. Son Jimmy was more jovial, a great deal more loquacious.

Together the Jones boys made one considerable duo—hardly dynamic, but totally clever and astute.

According to Arcaro, who always credited his mounts and their trainers, "You'd have to be some kind of nincompoop not to win with a horse trained by Ben or Jimmy Jones." Eddie's respect for the Jones boys remained unabated. "Listen, it was Ben who gave me both Lawrin and Whirlaway; and it was Jimmy who called me for both Citation and Hill Gail. My only regret is that they didn't convince me to ride either Pensive or Ponder, or both."

Eddie praised them continually. "They were the finest trainers I've ever been around, especially Ben. He wrote the book on trainers. Always controlled his feelings, never did anything rash, except, well, maybe once." Eddie recalled what happened in the paddock prior to the 1952 Derby, in which Calumet, the Jones boys, and Eddie would combine skills to win with Hill Gail. "Ben rarely got mad or frustrated, but Hill Gail was acting up real bad, and Ben just hauled off and clouted the colt right in the snout! That settled Hill Gail's hash once and for all. No more backtalk. Hill Gail just went out and won the Derby like he was supposed to."

The first time I saw "Canny" Max Hirsch, the fabled trainer was in a bad mood. He had saddled Triple Crown winner Assault for the 1946 Arlington Classic, then stood there dumfounded as the colt finished dead last to an unsung Illinois colt named The Dude. But Hirsch smiled more often than not during a sparkling 65-year training career. He developed a slew of stakes stars, starting out with Grey Lag as a 2-year-old. He also tightened the girth on handicap ace Sarazen. He won three Derbys—with Bold Venture (1936), Assault (1946), and Middleground (1950). Max's pride and joy was "the Club-footed comet," Assault, whose 1946 Triple Crown score, plus subsequent success as an outstanding handicap performer, guaranteed the elder Hirsch his rightful place in Thoroughbred racing's Hall of Fame alongside the Jones boys.

Max started out as a jockey prior to his teens, but he lost the battle of the bulge. By the time he was 20, he had distinguished himself as one of the youngest trainers of record. Before discovered by King Ranch, Canny Max was, like Ben Jones, well-known in racing. He had already won the Derby with Bold Venture, who would sire another Derby winner, the great Assault himself.

Max turned out to be quite a sire in his own right, developing his own racing family dynasty. His daughter Mary, who later married respected racetracker Charles McLennan, was a pioneer among women trainers. His son William J. "Buddy" Hirsch also became a conditioner of undeniable substance. Other father–son training teams included Charles and Mike Whittingham, Wayne and Jeff Lukas, and Marion and Jack Van Berg. It wasn't often, however, that the "chip off the old block" would surpass the old man. One exception may be the Van Bergs.

Marion Van Berg was a "horseman's horseman" who found the winner's circle quicker, and more often, than most of his contemporaries. It all started inauspiciously for the friendly farmer from Columbus, Nebraska, in 1937, when a 6-year-old mare, Dorothy R., lit up the tote board in victory at Fairmount Park in downstate Illinois. The mare's owner, Marion H. Van Berg, was no youngster; he was 41 at the time, debuting as a Thoroughbred horseman on his way to becoming one of the game's brightest stars—4,691 winners and $13,936,965 in purse earnings. And money was money in those days.

Marion's son Jack deftly grabbed the baton from his talented father and piled up thousands of winners himself as a racing Hall of Famer. In 1987, Alysheba thrust Jack Van Berg into the national spotlight. The burly conditioner basked in his colt's incredible Kentucky Derby victory. After clipping heels with Bet Twice in upper stretch, Alysheba recovered miraculously under masterful guidance by jockey Chris McCarron, scoring decisively. Van Berg saddled Alysheba for another clear-cut tally over Bet Twice in the Preakness, standing on the threshold of racing immortality, only to suffer defeat by Bet Twice in the Belmont. Alysheba, however, won the Breeders' Cup Classic in 1988 for Jack and was crowned Horse of the Year.

"I'm still looking for another Alysheba," Jack told me in 1998 while deputizing for his late father, who was being inducted in the Hawthorne Hall of Champions. "I'm a firm believer that lightning, if you're lucky enough, can really strike twice."

Two of my personal favorites among the trainers were Bill Molter and William Hal Bishop. Molter won the 1954 Kentucky Derby with little Determine. Always smiling, yet at times diffident to a fault, Molter had developed the fine colt Bobby Brocato, who aced the Santa Anita Handicap in 1956. But it was his close association with the Travis M. Kerr Stables' mighty Round Table that made Molter a trainer to be remembered.

William Hal Bishop, a former mule trader from Anna, Illinois, never had a horse to equal Round Table's prowess, but he did spring one of the upsets of the ages when he saddled the Illinois horse Bernburgoo to defeat Molter's Round Table in the 1958 Warren Wright Memorial at Arlington, the year in which Round Table reigned as both Horse and Grass Horse of the Year. "I never had that many stakes horses," Bishop always deplored, "but beating Round Table that day at Arlington is still my greatest thrill." In 1949, Bishop and Molter tied for national honors in races won. Bishop grabbed off a belated national title all his own in 1962 when he saddled 162 winners.

Bishop ruled the roost for many years as "king of the claimers." Horses passed through his hands so fast that, as he pointed out, he rarely got "to know the horse, let alone his name." A robust, gregarious man rarely seen without his trademark Stetson, he claimed copiously, assembly-lining his runners week after week, day after day, race after race. "I just loved the winner's circle," he boasted. Let the record speak for itself: Bishop won no fewer than seven Arlington training titles, including four straight (1951–1954). He topped Hawthorne a record 11 times. He was that good.

If one story could personify Bishop's zeal to claim and win, I have to go back to a Saturday–Monday weekend in the early 1960s at Hawthorne Race Course. I can't recall the horse's name, but the $2,500 claimer was owned I think by Emil Denemark; trainer Elmer Kalensky, I believe, had boldly entered the plug in both Saturday's and Monday's programs. We had no Sunday racing those days. The horse won Saturday's last race for Denemark and was claimed out of the race by Bishop, who surprisingly refused to scratch the plater from Monday's card. Bishop started him right back with only a single day's rest, and the horse won again! Such things just don't happen these days.

I wish I had had the chance to get to know Sunny Jim Fitzsimmons better. He was eastern-based, but he invaded Chicago occasionally, as he did with Nashua in 1955 for the Classic and the match race with Swaps. I saw him in Florida with another of his favorite trainees, the free-spirited Bold Ruler. By then he was bent over with painful arthritis, but he never belied his famous nickname.

Sunny Jim had reason to fret as his career neared a close. In October 1955, following Nashua's incendiary victory over Swaps, he was stunned by the accidental death of Nashua's young owner, William Woodward Jr., at his Oyster Bay, Long Island, home. It was a senseless tragedy that made news and sports headlines around the world. Confusion and controversy clouded the situation. According to the reports, Woodward's wife, awakened suddenly from slumber, grabbed a shotgun deliberately kept at bedside for protection and, mistaking her husband for a prowler, blew his head off. Shock resonated throughout the turf world.

The sport kept even keel, however, with the continued success of such trainers as Elliot Burch and Allen Jerkens. Burch saddled three Belmont Stakes winners: Sword Dancer (1959), Quadrangle (1964), and Arts and Letters (1969). Jerkens, like Burch a noted easterner, earned a deserved reputation as "giant killer," especially with Onion and Prove Out, both of whom took turns at quelling the Secretariat express in 1973. I was privileged to call several of Jerkens's top Hobeau Farm stars, including Beau Purple (1962) and Group Plan (1974), who galloped off with the Hawthorne Gold Cup. Jerkens also won the Hawthorne Derby twice, with Sensitive Prince (1978) and Handsome Boy (1966).

No Chicago history would be complete without conditioners Frank Whiteley Jr. and Charles "the Bald Eagle" Whittingham. The former's touch with both Tom Rolfe and Damascus remains legendary. Whittingham also was particularly visible at Arlington and Washington Parks. I was at the mike when he won the Arlington Handicap with both Paliharaki (1983) and Ifrad (1987). He also saddled Mister Gus to win the event in 1956. Arlington

International's Beverly D. reigned as the world's richest grass race for fillies and mares ($500,000). Its second running in 1989 was won by Whittingham's Claire Marine, who led from start to finish. I also called two of the Bald Eagle's Arlington Million scores—Golden Pheasant (1990) and the gallant mare Estrapade (1986).

The Million, of course, was presented on the grass, and turf coverage would be incomplete without mention of my two all-time favorite trainers, Harry Trotsek and Noel Hickey. On dirt they were good; on grass, spectacular! Round Table, John Henry, and Stan are the three greatest grass horses I've seen or called in the past half-century. Round Table was developed by Bill Molter; John Henry was conditioned by Ron McAnally; Stan was a trainee of Harry Trotsek, who called Cicero, Illinois, home.

Stan was the finest "foreign-bred" selected, purchased, and trained by Trotsek, for the formidable Hasty House Farms, the stable that pioneered grass racing in North America. The Reubens of Hasty House scoured England, Ireland, and especially South America to import their best horseflesh, among whom were Inseparable, Seaward, Platan, Mahan, Mister Black, Carteret, Lostato, Porvenir II, Unanime, Summer Solstice, and, of course the creme de la creme, Stan himself.

Stan won the Hialeah Turf and was a standout wherever tracks featured grass competition. His victory in the 1954 Arlington Handicap—my second year as a track publicist—was a masterpiece. Five lengths off the high-flying Brush Burn in midstretch, Stan inhaled that startled leader as if the latter were walking, then sprinted clear for a five-length victory all his own.

P. Noel Hickey was the Trotsek of his day, from the 1980s onward, and he was hottest during my final two or three seasons in Chicagoland. Fact is, in 1991 Hickey won something like nine Arlington stakes, with his turf runners (all of which he bred and owned) scoring at an amazing 49 success rate. In 1990 at Arlington, he won 28 of 85 turf races. An Irish-bred himself, the man has the Midas touch; just ask Buck's Boy, among others, whose versatility—a winner over dirt as well as grass—simply adds to the Hickey mystique. Buck's Boy has become something of a Chicago legend. The horse was bred in Illinois, won the 1997 Hawthorne Gold Cup on the dirt, then captured the $2 million Breeders' Cup Turf in 1998 at Churchill Downs.

Among the most celebrated trainers I've called are Lucien Laurin, of Secretariat fame; Carl Nafzger, whose Unbridled made him a TV star; and Woody Stephens, who broke all records when he saddled five straight winners of the Belmont Stakes.

A kindly, personable, highly skilled practitioner of the training art, Laurin came to my attention when I called his Clansman home first in 1965 Laurance Armour Handicap at Arlington. Nafzger won an Eclipse Award as America's top trainer of 1990, thanks to Unbridled's reign as 3-year-old of the year. Carl and I go back many years. I called his Fairway Phantom when he won the 1981 Arlington Classic, his first graded-stakes triumph. Carl started out as a nationally ranked rodeo rider. I'm glad he had the good sense to bump himself up to bigger and better things. He's a true big leaguer, and a decent person, which is all the more important.

Bold Bidder won the 1966 Hawthorne Gold Cup and the 1966 Washington Park Handicap for Woody Stephens. Other Stephens successes were the American Derby with Creme Fraiche (1985) and with Smarten (1979). His Clem won the 1957 Arlington Classic.

I'm only human, so I had favorites. I cheered inwardly for Nafzger; Bert Sonnier, whose Meadowlake was potentially one of the great equines of all time; Bud Delp, especially his marvelous work with Spectacular Bid; congenial Gerry McGrath; talented Harvey Vanier; a genuine Bobby Voelkner; jockey-turned trainer Wayne Catalano; jockey-turned TV producer Gerry Gallitano; Chicago regulars Gene Cilio, Rickey Harris, Tommy Tomillo, Richard Hazelton, Eddie Cole, and Charlie Vinci—I must cease now, or I'll never be able to stop.

One of my favorites, barely remembered these days, was the late William J. Schmidt. His friends called him Smitty, and he died too young, but he was among the first horsemen to support my ambitions and cheer me on after I called my first race in 1959.

How often experts and pundits have debated the question: what makes a good trainer? First, he must have the horse. Eddie Arcaro was the first of racing's star jockeys to credit "at least 95 percent" of the win to the horse. At the same time, he applauded the job turned in by the horse's trainer. There was a chain of "complementary command," which also included the owner. It's commonplace today to hear winning riders praise both horse and trainer. No rider today is that egotistical to think he alone should be credited for victory achieved.

Bill Schmidt, Smitty, provided one extraordinary example of the contribution an astute trainer can make to a winning effort. It was at Washington Park in the late 1950s, and Smitty was hounding friendly rival William Hal Bishop for training honors. Smitty already had in his care a sturdy, valiant 15-year-old named Fleet Argo. In those days any horse, no matter his class, could race into his 15th year, after which the horse's retirement was mandatory, unless the horse won as a 15-year-old, which meant he could race at 16; should he win again, then age 17 was also available. He could race as long as he could win in each succeeding year.

Smitty had another oldtimer named Sanders Road, a cheap but game campaigner. The gelding had an irreversibly bad, at times painful, left front ankle, so the old guy preferred racing on his right lead, though that often tired him out in the late going. Sanders Road's jockey was an old pro named Jimmy Nichols. Smitty confided in me before the race: "Phil, I'm gonna tell Jimmy not to use his horse's left lead that much, especially down the stretch. But if Sanders Road's close enough, say locked head-and-head with another near the wire, Jimmy's to get him to switch leads late, but only in the last 70 yards or so—not before—otherwise the old guy will really get the worst of it."

Sanders Road was a born speedball. He blasted to the front, but Nichols eased him back to third approaching the far turn. Once straightened away down Washington Park's long home lane, Nichols asked for his mount's best. Sanders Road responded, leaped from third in a bound, wrested command inside the eighth pole, and looked all over a winner. Just then another horse bolted from the pack, and the two of 'em were head and head with 100 yards to come. That's when the other horse put his head in front. Sanders Road looked beaten.

That's when Jimmy Nichols followed Smitty's orders to a T. He urged with whip and reins, coaxing Sanders Road to switch leads, going to his left for the final dash home. That lead was fresh; it added new life to Sanders Road, and it would take several yards before he'd start hurting. The maneuver did the trick! Sanders Road recoiled on command and, with immediate but temporarily renewed vigor, came back to regain the lead, and the victory! His ankle started to hurt, as Smitty knew it would, so he switched back to the other lead for a more comfortable stride, but the wire had been passed, the win secured.

In the winner's circle, Jimmy Nichols hailed Smitty as a genius. Smitty smiled, and he kissed Sanders Road above his right nostril. "He's the one who deserves all the credit," Smitty ceded, discounting his own know-how and experience.

Smitty and I celebrated over steak and ale that night. Jimmy Nichols dropped in for a calorie-free dessert; age was dogging his heels, and weight was a constant bugaboo. "Arcaro never rode better," Smitty said, slapping Jimmy's back, "and old Sanders Road must've thought he was Citation himself."

Sanders Road was a Thoroughbred, heart and soul. Old, battered, and weary, true. Nevertheless, he gave his best despite the onslaught of age and circumstances. He'd win another race two weeks later. But age and infirmity were catching up; Smitty retired the old guy, along with the aforementioned Fleet Argo, for a pensioned life of leisure at Smitty's big farm and breeding nursery in Northbrook, Illinois.

We've just about come to the end of our sentimental journey down Thoroughbred racing's memory lane. Forgive me if I greet its close with mixed emotions. What I saw and experienced since 1941 can never be repeated or duplicated, so I'm truly sad to close out this labor of love. At the same time, I'm proud to have been, if not always an actual eye-witness, at least a grateful bystander to history in the making.

I must confess that I didn't deliberately save what I considered the best for last; that is, the Sanders Road story of an unassuming Thoroughbred winning just another cheap race, trained by a horseman few fans remember, and ridden by just another run-of-the-mill jockey. But the story pierced my very marrow, not as something terribly profound or extraordinary, but as perfect commentary to end a personal opus embracing those unforgettable horses, people, places, and things I was privileged to view through these binoculars.

The essence of the Sanders Road story is that yes, indeed, Sanders Road very well might have been Secretariat, Man o' War, Kelso, Whirlaway, or Citation himself. Trainer Bill Schmidt could easily have been Ben Jones, Sunny Jim Fitzsimmons, Max Hirsch, Bob Baffert, or Wayne Lukas. And jockey Jimmy Nichols might well have been Bill Shoemaker, Bill Hartack, Jerry Bailey, Pat Day, or Eddie Arcaro.

They comprised what I proclaimed 96,131 times over the mike: "And in the winner's circle, ladies and gentlemen, the winning team!" As that "winning team," collectively they epitomize everything that was good, decent, exciting, and memorable during Thoroughbred racing's golden age. Please accept what I saw and related in these writings not merely as an old man's attempt to relive bygone days of "when racing was racing," but, equally important, as intimate insight into what this incomparable game of winning and losing is all about.

Epilogue

It bears repeating: I can't deny either my name or birthday. Phillip, in Greek, means "lover of horses." And I was born on January 1, which you know is the universal birthday of all Thoroughbreds. I don't believe in predestination, but it seemed only right that I'd spend more than two-thirds of my life in Thoroughbred racing.

But I'm also a cat lover. Only one year total—nine months on one occasion, three on another—during my 71 years have I lived without a pet cat to light up my life before and since marriage. The morning of the day that I write these exact words, my wife Bobbie and I spent an agonizing half-hour at our local veterinarian's office having our beloved 15-year-old Burmese—his name was Squirt—put down, or "humanely destroyed" in racetrack parlance.

I will remember his sweet ways to my dying day; he touched my heart deeply; I'll never forget my time with him—days and years which can be recalled fondly, but never repeated. Yes, there will be other wonderfully loving pets, to be sure, but never the same. Thankfully, however, that slice of life, though impossible to restore, can be relived in memory over and over again with love and affection.

I'm sure at times you've had your fill of what some regard as similar sentimental drivel by pet lovers, perhaps dismissing such feelings as overdone hogwash. But I feel that in the course of this book we've become good friends, that you can graciously empathize with my personal heartache of putting little Squirt to sleep, and that you can understand it as fitting parallel to my tender feelings about Thoroughbred racing's glory days.

They're gone, true. But life must go on. I can't help but conclude that for racing to really survive and, more importantly, thrive, the sport must not only celebrate history but add to it! One big-league insurance company used a similar rationale to advertise its services. They pointed out that a fire in your home may totally wipe out great memories, but your insurance company is there to help you, the client, start over and at the same time build new memories. Sounds logical. And encouraging. Perhaps that's what racing should be doing right now—remembering the old, while adding the new. At least, a dedication toward that objective is in order.

I'm no doomsday advocate, but I am deeply concerned about the sport's future. If I had a sure solution, I'd speak it now. But I do know this: I honor Thoroughbred racing's past as precious, as perfect as anything in an imperfect world can be. The game's present, however, is tense, since its future is so uncertain. I believe my concerns, and the problem's answer, lie somewhere between what the state of racing actually is and what some doomsday critics say it is.

In sports' evolution during the past two decades, Thoroughbred racing has been relegated to sub-par status. Its legitimacy may not be questioned, but its recognition on annual TV sports awards shows is given no more than a lick and a promise. Except for Cigar and Triple Crown tries by Silver Charm, Real Quiet, and Charismatic, and hoopla over Fusaichi Pegasus, it's not been enough.

It's bad enough the NTRA sells the game as some rock or theatrical concert, but TV announcers and commentators talk of their "picks," combining them with outsiders and longshots in an effort to nail down an "exacta" or a "trifecta," as if cashing a bet mattered most with the Derby, Triple Crown, or Breeders' Cup. Many couldn't care less about racing's heritage. The last time I eagerly showed a young racing fan the 1955 Swaps–Nashua match race, the first words out of his mouth were: "What did Nashua pay?" I realize gambling's longtime ties with racing. But here was a time when newspapers, radio, and TV covered it as genuine sports fare.

Forgive me if I appear testy, even picayunish, but should TV Thoroughbred announcers refer to their viewers as "horse players"? I remember a period in the 1960s when one Chicago racetrack dared to advertise "You *don't* have to bet—just come on out and enjoy Thoroughbred Racing." I have always considered myself "a racing fan." Now, I'm not so naive that I'd dismiss the importance of the mutual handle and its impact on purses as an essential lure for quality horseflesh and top-level competition. But somehow, somewhere, racing's sporting aspect has been lost or abandoned.

From what I've seen evolve in all sports, empty stadiums give the inevitable impression that a team or game is unpopular, certainly not successful enough to attract fan support. Given the growing number of gambling casinos, plus spiraling cable and satellite networking, fewer and fewer racing events are able to generate big TV audience ratings. Few networks see the need to pay out big fees to racetracks for fear the sport can't deliver either prestige or audience.

I cringe every time I recall Ben Lindheimer's blunder in 1955, failing to recognize the importance of TV coverage in spreading the news of Thoroughbred racing's unique appeal. The general feeling today among the sports business set is that Thoroughbred racing, except perhaps for the Triple Crown, is not a positive broadcast sport. Ratings for the Derby in particular, the Triple Crown in general, are okay. But the Breeders' Cup ratings each fall, from what I gather, are hardly half those of average baseball teams in August.

Many observers think we have too much racing, that the number of foals is declining each year, resulting in not enough good horses to go around. And if gambling is now the sport's sole savior, the game's simply no match for casino action. Slots, roulette, craps, and video games are easier on the eyes, brain, and heart, especially for young people, who often find the process of handicapping a race too intimidating.

The sport's modernity reminds me of high-tech computer animation, lacking the rich color and personal detail a person who was raised on Disney's Snow White, Bambi, and Pinocchio is used to. But then, audiences change too, don't they? They flock to sustained action. We're in the midst of a sky-rocketing electronic age. Prestigious tracks will continue to merge into multi-outlet conglomerates. Smaller tracks will either die off, or become little more than off-track wagering facilities. But it's hard to imagine that racing's real future is in the cold hands of high-speed technology.

I'm prepared to be accused by some as a race-caller who simply grew old and tired while on the job. Guilty as charged. But while on that job, I lived racing's glory days. And loved every moment. Maybe, as some say, you do have to go back to the future to appreciate not only racing's past glories, but what impact its history should have on the sport, today as well as tomorrow.

But then, it's been the unexpected that helped make racing so marvelous and intriguing. I still eagerly invite the sport into my living room via TV each spring and fall, and all exciting times in between. Tom Durkin's incomparable call "Annnd they're off!" and the thundering hooves and great stretch runs still excite me. And I know I can still call 'em the way I like 'em called. Yet it's not the same. Nor will it ever be.

Were they redeemable, I'd happily have racing's glory days again. Nevertheless, I'm grateful for this unique opportunity to put into words all the wonders I saw from 1941 onward—the horses, people, places, and things that I gloried in for an incomparable half-century. Just like my precious feline buddy Squirt, Thoroughbred racing's golden days are gone, but not forgotten.

I remember them as a sweet dream of innocence when all sports had soul. And Thoroughbred racing was its beating heart.